Private Capital Flows in the Age of Globalization

In memory of my sister
Aurélie Uzan

Private Capital Flows in the Age of Globalization

The Aftermath of the Asian Crisis

Edited by

Uri Dadush

Director, Development Prospects Group, World Bank, USA

Dipak Dasgupta

Principal Economist, Development Prospects Group, World Bank, USA

Marc Uzan

Founder and Executive Director, Reinventing Bretton Woods Foundation, New York, USA

IN ASSOCIATION WITH THE INTERNATIONAL BANK FOR RECONSTRUCTION AND DEVELOPMENT/THE WORLD BANK

Edward Elgar

Cheltenham, UK • Northampton, MA, USA

Published by
Edward Elgar Publishing Limited
Glensanda House
Montpellier Parade
Cheltenham
Glos GL50 1UA
UK

Edward Elgar Publishing, Inc.
136 West Street
Suite 202
Northampton
Massachusetts 01060
USA

A catalogue record for this book is available from the British Library

Library of Congress Cataloguing in Publication Data
Private capital flows in the age of globalization : the aftermath of the Asian crisis / edited
by Uri Dadush, Dipak Dasgupta, Marc Uzan.
    Includes index.
    "In association with the Organisation for Economic Co-operation and Development/
the World Bank."
    1. Capital movements—Asia, Southeastern. 2. Debts, External—Asia,
Southeastern. 3. Financial crisis—Asia, Southeastern. I. Dadush, Uri B. II. Das Gupta,
Dipak. III. Uzan, Marc. IV. Organisation for Economic Co-operation and
Development. V. World Bank.

HG5740.8.A3 P75 2000
332'.042—dc21   99–049034

ISBN 1 84064 214 9

Printed and bound in Great Britain by Biddles Ltd, www.biddles.co.uk

Contents

PART III   MORAL HAZARD AND SYSTEMIC RISK

Figures

Tables

List of contributors

Vinod K. Aggarwal, Berkeley APEC Study Center, University of California, Berkeley, USA
Michel Aglietta, University of Paris X-Mini Forum and CEPII, France
Roberto Chang, Federal Reserve Bank of Atlanta, USA
Uri Dadush, Director, Development Prospects Group, World Bank, USA
Dipak Dasgupta, Principal Economist, Development Prospects Group, World Bank, USA
Gerardo Esquivel, Assistant Professor, El Colegio de Mexico, Mexico
Ross Garnaut, Professor of Economics, The Research School of Pacific and Asian Studies, The Australian National University, Australia
Richard A. Gitlin, Hebb and Gitlin, Connecticut, USA
Gordon W. Johnson, Weil, Gotshal and Manges Law Firm, New York, USA
Felipe Larraín B., Robert F. Kennedy Visiting Professor of Latin American Studies, Harvard University and Director of the Central America Project, Harvard Institute for International Development, USA
Paul D. Leake, Weil, Gotshal and Manges Law Firm, New York, USA
Marcus Miller, University of Warwick, CSGR and CEPR, UK
Frederic S. Mishkin, Graduate School of Business, Columbia University and National Bureau of Economic Research, USA
Hak K. Pyo, Seoul National University, Korea and The University of Tokyo, Japan
Adam C. Rogoff, Weil, Gotshal and Manges Law Firm, New York, USA
Marc Uzan, Executive Director, Reinventing Bretton Woods Foundation, New York, USA
Andrés Velasco, Professor of Economics, New York University, USA
Dominic Wilson, Australia–Japan Research Centre, The Australian National University
Lei Zhang, University of Warwick, UK

Introduction

Uri Dadush, Dipak Dasgupta and Marc Uzan

In the second half of 1997, four East Asian countries, Thailand, Malaysia, the Republic of Korea and Indonesia, experienced a massive reversal of the large foreign capital inflows that they had enjoyed through much of the 1990s. The swing from net inflows to outflows amounted to more than US$100 billion and exceeded some 11 per cent of their GDP. This precipitated large fall in their currencies, severe stock market and other asset price declines, deep domestic financial crises, and severe output declines, rivalling those in the worst years of the debt crisis in Latin America, and comparable to that in the early years of the Great Depression in the United States. In a matter of months, countries within a region that had experienced unprecedented growth and prosperity over the past three decades were suddenly in deep trouble. These events have raised three central questions: what caused the Asian crisis, why did most analysts fail to anticipate the crisis, and why were the effects so severe?

Subsequent events in the world economy were no less remarkable, as the Asian flu became an epidemic. With surprising speed and succession, the Asian crisis spread to Russia and the former Commonwealth of Independent State countries, the Middle East and other oil-producing countries, Brazil and the rest of Latin America, and numerous others. The effects of the Asian crisis spread most to countries that were (a) heavily dependent on private capital inflows to finance their current account deficits, because of the drastic fall in such capital flows; and/or (b) those that relied heavily on primary commodities for export earnings, as commodity prices plummeted some 30–40 per cent in the aftermath of the Asian crisis; and/or (c) those countries that relied significantly on manufactures exports in which Asian producers specialized, as world trade and prices of such exports fell sharply. Since a list of potential candidates from such a scenario included many if not most developing countries, 1998 marked the worst economic slowdown in aggregate growth in developing countries since the debt crisis of the early 1980s. The aftermath of the Asian crisis thus showed how much more interconnected the global economy had become. Interventions by international financial institutions and G-7 governments were notable in their failure to stem or arrest the spread of the crisis. The central question in that context is what caused the failures in the

1

global economic architecture to prevent and/or deal better with the consequences of such crises.

The above set of questions formed the background for a conference held in
May 1998 in Washington, DC on the subject of 'The Aftermath of the Asian
Crisis'. Researchers from around the world, including the Asian crisis countries
themselves, were invited to present their views. A selection of the papers
presented at the conference form the basis of this book. Each of the papers
offers a different perspective on the issues, and every section has a slightly
different focus. As a result, the reader will be able to benefit from reading
through all the chapters and forming his or her own opinion about what is now
arguably the single most important topic regarding the perils of globalization.

CRISIS COUNTRY PERSPECTIVES

The first set of chapters are by researchers in the Asian crisis countries
themselves (or by those who analyse the effects of the crisis on other developing
countries) and who therefore offer a unique insight into the questions regarding
the causes, effects and possible solutions to the Asian crisis. As the authors of
the Indonesia and Korea papers suggest, the crisis arose fundamentally from
the combination of deep-seated weaknesses in domestic financial and corporate
sectors, with the volatility in private international capital flows. It is also illus-
trative that there were significant country differences.

In past currency crises in developing countries, the core of the crisis was
usually due to fiscal deficits combined with excessive borrowing by the
government (or its agencies), as in the case of the 1980s' debt crisis. While the
old type of sovereign borrowing crisis is still important – witness the Russian
and Brazilian public finance problems in the current round – the crisis in East
Asia was very different. All the affected countries had relatively prudent fiscal
policies in place and sovereign borrowing was actually in decline. The
problems arose instead from excessive private borrowing and inadequate
management of what were essentially private risks – which became all of a
sudden a public risk as these countries were dragged into an economy-wide
crisis caused by the large swing in private-to-private capital inflows. The
critical indicators of vulnerability to crisis in such private-to-private flows were
also very different from the usual type of sovereign debt crisis: excessive debt
to equity ratios, maturity mismatches and excessive short-term debt, and
unhedged currency exposures, not the usual macroeconomic country debt
indicators such as debt to GDP ratios, debt to exports ratios or current account
deficits. One implication is that most analysts were unable to predict the crisis
in Asia because they were looking at the wrong set of crisis indicators.

Elements of the private overborrowing story and its links to policies was key in the crisis in Indonesia. Corporate borrowing increased sharply during 1994–7, stimulated by relative macroeconomic stability (rather than instability) with a predictable depreciation of the rupiah, and financial sector regulatory weaknesses combined with earlier deregulation laid the groundwork for excessive foreign currency borrowing. The authors also show that much of the borrowing was by domestically oriented firms in non-tradable sectors (that had few direct or indirect export earnings, such as property and infrastructure sectors), a result of an implicit bias in policies favouring investment in such sectors. The combination with a failure to hedge foreign currency exposure was disastrous. Another important part of the story is how willing lenders were to expose themselves to high risks: despite being rated among the worst in terms of accounting integrity, Indonesian corporate borrowers were able to acquire massive loans and bonds from abroad. All was well so long as a favourable international climate existed; but once the cycle turned, inflows turned to massive outflows and vastly amplified the effects. Only about 17 per cent of the total debt can be serviced sustainably, according to their analysis. As a result, the voluntary work-out of such a debt between creditors and debtors may hold the key to an eventual recovery in Indonesia.

Hak Pyo's chapter on Korea, in some contrast, discusses the origins of the crisis in Korea in terms of long-standing problems in that country's banking system that became suddenly exposed with the opening of the Korean banking system to foreign borrowing and the sudden large reversal of capital flows. Moral hazard (state guarantees on bank debt) and lax banking regulation are thus blamed as the fundamental causes of the crisis, accompanied by a transition to what Pyo terms as 'excessive competition' among the chaebols (large conglomerates) in similar or same product lines that only drove their fortunes (and those of the banks) down with them – as in motor cars or semiconductors. The accumulated problems resulted in high leveraging and rising non-performing loans, and with them the eventual loss of confidence in the banks. Looking to the future, Pyo argues that financial sector reform, as opposed to a focus on 'chaebol' restructuring, is vital, and that it would be desirable for mergers to take place so that stronger banks can eventually emerge.

COMPARING THE ASIAN CRISIS WITH THOSE IN LATIN AMERICA

Was the Asian crisis unique or new? And what can we learn by contrasting the Asian crisis with crises that have happened before, especially in Latin America? In order to explore this, the book presents two contrasting chapters. The first is by Roberto Chang and Andrés Velasco who argue that, each time a crisis happens, there is tendency to attribute it to a new set of causes, but that there is usually a much greater commonality.

Chang and Velasco suggest that there is nothing necessarily new about the Asian crisis. The fundamental factor behind this crisis, as in others before in Latin America, is international illiquidity, resulting in the outright collapse of the financial system. This illiquidity is almost always rooted in a previous bout of financial liberalization, which accentuates a maturity mismatch in borrowing. A creditors' panic and refusal to roll over short-term loans allows a self-fulfilling bank run. The central banks cannot stabilize both domestic banks and the exchange rate peg, hence we observe the traditional 'twin crisis' of balance of payments and finance. The punishment is much larger than the crime as small changes in exogenous circumstances can cause large changes in asset prices and exchange rates, the magnifying effect being the financial system. Chang and Velasco demonstrate in these terms the similarities between the Asian crisis and those in Chile in the early 1980s and Mexico in 1994–5. Their conclusions are strikingly different from the chapter by Esquivel and Larraín, in that they argue that small exchange rate appreciations and deterioration of other economic fundamentals are not enough to explain the crises. What is essential is international illiquidity, measured in terms of the high proportion of short-term debt to international reserves. The policy implications are clear: preventing such crises requires limiting short-term debt and not following pegged exchange rates.

Esquivel and Larraín compare the earlier Latin American experience with the Asian crisis. They point to the evidence that the early 1980s' Latin American crisis was mostly distinguished by classical balance of payments problems and unsustainable exchange rates, following the so-called 'first-generation' models of balance of payments problems. Here, with the exception of Chile, the problems arose because of unsustainable domestic policies of excessive government expenditures that eroded external balances and, eventually, the sustainability of fixed exchange rates. In that sense, such crises were also highly predictable. In contrast, they argue that the causes of the Asian crisis, the Chilean crisis in the early 1980s and the Mexican crisis of 1994–5 were different: fiscal balances were sound, countries were generally rated as good on fundamentals and prospects, but the crises nevertheless occurred primarily because of two key factors: large real exchange rate appreciations and credit/spending booms (whether for investment or for consumption) that widened current accounts unsustainably. To this extent, fundamentals were deteriorating prior to the crises and the crises were still predictable. Esquivel and Larraín then focus on the current situation in Latin America and presciently argue that Brazil represents the greatest weakness, since it has both the most appreciated currency and the largest twin deficits (public deficits and external deficits).

DEALING WITH THE ASIAN CRISIS: PRIVATE DEBT WORK-OUTS

If the heart of the Asian crisis was private-to-private transactions, and not necessarily macroeconomic issues, would it not be more appropriate for solutions to the crisis to concentrate upon microeconomic issues? The corporate lawyers' answer is a resounding 'yes', and offers a very different perspective from those usually proffered by economists. Two chapters shows why.

Gitlin, using the implicit role model of the legal system in the United States where bankruptcy and corporate restructuring practices are most advanced, suggests that the traditional solution to sovereign crises of injecting large amounts of external public funds is fundamentally flawed. Instead, the search for effective solutions should concentrate on resolution mechanisms for troubled commercial obligations within the affected country itself. This would reduce the size of the financial crisis, accelerate recovery and cause lenders and investors to share a greater proportion of the risks of their initial lending decisions. If business failure is at the heart of this crisis, Gitlin argues that the best rescue system should involve the efficient liquidation of businesses that should be allowed to fail, and saving others that can be saved, and be based on efficient, fair and predictable bankruptcy processes. He goes on to outline the possibilities, using both out-of-court procedures and in-court approaches. The critical role of such microeconomic approaches is to bring in secondary market purchasers for distressed assets in a banking crisis.

Goldstein, Rogoff and Johnson use a similar line of reasoning, but their solution is an international bankruptcy court. The thrust of their argument is that, just as national bankruptcy institutions perform an invaluable function for capitalism – by setting efficient equity rules, reducing waste in 'grab races' for assets, balancing the interests of other claimants such as employees, maintaining public confidence and reducing the risks of insolvency – international bankruptcy courts can achieve similar goals. The absence of such a court creates enormous problems, and the typical insolvency approach which involves debtors and creditors working under different systems and jurisdictions is impractical. The basic conclusion of their chapter is an attempt to remedy the current existing patchwork of conventions by drawing up the institutional modalities of a unified international bankruptcy court.

PREVENTING CRISES: INTERNATIONAL ARCHITECTURE ISSUES

A number of suggestions on ways to prevent such crises as in Asia (and its spread by contagion) are being currently debated in international forums. It is also suggested that the existing system, comprising the Bretton Woods international financial institutions and backed by the direct or indirect interventions of the most powerful industrialized countries, does not work well in preventing or dealing with crises. And the lack of much progress despite innumerable committee reports and meetings suggests that it is not easy to develop an international consensus on what improvements need to be made. In this context, the contributions in the present book are a refreshing antidote.

Vinod Aggarwal offers a refreshing historical and political perspective. He suggests that reform in relations between lenders and debtors in the international arena is nothing new. But his most important conclusion is that a critical role is played, not by international agencies or international consultations, but by the principal creditor countries themselves. Their role has almost always been a critical factor in resolving past debt crises. Thus, contrary to conventional wisdom, government intervention has always been a key. Further, the role played by the United States as a principal creditor government has usually been a decisive factor. Various historical precedents are analysed by Aggarwal to provide evidence for this, including the evolution of the Brady bonds in the 1980s as a solution to the Latin American debt crisis, the Mexican rescue package in 1995 and the interventions in the current Asian debt crisis.

Ross Garnaut and Dominic Wilson, in contrast, take a much more conventional line of argument. As they suggest, there is the need for a 'cool' assessment of the situation. For example, should there be a better balance between regional and global solutions? They argue that the critical need is for complementarity, and that new institutions should not be invented if existing ones work reasonably well. Regional agreements should concentrate, for example, on financial standards, but be complementary to international efforts. Further, the first line of defence ought to be better policies by countries themselves. Here they argue that fundamental causes of the Asian crisis were financial sector weaknesses, unhedged foreign debt, bursting of asset-price bubbles and pegged exchange rate systems (exacerbated, of course, by some changes and herd behaviour in global financial markets). Their conclusion is that better surveillance and greater transparency is the first order of business in international architecture issues. Good governance issues are second. Third, there are some issues concerning the challenges of coping with volatile capital flows, and some degree of caution over capital account opening is probably appropriate.

Marcus Miller and Lei Zhang take a more theoretical approach. The critical question is whether throwing more public money after crises simply leads to greater moral hazard and is therefore self-defeating, or whether it serves a useful purpose in addressing international illiquidity issues. Their answer is that it is vital to know first whether a crisis is one of insolvency or one of illiquidity. On the basis of their analytical exercises and arguments, they conclude that improved surveillance is important, that capital flow regulatory procedures are probably also important to reduce the vulnerability of many emerging markets to market volatility, that debt roll-overs and work-outs are essential to resolve liquidity crises (and not simply by handing over more money that creates more moral hazard), that moral hazard within domestic financial systems should also be reduced and, finally, that full capital account liberalization should not be pursued recklessly.

Michel Aglietta argues that the Asian financial crisis is only one in a long series of historical turmoils, with the critical suggestion that market failures in international cross-border lending are extensive and endemic. Deficiencies happen, not just on the depositor's side, but also among lenders. And they result in systemic risk and socially inefficient outcomes. What might be the solutions? On the debtor's side, the solution is mainly long term and structural: improving financial regulation and not undertaking ill-conceived financial and capital account opening. On the creditor's side, the keys are better surveillance of risk-taking activities by lenders, and true and effective lender-of-last resort activity to avoid panic sales and contagion effects of crisis. But Aglietta concludes that such roles can only be played by a club of powerful central bankers (and supervisors), not by a single international agency acting on its own.

The chapter by Frederic Mishkin raises the question of whether an international lender of last resort is needed to reduce the spread of these crises. If that is the case, what are the basic principles that should guide its operation? For Mishkin, an international lender of last resort may be needed to limit the damage from financial crises of the type that have been experienced in Asia. But it needs to focus on the microeconomics of financial markets in crisis countries by imposing a strong conditionality.

CONCLUSIONS

The contributions to this book provide some answers to the initial questions that were framed. While more debate and research on the subject of the Asian crisis and its aftermath will and should continue, certain answers are already possible.

What caused the crisis in Asian countries? A combination of domestic financial sector weaknesses, itself engendered by ill-conceived and ill-sequenced financial liberalization, and failures in international capital markets marked by cycles of euphoria followed by panic.

Why did most analysts fail to anticipate the crisis? Because most analysts were looking at the wrong set of crisis indicators suggested by past sovereign debt crises, instead of financial fragility indicators in private-to-private borrowing that were at the heart of this crisis. In this sense, this crisis was very different from the earlier Latin American debt crisis of the early 1980s. But the Asian crisis is not in any way new or unique either. Crises that happened before in Chile in 1982 and Mexico in 1994–5 have strong parallels with the crisis in Asia, especially in terms of a crisis precipitated by international illiquidity.

Why were the effects of the crisis so severe? Because they were accompanied by deep systemic crashes of the financial system, where such crashes amplify the shocks and initial triggering events, similar to the effects of the Great Depression.

What is the key now to recovery in Asian and other crisis countries? The rebuilding of the domestic financial system, which critically involves restructuring of the debts of the domestic corporate and banking sectors. Microeconomic solutions relying on voluntary private-to-private debt workouts are essential, where the state (both in crisis countries and in principal creditor countries) plays a crucial role in helping to set the institutional parameters of such transactions. Standard macroeconomic solutions, such as countries exporting their way out of crisis, are less critical or helpful.

Where did the international architecture fail in dealing with this crisis? The principal failure was in throwing money after the crisis in order primarily to bail out international private lenders, and, in turn, creating major moral hazard problems. After the experience of Russia, this was no longer credible. And the second key failure was in not promoting a private-to-private work-out of debts where lenders who took risky decisions should have been more accountable. A third failure was in not being able to stop or stem international contagion. It is also readily apparent that collective actions by principal creditor countries to resolve the crises needed to have been at the forefront.

How do we prevent such crises from happening in the future? Because the causes are failures both in domestic financial markets and in international capital markets, there is no simple recipe for avoiding such crises. They have happened before and will continue to happen in the future. But much can be done to reduce their incidence and the severity of costs. First, developing countries with weak financial settings and regulatory practices need to worry much more about the pacing and sequencing of financial deregulation and capital account opening. Second, traditional lessons still apply in avoiding large fiscal deficits and fixed and overvalued exchange rates. Third, curbing volatile short-term capital inflows prone to sudden reversals is important, especially where domestic financial settings are fragile. These three lessons will do much to insulate developing countries from such disasters in the future.

In the international arena, there is much less clarity. One set of answers looks to increased surveillance and regulatory oversight by international institutions. This is somewhat problematic in terms of practical possibilities and efficacy. A second envisages enhanced lender-of-last resort activities by a powerful new club of central banks. Again, this is of doubtful value without the backing and intervention of principal creditor countries and, since there is such an uncertain political climate for this, it is unlikely to be practical. A third is the search for more modest institutional approaches that rely essentially on voluntary private debt work-outs and the application of bankruptcy practices to international settings in the event of a crisis (including an internationally sanctioned temporary moratorium on external debt). While equally uncertain, this might eventually be the more desirable direction to take in preventing future crises since it reduces the problems of moral hazard implied in international bailouts.

PART I

The Asian Crisis in Perspective

1. Excess competition, moral hazard and industrial trauma in Korea, 1997–8[*]

Hak K. Pyo

INTRODUCTION

One of the most intriguing features of the recent Asian economic crisis was the interaction between financial collapse and industrial failure. The sudden exodus of foreign capital made both the abrupt currency depreciation and the sharp decline in stock prices inevitable, which in turn caused both firms and financial intermediaries to become insolvent as the central banks could no longer bail them out because their foreign reserves had already been depleted. In particular, large-scale corporate bankruptcies created massive amounts of non-performing loans. Then the banking sector which was suffering from lack of liquidity had to offer higher interest rates to avoid bank runs and to lure back foreign investment. The high interest policy invited further corporate bankruptcies, resulting in a circular causation of industrial trauma. At the same time, severe layoffs in both the industrial and the financial sector have depressed domestic demand severely so that most small and medium enterprises are either bankrupt or close to bankruptcy.

The current industrial trauma in the Republic of Korea (hereafter called Korea), Malaysia, Thailand and Indonesia must have deep roots in their endogenous systems, which on the surface may not look that different across the entire East Asian region including Japan and China. The problem of non-performing loans in domestic banking industries in both these countries is well known. Japan is dealing with it in a phased-out way going through a prolonged period of restructuring and recession-like economic environment: it can afford to do so because it is still the largest creditor nation after accumulating a balance of payments surplus over almost three decades. China still maintains tight control and regulations over domestic banking and foreign exchange

[*] The earlier version of this paper was presented at the Global Economic Prospects 1998 Workshop: 'The Aftermath of the Asian Crisis', 13–14 May 1998, Embassy Suites Hotel, Washington, DC, organized by the World Bank and the Reinventing Bretton Woods Committee. The present version was presented at a seminar at the Institute of Social and Economic Research, Osaka University and at Development Economics Workshop of Institute of Economic Research, Hitotsubashi University.

operations and, therefore, has managed to remain free from the contagion so far. Both Singapore and Hong Kong have maintained much more open trade regimes and liberal financial systems, so that the impact of the contagion could be contained to some extent. Taiwan has not had a chronic balance of payments problem in the past and accumulated enough foreign reserves to protect its currency from the contagion. Furthermore, its well-diversified industrial structure, based on small and medium enterprises and an unorganized but efficient money market, has kept the economy in check. Thus, the countries that have been most severely affected by the spread of the contagion were those with relatively weaker economic fundamentals in terms of industrial structure and financial resources. In other words, those countries' currencies became subject to speculative attacks when investors realized that they had not assessed their economic fundamentals properly.

As the corporate bankruptcies and massive layoffs began to spread under the International Monetary Fund-(IMF)-mandated programmes in Thailand, Indonesia and Korea, the crisis which started out as a currency crisis has now become a full-scale social and political crisis. Their political regimes were weak and fragile in conflict resolution and their social safety nets are almost non-existent. Unless it was contained at the point where the contagion had spread to Korea, which was the eleventh largest economy in gross national product (GNP), there was no guarantee of avoiding the second-round currency crisis and a devastating expansion to the rest of Asia and the rest of world through another round of competitive devaluation. Considering the speed and the magnitude of social unrest in the crisis economies, it was premature to claim that the crisis would be over soon and that a reasonable recovery was expected.

The crisis seems to be much more deep-rooted than commonly believed and, therefore, we have to pay more analytical attention to the real cause of the crisis. We also have to weigh up whether the IMF mandates are appropriate and, if there are rooms for improvement, what policy options can be explored.

The purpose of this chapter is twofold: to trace the real cause of the current industrial trauma in Korea and to assess the aftermath of the currency crisis since December 1997 in order to draw policy implications. A more detailed analysis of the Korean experience seems warranted, because we need to explain why the eleventh largest economy in the world had to rely on the record amount (US$57 billion) of IMF-led bailout to avoid national insolvency when the contagion from Southeast Asia hit the country in November 1997. As emphasized in Pyo (1997), we need more than a simple model of moral hazard or cronyism to identify factors which ultimately contributed to the current turmoil.

The chapter is organized as follows. The next section explores a theoretical framework in which the excess competition combined with moral hazard and lax banking regulation becomes a dominant cause of the currency crisis. This is followed by an empirical examination of the industrial structure in Korea to characterize it as a monopolistic competition across industries. The penultimate section highlights a policy dilemma in the current structural reform efforts under IMF-mandated programmes. The last section is devoted to policy implications and prospects of corporate restructuring in Korea.

A MODEL OF MONOPOLISTIC COMPETITION ACROSS INDUSTRIES

It is well known in the modern theories of industrial organization such as Scherer (1980), Okuno-Fujiwara *et al.* (1980), Okuno-Fujiwara (1988), Stiglitz (1981), Suzumura and Kiyono (1987) and Itoh *et al.* (1988) that measures taken to stimulate competition could result in inefficient equilibrium. In particular, Itoh *et al.* (1988) have shown that, from the standpoint of national economic welfare, it may be desirable for government to regulate entry to the industry if the industry is characterized by a Cournot–Nash oligopoly. Assuming that each firm in the industry behaves in a Cournot–Nash fashion and that the government can regulate the entry to the industry but cannot enforce marginal-cost pricing for each firm, the authors show that the number of firms established in the long-run Cournot–Nash equilibrium with free entry and exit exceeds the so-called 'second-best' number of firms established as a result of maximizing total social surplus (the sum of consumers' and producers' surplus). They define this as excess competition and distinguish it from excessive competition, which refers to a competitive (not oligopolistic) industry with free entry, but where when excess capacity arises, exit does not rapidly occur and in which labour mobility is low.

The excess competition model implies that, when the number of firms in a Cournot–Nash oligopoly increases, the change does not always improve welfare. It also implies that, as a result of the autonomous entry and exit of private firms, there is the possibility of excessive entry relative to the second-best number of firms. The model has served as a justification for cartels and government regulations on entry to particular industry in Japan since the end of the Second World War. It can also be applied to the industrial development in Korea. But we should note that such a second-best Counot–Nash equilibrium becomes an optimal one if and only if the government knows when and how to regulate the entry and exit. If for some reason, there is a policy failure, the second-best equilibrium is not necessarily a welfare-maximizing equilibrium, even under the oligopoly. Suppose, for example, that the Japanese model of regulation was more consensus-based among bureaucrats and industrialists than the Korean model. Then it would be more likely for the Korean regulatory system to be managed on an ad hoc basis rather than on consensus building. In addition, the excess competition model implicitly assumes a perfect capital market so that, once the optimal number of firms is established, each firm has a ready access to a capital market or is bailed out if it runs into financial trouble. In other words, in such an equilibrium, it will be optimal to bail out such a firm because the government is supposed to keep the optimal number of firms in the oligopolistic industry. The other alternative would be to allow an exit of the firm and simultaneously allow an entry of another firm, which will entail transaction costs. Such an implicit assumption of a perfect capital market limits the usefulness of the excess competition model. If the financial sector is operating under moral hazard and if the government is lobbied or bribed by interest groups, the second-best equilibrium cannot be maintained. In this regard, it is not surprising to observe the collapse of such a regulatory equilibrium in a period of transition from an authoritarian regime to a less authoritarian or democratic one.

EXCESS COMPETITION WITH MORAL HAZARD AND WEAK GOVERNMENT

A distinguishing feature of export-led growth in South Korea is its unique industrial structure and corporate governance. The Korean model of economic development in the past can be defined as a model of monopolistic competition across industries where government acts as both competition promoter and project monitor. In the literature of industrial organization, a monopolistic competition is usually defined within an industry. It is frequently characterized by the competition among a limited number of firms producing differentiated products. The existence of monopolistic competition is due to scale economies, entry barriers and discriminating tastes.

In the case of Korea, the government has deliberately introduced limited competition by lowering entry barriers over time and by monitoring market failures by major conglomerates in order to maximize efficiency of limited resources. In other words, the government has played the role of competition promoter and supervisor through government-controlled banks which are part of a quasi-internal organization. In this regard, the system has promoted monopolistic competition across industries. That is why one observes in Korea a larger number of motor car manufacturers, shipbuilders, airlines, oil refineries, semiconductor manufacturers, telecommunication equipment producers, mobile phone companies and so on than those normally observed in many developing countries or smaller advanced countries.

The government policy protected bureaucrats from accusations of being linked to one or two conglomerates' interest but, at the same time, provided big conglomerates with irresistible incentives for horizontal diversification. The phenomenon of 'too big to be failed' set in because big conglomerates themselves were stockholders of many financial institutions and the moral hazard in financial institutions started eroding their competitiveness. The top 30 conglomerates are producing over half of Korea's GNP and the top five con-glomerates' share is as much as one-third of the country's total production.

The business groups called 'chaebol' in Korea may look quite similar to the Japanese 'zaibatsu', but they are different in many respects. First, Korean chaebols had to rely on developing the export market more intensively than the Japanese firms because their domestic market size was less than 5 per cent of the Japanese domestic market size in 1975 (US$20.9 billion, as against US$499 billion, in terms of GNP) and less than 9 per cent in 1995 (US$453 billion, as against $5156 billion, in terms of GNP). As a result, there could coexist in Japan two types of zaibatsu: one is a highly specialized technology leader in multinational markets (for example, Toyota, Sony and Toshiba) and the other is a business group of horizontally diversified firms (for example, Mitsubishi group, Mitsui group, Sumitomo group and Fuji group). But, in Korea, only the latter type (for example, Samsung, Hyundai and Lucky-Goldstar) could be established because specialization was riskier than diversification under the oligopolistic setting with the government regulation on entry and exit. In addition, diversification through cross-shareholding could generate higher economies of scale in a limited domestic market. Second, the way the business groups are governed in Korea is quite different from that in Japan. As a result of dissolution of zaibatsu under the MacArthur administration, there were few dominant family groups which could own and manage zaibatsu. The corporate ownership structure in Japan is a more diversified one than that in Korea and the role of institutional investors is much more important in Japan than in Korea. As a result, the decision-making process and the corporate governance in Japan are much more consensus-based than those in Korea. Such a difference in ownership structure and governing pattern could make a substantial difference to the outcome of the excess competition because a more consensus-based system can survive better than an authoritarian owner-management system at the time of policy failure and can protect itself from overextension through a built-in system of checks and balances.

But now the model of monopolistic competition across industries in Korea has been subject to change both domestically and internationally. First of all, the so-called 'Lipset phenomenon' has arrived on the sociopolitical scene of Korea, as outlined in Pyo (1993). The country's success in export-led growth has brought about increasing demands for democracy and the transition from an authoritarian regime to a democratic one has been turbulent rather than smooth. The increasing demand for higher wages and benefits by organized labor through, at times, violent disputes and strikes has placed an extra burden on firms' efforts at restructuring and 'downsizing'. But most important of all, in the face of increasing domestic and foreign competition, some monopolistic competitors have carried out a series of ill-fated pre-emptive strategic investments. As anticipated in Pyo *et al.* (1996), the potential impacts of the World Trade Organization (WTO) in a general equilibrium context have become much greater than those in a partial equilibrium context. One typical manifestation of such impacts is overinvestment in non-tradable sectors and pre-emptive investment in some tradable sectors.

The Kia Group expanded its car production capacity drastically and, at the same time, pursued both unchecked vertical integration (Kia Special Metals Co.) and unconventional horizontal diversification into the construction and financing business. Later on, even the Samsung group, which was one of the most widely diversified groups, entered the car manufacturing business in 1996. The New Core group made strategic investments in a retail and large merchandise distribution network in anticipation of domestic conglomerates' and foreign multinationals' entry into retail business after the inauguration of the WTO. But the slow business in retail sales could not pay off the high cost of borrowed funds, resulting in the company's application for court protection. The Hyundai group announced its intention to enter steel manufacturing, which had been monopolized by the Pohang Steel Co., just a few months before the failure of the Hanbo group in 1997. Considering the current market trend towards deregulation and privatization, it was difficult for the government to discourage the entry. Even though it has not materialized owing to the objections by the government and the subsequent financial turmoil, we could have seen another pattern of oligopolistic competition in the steel industry, too.

Many Korean firms in the motor industry and the semiconductor industry have tried to put themselves in strategic positions in the global market. They seemed to take the view that there was increasing demand for their products from emerging markets and transition economies. They regarded their products as not necessarily top-quality goods but as reasonably priced, competitive products in such markets. Their success or failure depended on their income-generating capacities because they had to pay back interests and principals of the loans they had borrowed from domestic and foreign banks. This game of high-yield high-risk in strategic markets was to determine the substantiality of export-led growth in Korea. Such a game could not have been maintained if there was no moral hazard in the financial sector and if the government was strong enough to insulate its bureaucrats from the distributive politics among chaebols and other interest groups, including labour unions. But neither condition was met. In addition, the owner-management corporate governance without consensus building and internal checks and balances resulted in overinvestment in existing business and caused excessive competition against a background of moral hazard in the financial sector and lax banking supervision by weak government. In my judgment, this was the most fundamental cause of the financial crisis in Korea.

Many economists watching the recent financial turmoil in South Korea were disturbed by the fact that the economy's macroeconomic indicators did not warrant massive market failures, as shown in Table 1.1. In the midst of continuing Won depreciation and stumbling stock prices during the first half of 1997, the GNP managed to grow at an annual rate of 5.4 per cent. But it should have been noted that the growth rate was a significantly lower one than that in the previous years: 8.4 per cent in 1994, 4.6 per cent in 1995 and 7.2 per cent in 1996. As a result, the conglomerates which had a higher debt–equity ratio started being squeezed out and the failure of the Hanbo Steel Group and the Kia Motors Group had caused the financial industries' ratio of non-performing loans to climb even higher than before.

Table 1.1   Major economic indicators: Korean economy (1991–7)

	1991	1992	1993	1994	1995	1996	1997
1. Per capita income (US dollars)	6 745	6 988	7 484	8 467	10 037	10 543	9 511
2. Real GNP growth (%)	9.1	5.0	5.8	8.4	8.7	6.9	5.5
3. Gross savings rate (%)	36.1	34.9	35.2	35.4	36.2	34.8	34.6
4. Real consumption (%)	9.3	6.8	5.3	7.0	7.2	6.9	3.5
(Private consumption)	(9.5)	(6.6)	(5.7)	(7.6)	(8.3)	(6.8)	(3.1)
5. Real investment (%)	12.6	–0.8	5.2	11.8	11.7	7.1	–3.5
6. Nominal wage (%)	17.0	15.0	12.2	12.7	11.2	11.9	8.1
7. Consumer price (%)	9.3	4.5	5.8	5.6	4.7	4.9	6.6
8. Current account balance (billion US dollars)	–8.3	–3.9	1.0	–3.7	–8.5	–23.0	–8.6
Exports growth (%)	10.5	6.6	7.3	16.8	30.3	3.7	5.0
Imports growth (%)	16.7	0.3	2.5	22.1	32.0	11.3	–3.8
9. Stock price index* (7 January 1980:100)	610.9	678.4	866.2	1,027.4	882.9	651.2	376.3

Note: * End of period.

Sources: The Ministry of Finance and Economy, *Monthly Economy*, April 1999; The Bank of Korea, *National Accounts 1998* (preliminary), April 1999.

As shown in Table 1.1, major economic indicators of the Korean economy in 1996 were already pointing to a significant downturn, with the current account deficit at a record US$23 billion. Real consumption and investment declined from a growth rate of 7.2 per cent and 11.7 per cent in 1995 to 6.9 per cent and 7.1 per cent, respectively in 1996. But the growth rate of the nominal wage rate and inflation rate continued to increase, from 11.2 per cent and 4.7 per cent in 1995 to 11.9 per cent and 4.9 per cent in 1996, respectively. During 1996, the stock price index fell by 26 per cent, from 882.9 to 651.2. Entering 1997, there was a brief sign of improvement in macroeconomic indicators. The current account deficit during the first half of 1997 was cut drastically, to 242 million dollars from US1305 million during the corresponding period of 1996. Between the first half of 1996 and the first half of 1997, the growth rate of the consumer price index had declined from 3.3 per cent to 2.4 per cent and that of the nominal wage index in all industries had also declined from 9.8 per cent to 6.3 per cent. Therefore one could have concluded that the South Korean economy was following a typical pattern of slowing down, but not a drastic one that would bring about massive corporate failures in the immediate future. However, it was apparent that there would be further corporate failures in the process of reducing speculative bubbles and restructuring across industries by major conglomerates. By the end of October 1997, seven out of the nation's top 30 conglomerates, including the Kia Motors Group, filed for court-mediated protection or court-ordered receivership. The net consequence of excess competition with moral hazard and weak government started to manifest itself long before the financial crisis.

The signs of accumulated inefficiency in Korea's industrial sector can be detected in many areas. According to a recent report by the Korea International Trade Association, the foreign exchange earnings ratio of Korean exports, which is defined as the ratio of value-added created net of export-induced import to the total value-added, started to decline continuously from the peak of 67.9 per cent in 1989 to the level of 55.9 per cent in 1997. The 1995 Input–Output Table published by the Bank of Korea (1998) indicates that the ratio of external dependence, defined as the ratio of export and import in total domestic demand, declined from 25.8 per cent in 1985 to 23.4 per cent in 1990, but started increasing again, to 24.9 per cent. This is about three times the ratio of Japan (8.9 per cent). In particular, Korea's ratio of import dependence (13.2 per cent) is much higher than Japan's ratio (4 per cent). The table also compares the investment requirement for producing 1000 Won of value-added: Japan (294 Won), Taiwan (234 Won) and Korea (390 Won) in 1995. It had been 301 Won in Korea in 1985. The recent time-series estimates of economy-wide gross real rate of return in Pyo and Nam (1998) show a secular pattern of decline, from the 18 per cent level in the early 1980s to the 9 per cent level in the mid-1990s, which was lower than Japan's (12 per cent). Pyo and Ahn (1998) estimate that the average price–cost margin of Korean manufacturing industries increased from 0.279 to 0.372.

It is not surprising to observe that the accumulated inefficiency in the industrial sector ultimately shows up in the form of a higher debt–equity ratio in the balance sheet and an increasing volume of non-performing loans in the banks. According to a report released by the Fair Trade Commission, the average debt–equity ratio of the top-30 business groups deteriorated drastically, from 386.5 per cent in 1996 to 518.9 per cent in 1997. The Korea Development Institute reports that, if corporate restructuring is postponed, the total amount of bad loans could reach 100 trillion Won (US$71.4 billion at the exchange rate of 1400 Won per dollar), which is about 25 per cent of GDP. The Bank Supervisory Board also reports that the nine business groups which have filed court-mediated or court-ordered receivership so far have a total loan amount of 20.3 trillion Won (US$14.5 billion) which represents about two-thirds of total bad loans outstanding in the entire banking sector (9.6 trillion Won by the banks and 10.7 trillion Won by non-bank financial institutions). According to the Security Supervisory Board, the total amount of operating loss by 92 major companies of the top-30 business groups in 1997 reached 509.5 billion Won (US$ 363.9 billion). When their accounts are combined, eliminating double counting of the sales amount within the same business group as required in submitting to the authority, the loss amount increased sevenfold to 3584 billion Won (US$2560 billion).

UNEMPLOYMENT AND INDUSTRIAL RESTRUCTURING: A POLICY DILEMMA

In order to assess the magnitude of industrial trauma after the announcement of the IMF bailout of 3 December 1997, we need to look at the movement in key macroeconomic indicators: interest rates, unemployment rate, industrial production and investment trend, balance of payments and foreign exchange reserves. As shown in Table 1.2, the high interest rate policy as mandated by the IMF continued throughout the first two quarters of 1998. The imposition of the Bank for International Settlements (BIS) standards on the banks and the closing of several merchant banks created a tremendous credit crunch. Many banks refused to open letters of credit for importers to meet the BIS standards. As a result, there have been widespread corporate bankruptcies and layoffs. The foreign exchange market restored some confidence as more than 95 per cent of Korea's short-term loans were rescheduled by its creditor banks and the Foreign Exchange Stabilization bond of US$4 billion was successfully issued during the first quarter of 1998. The Won–dollar rate, which at one time during December 1997, soared to the level of 1950 Won per dollar, had been stabilized to the level of 1350–1400 Won per dollar by the end of April 1998. This enabled the Korean government to lower interest rates below the 20 per cent level after consultation with the IMF.

Table 1.2   Economic indicators of Korea after the currency crisis of December 1997

	1997 Dec	Jan	1998 Feb	Mar
1. Interest rates (%)				
Merchant bank prime rate	21.4	34.2	25.4	20.1
Corporate bond yield	28.9	18.5	20.5	18.3
Call rate (overnight)	21.3	25.3	23.4	22.1
2. Banks' loan amount (billion won)		7 285	2 371	527
1996 March				2 045
1997 March				4 685
3. Unemployment rate	3.1	4.5	5.9	6.5
1,000 persons	658	934	1 235	1 378
4. Production and investment (growth rate %)				
Production	3.0	−10.8	−1.7	−10.1
Investment	−2.1	−31.8	−26.2	−36.7
5. Export and trade balance				
Export growth rate (%)	9.3	0.3	21.6	7.0
Trade balance	−8 452	1 510	3 283	3 737
6. National accounts	1997	1997 1/4	1998 1/4	
GDP	5.5	5.7	−3.8	
Consumption	3.5	4.4	−9.5	
(Private)	3.1	4.2	−10.3	
(Government)	5.7	5.1	−4.3	
Investment	−3.5	0.3	−23.0	
(Structure)	2.7	0.8	−7.7	
(Equipment)	−11.3	−0.2	−40.7	
Exports	23.6	13.5	27.3	
Imports	3.8	8.1	−25.4	

Sources: The Bank of Korea, Principal Economic Indicators, May 5 1998. The Bank of Korea, *National Accounts 1998* First Quarter (Preliminary), May 21 1998.

As shown in Table 1.2, both the call rate and the corporate bond yield had come down from the 30 per cent level at the time when the crisis broke, to 18.4 per cent by the end of April 1998. However, the magnitude of the credit crunch was so severe that many exporters could not negotiate letters of credit. The total amount of bank loans in March declined drastically, from 2045 billion Won in 1996 and 4685 billion Won in 1997 to 527 billion Won in 1998. The unemployment rate started to climb very rapidly, from 3.1 per cent in December 1997 to 6.5 per cent in March 1998. The number of unemployed increased from 658 000 persons to 1 378 000 persons during the same period. According to a survey conducted by the Korea Federation of Industries, the top-30 business groups have reported having from 5 per cent to 30 per cent excess manpower which will have to be trimmed in the restructuring process. The Korea Association of Managers predicted that there would be 30 000 layoffs by large enterprises (above 300 full-time employment) in 1998 and 340 000 layoffs in 1999. By the end of 1998, the actual unemployment rate reached 7.4 per cent.

As the austerity measures continued, both industrial production and investment fell by record amounts during 1998, by 7.3 per cent and 21.1 per cent, respectively. According to a nationwide business survey conducted in 2321 firms by the Korea Development Bank, the investment plan for 1998 declined by 30.6 per cent from 1997, which is the largest reduction of investment since 1973.

According to the balance of payments statistics released by the Bank of Korea, the balance of payments surplus during 1998 reached US$40 billion. In terms of the customs clearance base, exports decreased by 2.8 per cent, while imports decreased by 35.4 per cent. In fact, the Bank of Korea reports that the average unit price index of exports during the first quarter of 1998 declined by 19.4 per cent from the corresponding period of 1997, which is a clear indication of worsening terms of trade. The unit price reductions by representative export items were semiconductors (48.6 per cent), electronics (38.6 per cent), fine instruments (25.9 per cent) and chemical products (19.5 per cent). Therefore, even though the balance of payments situation improved during the first quarter of 1998, this was mainly due to the heavy reduction of imports rather than to the real growth of exports. In addition, if we note the fact that Korean exports are still dependent on imported raw materials and intermediate goods with a lower ratio of foreign exchange earnings capacity, then the prospects for export growth are not that bright.

While the Korean government succeeded in restoring some confidence in the currency market by sticking to IMF-mandated reform programmes, it now faces a policy dilemma: it is forced to choose between a massive spread of unemployment and a wide-ranging restructuring in both the financial and the industrial sectors. At the beginning, there was an expectation that a quick and sharp restructuring would be better than a prolonged one and that the spread of unemployment would be inevitable but could be contained, too. But the actual magnitude of industrial trauma turned out to be much greater than expected and therefore, at the present time, there is an intense debate in Korea on the speed and the scope of restructuring and on the optimal sequencing of financial and industrial restructuring.

PROSPECT AND POLICY IMPLICATIONS

According to recent debt statistics confirmed by both the Korean government and the IMF, the total foreign debt increased by almost three times between the end of 1992 and the end of 1997, from US$42.8 billion (US$18.5 billion short-term and US$24.3 billion long-term debt) to US$120.8 billion (US$51.3 billion short-term and US$69.5 billion long-term debt). Assuming an average interest rate of 8 per cent, the estimated payments of interest alone could amount to US$9.7 billion. With such a large amount of debt overhang, it will be very difficult to regain growth momentum, unless Korea succeeds in going through a painful but extensive restructuring programme. Now the question is the mode and the scope of such a programme.

The Organization for Economic Cooperation and Development (OECD) predicted in its quarterly economic outlook (1998, first quarter) that Korea's real growth rate in 1998 and 1999 would be –0.2 per cent and 4 per cent, inflation rate 10.5 per cent and 6.6 per cent, current account surplus US$15 billion and greater than US$15 billion, and unemployment rate 5.7 per cent, and 6.3 per cent respectively. They noted that, even though the exchange rate and interest rates would be stabilized in time, there would remain a danger of social unrest from massive layoffs and further corporate bankruptcies.

The Korea Development Institute (KDI) released two alternative projections. One scenario, which is likely after a quick successful restructuring, forecasts a growth rate of –1.4 per cent (1998), 3.1 per cent (1999) and 5.1 per cent (2,000) with unemployment rates of 6.3 per cent, 7.0 per cent and 6.1 per cent, respectively. The other scenario, which is to follow if such a restructuring programme fails, estimates a growth rate of –3.1 per cent, –0.4 per cent and 1.4 per cent with unemployment rate of 6.3 per cent, 8.4 per cent and 8.4 per cent, respectively. KDI recommends a bond-financed restructuring package of 10 trillion Won.

At the present time, the Korean government seems to favour a quick and sharp simultaneous restructuring of both the financial and the corporate sector during the period of five months starting May 1998. However, in my judgment, the reform process needs to be sequenced, in such a way that the financial sector reform precedes the corporate restructuring reform, because the former is more controllable and does not endanger the property right. Under the current average debt–equity ratio of 5–6:1 and the effective interest rates well above 20 per cent, few companies will survive unless they go through restructuring on their own. Therefore the government needs not to intervene in the process of corporate restructuring. In addition, the restructuring of the financial sector itself should be based on an incentive system rather than a penalty system and it would be more desirable to provide incentives for M&A among good banks. The M&A among bad banks and weak non-bank financial institutions should be imposed, with necessary fiscal assistance to mitigate negative impacts. Most of all, it is important to be patient and to have a realistic picture of recovery. Instead of forcing a premature recovery within a year or so, it would be more optimal to go through a sequenced but steady and firm restructuring programme, because the social unrest which is likely to follow such a devastating financial crisis and a too harsh reform programme could endanger the entire recovery effort. While we have seen the danger of being too slow in Japan's recovery effort, we also see a quite opposite danger in Korea's recovery effort. Since the economy is not a transitional economy, international institutions such as the IMF and the World Bank should pay more respect to the endogenous system and should not discredit it entirely as a nepostic system. After all, it was the system which succeeded in pulling the country out of a state of absolute poverty.

REFERENCES

The Bank of Korea (1998), *1995 Input–Output Table*, Seoul.

Itoh, M., M. Okuno, K. Kiyono and K. Suzumura (1988), 'Industrial Policy as a Corrective to Market Failures', in Komiya *et al.* (eds) *Industrial Policy of Japan*.

Krugman, Paul (1998), 'What happened to Asia?', mimeo from Paul Krugman home page, January.

Okuno-Fujiwara, M. (1998), 'Interdependence of Industries, Coordination Failure and Strategic Promotion of an Industry', *Journal of International Economics*, **25**, 25–43.

Okuno-Fujiwara, M., A. Postlewaite and J. Roberts (1980), 'Oligopoly and Competition in Large Markets', *American Economic Review*, **70**, 22–31.

Pyo Hak K. (1993), 'The Transition in the Political Economy of South Korean Development', *Journal of Northeast Asian Studies*, **12** (4), Transaction Periodical Consortium.

Pyo, Hak K. (1996), 'Sustainability of Export Growth in East and Southeast Asia', invited paper at Asian Development Outlook Conference, Asian Development Bank, Manila, November.

Pyo, Hak K. (1997), 'Is Export-Led Growth in South Korea Sustainable?', paper presented at East Asian Seminars of East Asian Institute, Columbia University and Asia Society Meetings in Washington, DC, November.

Pyo, Hak. K. and S. Ahn (1998), 'The Differential Impacts of Exchange Rate Variations on Investment in Manufacturing by Industries: Korea (1985–96)', mimeo, Seoul National University, May.

Pyo, Hak K. and Kwang-Hee Nam (1998), 'Estimation of Cross-national Rates of Return and the Test of Convergence Hypothesis', Research Report, Korea Economic Research Institute.

Pyo, Hak K., K.H. Kim and I. Cheong (1996), 'Foreign Import Restrictions, WTO Commitments, and Welfare Effects: The Case of Republic of Korea', *Asian Development Review*, **14** (2), Asian Development Bank.

Scherer, F.M. (1980), *Industrial Market Structure and Economic Performance*, 2nd edn, Chicago: Rand-McNally.

Stiglitz, J.E. (1981), 'Potential Competition May Reduce Welfare', *American Economic Review*, **71**, May.

Suzumura, K. and K. Kiyono (1987), 'Entry Barriers and Economic Welfare', *Review of Economic Studies*, **54**, January.

2. The Asian financial crisis in perspective

Roberto Chang and Andrés Velasco[*]

AN OLD TYPE OF CRISIS

Whenever another crisis erupts in the world, it is tempting to identify it as an unprecedented syndrome and to develop a new theory to go with it. This has happened in the aftermath of the Asian crash. Some analysts have claimed that it is a new type of crisis in that it was not caused by an irresponsible government running large deficits and printing money to finance them. Others have claimed that it is also a new type of crisis, but for the opposite reason: an irresponsible government provided banks with guarantees, causing moral hazard, overinvestment and inflated asset prices that finally had to come tumbling down. In both cases, *novelty* is the operative concept.

These claims miss a central lesson from the Asian crisis. This crash is not a new and frightening creature just emerging from the depths of the Gulf of Borneo, but a *classic financial crisis*, the likes of which we have seen before in so-called 'emerging markets'. Chile in 1982 and Mexico in 1994 provide the clearest, but by no means the only, precedents. These classic crises have five distinguishing elements. First, *international illiquidity*, which sometimes results in outright collapse of the financial system (often but not always the commercial banks), is at the centre of the problem. The key issue is a mismatch of assets and liabilitites: a country's financial system is internationally illiquid if its potential short-term obligations in foreign currency exceed the amount of foreign currency it can have access to on short notice. As we shall discuss later (and as has been argued at length in Chang and Velasco, 1998a, 1998b), the concept of international illiquidity is crucial, for it involves a fragile situation: it is a necessary and sufficient condition for financial crashes and/or balance of payments crises.

* We are indebted to Will Roberds and conference participants for useful comments and suggestions, and to Mike Chriszt and Vincenzo Guzzo for their able assistance in assembling data. The views expressed here are ours and not necessarily those of the Federal Reserve Bank of Atlanta or the Federal Reserve System. In particular, any errors and omissions are ours alone.

Second, the illiquidity of the financial system is almost always rooted in a previous bout of financial liberalization, which accentuates the maturity mismatch between international assets and liabilities. In addition, capital flows from abroad, caused by an opening of the capital account and/or falls in world interest rates, magnify the problem by making available huge amounts of resources that can be intermediated by domestic banks. If short in maturity, as they were in the latter stages of the Mexican and Asian episodes, additional foreign loans can sharply increase the vulnerability of domestic banks: a creditor's panic, that is, a creditor's refusal to roll over these short-term loans, may render a self-fulfilling bank run possible.

Third, bad policy, in the conventional sense of unsustainably large, money-financed deficits, is not to blame. A striking fact shared by Chile (1982), Mexico (1994) and Asia (1997) is that governments in all of them were running either surpluses or small deficits. The problem may only become fiscal ex post, in the sense that the cost of the bailout deteriorates the fiscal position.

Fourth, the collapse of fixed exchange rates occurs because stabilizing banks and keeping the exchange rate peg become mutually incompatible objectives. To help the banks, the central bank must pursue an expansionary policy, either to keep interest rates from rising (and further wrecking the banks) or to provide lender-of-last-resort funds. But in either case private agents will use the additional domestic currency to buy reserves, eventually causing the collapse of the fixed exchange rate. It is in this sense that we observe 'twin crises': a financial crisis and a balance of payments crisis.

Finally, the punishment is much greater than the crime. Moderately weak fundamentals (especially real exchange rate overvaluation) and small changes in exogenous circumstances (terms of trade, world interest rates) can cause large changes in asset prices and economic activity. The magnifying mechanism is the financial system, whose collapse causes costly asset liquidation and an unnecessarily large credit crunch.

In previous work (Chang and Velasco, 1998a, 1998b) we have discussed the theoretical aspects of classic financial crises in open economies.[1] In this chapter we shall argue that, by and large, the recent Asian crises fit the patterns just described and resemble in many ways the experience of countries like Chile in 1982 and Mexico in 1994. Fiscal policy was cautious in the preceding years. While real fundamentals, such as the real exchange rate and the current account deficit, did weaken in the run-up to the crises, the degree to which this happened varied substantially across the Asian economies in trouble. What these countries had in common, and to a striking degree, was a situation of international illiquidity evidenced by sharply rising ratios of hard currency short-term liabilities to liquid assets. Consequently, they were extremely vulnerable to a reversal of capital inflows, which occurred (and massively) in the second half of 1997. Bankruptcies, payments moratoria and asset-price collapses (including the exchange rate, the price of domestic money) proliferated. The financial panic fed on itself, causing foreign creditors to call in loans and depositors to withdraw funds from banks – all of which magnified the illiquidity of domestic financial institutions and forced yet another round of costly asset liquidation and price deflation.

This financial fragility had its roots in inappropriate microeconomic policies followed during previous years. As we document below, financial liberalization measures in Asia resulted in a deterioration of the international liquidity position of the financial system, much as happened in Chile and Mexico. These measures, carried out at a time of large capital inflows, created the conditions for a crisis. Much of the borrowing was in dollars and, especially in the period right before the crisis, short term. These two factors left domestic banks exposed to exchange risk and to the mood swings of lenders who had to roll over large loan volumes at short intervals.

The financial nature of the Asian crisis has confronted policy makers with a number of difficult tradeoffs in designing an appropiate response. The potential conflicts had, once again, been confronted by some of the financially distressed Latin countries. One difficulty has to do with the management of monetary policy and the exchange rate. On the one hand, loose money (much of it aimed at supplying liquidity to banks) may help forestall the panic and a depreciated exchange rate may improve competitiveness; on the other hand, depreciation fears may feed on themselves and spiral out of control, making it increasingly expensive for domestic firms to service foreign currency-denominated loans. A second conundrum has to do with how forcefully to proceed in closing insolvent banks and forcing weak ones to recapitalize. Swift bank closures minimize moral hazard dangers but, if depositors have difficulty distinguishing sound from unsound institutions, may trigger runs on healthy banks. Forced recapitalization (expressed in higher capital–asset ratios) may force banks to curtail credit, in turn exacerbating the illiquidity of troubled borrowers and possibly worsening the quality of banks' loan portfolios.

Finally, the recent wave of financial meltdowns forces us to revisit some policy lessons for emerging markets. The first has to do with the dangers of fixed exchange rates in a context of large capital inflows and potential financial fragility. The second stresses the fragility of financial liberalization that is not coupled with much improved regulatory oversight. The third ponders the potential benefits of policies that discourage short-term foreign borrowing, particularly by domestic banks. The fourth underscores the importance of an international lender of last resort in circumstances in which coordination failure on the part of creditors can cause a bank and/or a balance of payments crisis.

The chapter is organized as follows. The next section discusses two cases of crises, Chile (1982) and Mexico (1994) that in many ways resemble recent Asian episodes. The third section reviews the 'conventional' macroeconomic fundamentals in Asian countries before their recent crises. The fourth section presents the key concept of international illiquidity and discusses evidence showing that such a condition did in fact characterize the Asian pre-crisis situation. The fifth section discusses three factors (financial liberalization, shortening of the foreign debt structure and the currency denomination of assets and liabilities) that explain how the Asian countries became internationally illiquid. The sixth section discusses how the potential for a crisis implied by international illiquidity was translated into an actual financial crash and the collapse of fixed exchange rates in Asia, while the concluding section discusses lessons for policy.

THE PRECEDENT FROM LATIN AMERICA: CHILE (1982) AND MEXICO (1994)[2]

Before their respective crises in 1982 and 1994, Chile and Mexico were seen as examples of successful economic reform. The two were highly market-oriented economies that had liberalized internal and external markets, and had gone through successful stabilization, deregulation and privatization of state-owned enterprises. Tables 2.1 and 2.2 show some results. Economic growth was impressive in Chile and moderate in Mexico; in both countries, inflation was falling. Most importantly, they were both paragons of fiscal rectitude, having rectified the fiscal populism of earlier governments. Chile ran a fiscal surplus every year between (and including) 1976 and 1981. Similarly, Mexico's operational balance was in surplus every year between 1990 and 1994.[3]

International markets amply rewarded both countries for their virtuous behaviour. Capital inflows were massive, averaging more than 6.7 per cent of Mexican gross domestic product (GDP) in 1990–94. The large inflows pushed the real exchange rate (RER) up, as shown by Tables 2.1 and 2.2. Chile's appreciation was 30 per cent between 1978 (the year an exchange rate stabilization was adopted) and year-end 1981. Estimates for Mexico's varied, but common opinion put the real appreciation accumulated in 1988–93 at 15–20 per cent. In neither country was there agreement that the observed appreciation constituted misalignment. Both governments (and many observers) argued that the bulk of such relative price changes was an equilibrium phenomenon due to trade liberalization, deregulation and other competitiveness-enhancing structural reforms. The current account (CA) deteriorated nonetheless, and reached alarming proportions in both countries (14 per cent of GDP in Chile in 1991, nearly 7 per cent in Mexico in 1994). But markets seemed not to mind, and capital inflows continued at constant (and even falling) interest rate spreads until shortly before the collapse. As a result, and in spite of the large external deficits, international reserves were rising until late 1981 in Chile, and early 1994 in Mexico.

Table 2.1   Chile macro indicators

	Growth (%)	Inflation (%)	Fiscal surplus (% of GDP)	RER	CA (% of GDP)	Reserves (mn US$)
1979	8.28	33.33	4.8	140.2	−5.72	1 938
1980	7.78	33.33	5.5	169.9	−7.15	3 123
1981	5.53	18.75	0.8	175.1	−14.49	3 213
1982	−14.09	10.53	−3.4	134.8	−9.48	1 815
1983	−0.73	23.81	−2.8	144.9	−5.65	2 036

Note: An increase in the RER denotes real appreciation.

Sources: IFS, JP Morgan.

Table 2.2   Mexico macro indicators

	Growth (%)	Inflation (%)	Fiscal surplus (% of GDP)	RER	CA (% of GDP)	Reserves (mn US$)
1991	4.17	22.7	2.9	103.8	−5.13	17 726
1992	3.59	15.48	2.9	111.6	−7.31	18 942
1993	2.00	9.74	2.1	120.8	−5.81	25 110
1994	4.44	6.95	0.5	97.7	−6.98	6 278
1995	−6.13	35.00		101.7	−0.23	16 847

Sources: IFS, JP Morgan.

During the upswing, domestic financial markets boomed. This was a result of both deregulation and the intermediation of large capital inflows from abroad. Both countries privatized their largest banks (Chile in the mid-1970s and Mexico in the early 1990s) while engaging in a fully-fledged round of financial liberalization. Interest rate ceilings were abolished, required reserve ratios lowered, regulations concerning foreign currency-denominated assets and liabilites relaxed, boundaries between banks and other financial institutions redrawn. Indicators of 'financial deepening', such as the ratio of M2 to GDP, rose quickly. So did lending by both banks and non-banks: in Chile, the share of financial system loans to the private sector in GDP rose from 5 per cent in 1974 to over 82 per cent in 1982; for Mexico, this share went from 26 per cent in 1991 to 41 per cent in 1994 (see Table 2.3). Predictably, asset prices boomed in both countries. The real stock price index nearly quadrupled in Chile in the three years after 1978; similarly, prices of land and urban real estate skyrocketed.

Several factors – which reappear with a vengeance in the more recent experience of Asian countries – conspired to transform the financial boom into a particularly dangerous phenomenon. The first was the currency denomination of assets and liabilities. Domestic banks borrowed abroad and in foreign currency, and also took an increasing stock of dollar-denominated deposits at home. In turn, they lent at home, mostly in domestic currency. This meant that banks were very exposed to exchange risk, not a concern early on, when promises to sustain fixed exchange rates indefinitely enjoyed some credibility, but troublesome later when devaluations became a fact. It also meant that central banks were hindered in their ability to serve as lenders of last resort vis-à-vis the domestic financial system: monetary authorities could print pesos but not dollars, and their own reserves of foreign currency were limited.

Table 2.3   Credit to private sector (% of GDP)

Chile		Mexico	
1979	34.09	1991	26.13
1980	43.38	1992	32.67
1981	51.08	1993	33.51
1982	82.55	1994	41.47
1983	74.11	1995	30.44

Source: IFS.

A second factor was the large (and, over time, growing) share of short-term loans abroad. What is striking is that, in spite of all the bullish rhetoric about successful economic reform, long-term flows (including foreign investment: FDI) constituted a small portion, while short-term portfolio flows took the lion's share. Table 2.4 shows that the behaviour of private capital inflows was largely dominated by non-FDI flows, which are likely to reflect the ins and outs of hot money . In Mexico, short-term borrowing was, in addition, a large problem for the government; this matters because, if the government is called upon to serve as lender of last resort to the banks, the real resources available for this purpose are its international reserves net of the short-term government liabilities which may be called in at a time of trouble. As Sachs *et al.* (1996a) discuss in some detail, government debt arose, not because of fiscal deficits, but because of the Bank of Mexico's attempt to sterilize capital inflows, starting in 1990. Then, when world interest rates rose in 1994, the authorities attempted to play on a very steep yield curve, borrowing short on the expectation that the international rate hike (compounded domestically by increased political risk) would be temporary. The Mexican government's inability to roll over its large stock of short-term debt (in particular, the infamous *Tesobonos*) was to prove crucial in triggering the financial crisis in December 1994.

Table 2.4   Private capital inflows (% of GDP)

	Chile			Mexico	
	Total	Non-FDI		Total	Non-FDI
1980	12.3	11.5	1992	7.5	6.2
1981	14.9	13.7	1993	8.0	6.8
1982	4.1	2.4	1994	3.1	0.2
1983	5.6	4.9	1995	0.4	−3.5

Source: World Bank.

In both Chile (1982) and Mexico (1994), the net effect of the trends just described was to make their financial system internationally illiquid: short-term claims on the consolidated financial system (including the central bank), either in foreign currency or readily convertible to foreign currency at the fixed exchange rate, far exceeded available liquid resources. As we discuss in more detail below, illiquidity is partially captured by the ratio of M2 to international reserves; Table 2.5 reveals that this ratio not only exceeded one in both cases, but it also rose rapidly in the build-up to the crisis.

In both cases, the boom in financial intermediation continued unabated, in spite of some deterioration of fundamentals, until a sharp break in expectations. The loss of confidence was partially triggered by exogenous events, such as the 1982 South Atlantic War and the 1994 political violence in Mexico, and precipitated a reversal in the direction of capital flows. In both cases, and particularly in Mexico, the degree to which the eventual collapse seems to have been unanticipated by investors is striking. Interest rate spreads on Mexican assets, for instance, were essentially constant between March 1994 and the outbreak of the crisis in December.[4]

Authorities reacted to the mounting troubles in similar ways. On the one hand, they were extremely reluctant to give up the fixed exchange rate systems in which so much credibility and so much political capital had been invested. The Central Bank of Chile and the Bank of Mexico spent large quantities of reserves defending the peg and held on to the bitter end. Mexico, for instance, allowed its international reserves to fall from nearly US$30 billion in early 1994 to US$6 billion at the end of the year. On the other hand, central banks were hindered in their defence of the peg by the fragility of banks, and by the expectation on the part of the public (correctly, it turned out) that growing bank losses would be partially monetized. The Bank of Mexico recognized as much in its 1995 Monetary Programme, arguing that, if capital outflows had not been sterilized (by increasing domestic credit), 'interest rates would have reached exorbitant levels, which would have affected debtors, including financial intermediaries, in an unfavourable way' (Banco de Mexico, 1995).

Table 2.5   M2 as a fraction of reserves

Chile		Mexico	
1979	2.39	1991	4.60
1980	2.29	1992	5.16
1981	2.87	1993	4.43
1982	5.24	1994	19.90
1983	3.67	1995	5.20

Source: IFS.

Liquidity crises occurred in both countries. Emblematic of the liquidity squeeze was the Mexican government's inability to find new takers for its maturing tens of billions of dollars in short-term bonds, forcing several auctions to be cancelled.[5] In Mexico, the abandonment of the peg, which finally came in late December, contributed to worsening investors' expectations even further. A financial panic set in.

The abandonment of the fixed parities brought into the open the financial crises that had been long in the making. Bank deposits fell as investors rushed to restructure their portfolios away from peso-denominated assets. Open bank runs were only prevented by the blanket government guarantees on deposits. As mentioned earlier, in the case of Mexico a run on government debt did take place, with investors refusing to roll over short-term bonds as they matured. Asset prices took a spectacular hit, with the stock market falling precipitously in both instances.

In the aftermath of the crash, domestic banks were revealed to be in very bad shape. Sharp devaluations and the fall in economic activity did much harm to bank health. As Table 2.6 reveals, the share of non-performing loans in bank assets rose sharply. In Chile, bank troubles forced the government to take direct action. By early 1983, 11 commercial banks (including the country's two largest private commercial banks) and five finance companies (so-called 'financieras') were under government intervention or had been liquidated.[6] In both countries sizable programmes of loan rescheduling for debtors and asset swaps with troubled banks were implemented by the authorities. The total costs of these bailouts remain unclear, but they have been estimated to be as high as 12 per cent of GDP for Mexico and 20 per cent for Chile.

Table 2.6   Non-performing loans (% of total loans)

Chile		Mexico	
1980	0.9	1993	7.26
1981	2.4	1994	9.02
1982	8.2	1995	12.26
1983	18.7	1996	11.98

Sources: Velasco and Cabezas (1998), Banco de Mexico.

One last peculiar feature of these episodes concerns the behaviour of output and asset prices. Financial turmoil, a sharp credit crunch and high interest rates took a large toll: output fell by 14.2 per cent in Chile and nearly 7 per cent in Mexico in the year of their respective crises. Pessimism was rife, and for the same reasons as in Asia today: talk of inefficient investments, excessive allocation of capital to the non-traded goods sector (shopping malls, luxury office buildings and the like), lack of transparency, corruption and so on. A protracted recession was commonly forecasted. But these pessimistic expectations were wide of the mark. After a decline of about a year or so, both economies began growing very quickly, with Chile's expanding by 4.8 per cent per annum between 1984 and 1987, and Mexico expanding by an average of 6.1 per cent in 1996–7. Asset prices recovered rapidly as well.

MACROECONOMIC FUNDAMENTALS IN EAST ASIA

The classic Krugman (1979) model blamed money-financed budget deficits for reserve erosion and the eventual collapse of an exchange rate peg. This focus corresponded well to the facts in some currency crisis in emerging markets – Mexico in 1976 and Argentina, Brazil, Peru and (again) Mexico in the early and mid-1980s – which could readily be attributed to fiscal irresponsibility. A first and striking characteristic of the Asian economies is that their fiscal performances were rather far from this conventional account, and rather close to the Chilean and Mexican experience discussed in the previous section.

Table 2.7 summarizes the conventional macroeconomic fundamentals in the so-called Asean-5 countries (Korea, Malaysia, Indonesia, Thailand and the Philippines), the countries hardest affected by recent crises. Moderate fiscal

Table 2.7 Asean-5 countries: basic macroeconomic data (percentage points)

	Real GDP growth		Inflation		Govt. surplus		Savings/GDP		Investment/GDP	
	90–96 avg.	1996	90–96 avg.	1996	90–96 avg.	1996	90–96 avg.	1996	90–96 avg.	1996
Indonesia	7.3	8.0	8.6	6.4	–0.2	0.0	28.4	30.6	33.4	32.7
Korea	7.7	7.1	6.4	4.9	–0.5	0.2	35.4	33.9	36.5	36.8
Malaysia	8.8	8.6	4.0	3.6	–0.4	–0.5	34.6	40.6	37.0	42.2
Philippines	2.8	5.7	10.7	8.4	–2.2	–0.5	19.1	22.7	22.5	23.9
Thailand	8.5	5.5	5.1	5.9	2.6	1.5	28.6	31.5	40.3	42.5

Sources: IMF, JP Morgan.

deficits in a few countries (Korea, Malaysia and, especially, the Philippines) in the early 1990s were virtually eliminated by 1996. In fact, these countries were so prudent that they were often lauded for their tightening fiscal policy in response to capital inflows and incipient overheating.[7]

Two other reassuring features of the Asian economies resulted from this strong fiscal stance. The first (see Table 2.8) is that public debt as a share of GDP was low, if compared both to other emerging markets and to OECD countries. The other is that monetary growth could be kept reasonably tight, resulting in low inflation: Table 2.7 shows that inflation in the 1990s was held at 10 per cent or below, with no clear tendency to increase in any of the countries. Finally, international reserves were either stable or growing in all countries, as shown by Table 2.9. In short, we have a picture far removed from the crisis syndrome described by the so-called 'first-generation' models à la Krugman.

Table 2.8   Public sector debt (% of GDP)

	Indonesia	Korea	Malaysia	Philippines	Thailand
1990	45.7	8.3	81.3	51.3	18.4
1991	40.3	11.5	76.4	49.7	13.3
1992	42.7	11.5	66.1	52.8	10.9
1993	37.5	10.9	59.3	67.1	8.4
1994	36.6	10.0	50.1	56.4	5.8
1995	30.9	9.0	42.8	n.a	4.7
1996	24.1	8.6	n.a	n.a	3.7

Source: World Bank.

Table 2.9   International reserves (mn US$)

	Indonesia	Korea	Malaysia	Philippines	Thailand
1990	7 459	14 793	9 754	924	13 305
1991	9 258	13 701	10 886	3 246	17 517
1992	10 449	17 121	17 228	4 403	20 359
1993	11 263	20 228	27 249	4 676	24 473
1994	12 133	25 639	25 423	6 017	29 332
1995	13 708	32 678	23 774	6 372	35 982
1996	18 251	34 037	27 009	10 030	37 731

Source: IMF.

Also revealing is the behaviour of output in the Asean-5 countries. Some currency crises, especially the exchange rate mechanism (ERM) collapse of 1992, have been blamed on stagnation and mounting unemployment, which arguably undermined the credibility of fixed exchange rates and eventually caused a run by panicky investors trying to protect themselves from an impending devaluation.[8] It has even been argued that models in this 'second generation' can explain the 1994 episode in Mexico, where the combination of a slow-growing economy and a highly contested presidential election probably kept the authorities from raising interest rates enough to defend the peg. Anyway, the current Asian episode could not be more different. As Table 2.7 shows, Asian growth rates were very fast throughout the 1990s, including 1996. In this they resemble Chile in the early 1980s, where growth averaged 7.9 per cent in the five years leading to the 1982 crash.

Table 2.10   Current account surplus (% of GDP)

	Indonesia	Korea	Malaysia	Philippines	Thailand
1990	−2.8	−0.9	−1.9	−6.1	−8.5
1991	−3.7	−3.0	−8.5	−2.3	−7.7
1992	−2.2	−1.5	−3.4	−1.9	−5.9
1993	−1.2	0.1	−4.2	−5.5	−5.3
1994	−1.4	−1.2	−5.7	−4.8	−8.1
1995	−3.2	−2.0	−7.7	−2.6	−7.6
1996	−3.3	−4.8	−6.5	−3.2	−7.5

Source: IMF.

As shown by Table 2.7, the Asean-5 countries saved a lot, and invested even more. Correspondingly, their current accounts were generally in deficit, as seen in Table 2.10. The interpretation of this performance was and remains ambiguous. While there is no clear theoretical reason why sustained current account imbalances should lead to a crisis, in the aftermath of the Mexican 1994 collapse both private investors and Washington multilaterals have regarded deficits exceeding a rule of thumb threshold (often 5 per cent of GDP) as a source of potential trouble. But the caveats are many. Table 2.10 shows that the Asian economies did indeed post some large deficits in 1990–96, but the deficits are only very large (systematically above 5 per cent) in Malaysia and Thailand. Paradoxically, Korea and Indonesia, arguably the hardest hit by the crisis, had the smaller deficits.[9] Moreover, formal econometric work fails to confirm the validity of the 5 per cent rule of thumb. In the Frankel and Rose (1996) study of 117 currency crises, the current account is no larger on average in crisis times than in tranquil times. Sachs *et al.* (1996c) also find that the current account is a poor predictor of trouble – in their case, of which countries were hit by the contagion effect of the Mexican crisis.

Sustained current account deficits may become 'unsustainable' once accumulated foreign debt becomes large,[10] but, as Table 2.11 shows, total foreign debt levels were moderate for all Asian countries in the sample, except for Indonesia, and even Indonesia's debt was not substantially greater than that of comparable countries. Latin American countries such as Chile and Peru ran much higher current account deficits in the 1990s, and had similar or worse debt situations, but nonetheless came out unscathed.

Table 2.11   Foreign debt exports

Year	Indonesia	Malaysia	Philippines	Thailand
1990	2.34	0.44	2.30	0.90
1991	2.37	0.43	2.19	1.00
1992	2.30	0.43	1.87	0.97
1993	2.13	0.48	1.87	1.06
1994	2.32	0.43	1.63	1.12
1995	2.34	0.40	1.19	1.12
1996	2.21	0.42	0.98	1.21

Memo	Argentina	Brazil	Chile	Mexico	Peru
1989	5.42	2.94	1.84	1.97	4.07
1996	2.96	2.94	1.41	1.36	3.52

Source: Global Development Finance 1998, World Bank.

Several observers contend that the Asian current account deficits were problematic in that they were caused by a loss of competitiveness. This view is consistent with the behaviour of the real exchange rate: as Table 2.12 shows, most of the Asean-5 economies experienced appreciation relative to 1990. This tendency sharpened in late 1995, as the US dollar (to which these countries' currencies were, de facto or de jure, pegged) gained on the Japanese yen.[11]

Real exchange rate appreciation is in fact a good predictor of currency crises in the making, as found for instance by Sachs *et al.* (1996b) and Frankel and Rose (1996). Yet several caveats are in order to interpret the Asean-5 data. The first is that there is a great deal of heterogeneity accross country experiences. Numbers for the period between 1990 and year-end 1996 range from a 13 per cent real *depreciation* for Korea to a 16 per cent real *appreciation* for the Philippines. A second is the usual question of whether the observed

Table 2.12 Real effective foreign exchange rates

	Indonesia	Korea	Malaysia	Philippines	Thailand	Mexico	Argentina	Brazil	Chile
1987	101.1	87.0	111.1	99.0	95.2	95.1	86.2	61.9	100.2
1988	98.8	101.9	100.5	101.7	97.3	110.6	117.7	69.2	98.5
1989	101.9	106.2	102.9	108.2	99.3	101.7	70.2	93.1	97.8
1990	97.4	96.1	97.1	92.4	102.2	100.3	138.0	76.3	100.9
1991	99.6	91.5	96.9	103.1	99.0	103.8	112.0	71.7	106.2
1992	100.8	87.7	109.7	107.1	99.7	111.6	114.0	77.5	115.7
1993	103.8	85.2	111.0	97.4	101.9	120.8	114.7	86.2	112.7
1994	101.0	84.7	107.1	111.7	98.3	97.7	109.2	108.7	120.1
1995	100.5	87.7	106.9	109.5	101.7	77.2	110.6	96.6	120.8
1996	105.4	87.1	112.1	116.3	107.6	95.5	115.4	99.6	128.5
1997	62.3	59.2	84.8	90.8	72.3	106.1	123.0	107.4	133.4

Note: Data are for the end of period. Average 1990 = 100.

Source: JP Morgan.

appreciations do reflect misalignment. For standard Balassa–Samuelson reasons, one would expect rapidly growing economies such as these to experience substantial equilibrium appreciation, and that is precisely what more careful studies show.[12] The third caveat comes from comparisons with other countries as well as other times, which suggest that real appreciation in Asia was not a such a large problem. Table 2.12 shows that, in the last decade, emerging economies such as Argentina, Brazil and Chile experienced much greater appreciations, yet no crisis struck. Also, Table 2.12 shows that the change in the real exchange rate in the Asean-5 countries is much smaller if the reference point is taken to be 1988 or 1989 instead of 1990. All of this suggests that real overvaluation in Asia was neither so large nor a sufficient condition to trigger a financial crash.

Finally, the deterioration of conventional fundamentals in Asia seems too small to explain the magnitude of the subsequent crisis. As Calvo and Mendoza (1996) suggested about Mexico, we are sceptical that the size of the punishment was justified by the hideousness of the sins. As estimated by Radelet and Sachs (1998), the Asian economies experienced a capital outflow of US$34 billion in the second half of 1997, equivalent to a negative shock of 3.6 per cent of GDP. Growth has fallen from highly positive to negative. Currencies trade for as little as 25 per cent of their mid-1997 value vis-à-vis the US dollar; the prices of stocks and real estate have fallen just as far. It is hard to understand the magnitude of this collapse without reference to the severe turmoil in the Asian financial sector. To that subject we now turn.

FINANCIAL FACTORS AND INTERNATIONAL ILLIQUIDITY IN ASIA

Financial collapse has clearly been the most spectacular aspect of the Asian meltdown.[13] Bank failures and closures have taken place in each of the Asean-5 nations. In Indonesia, 16 commercial banks were closed; in Korea, 14 out of 30 merchant banks were suspended; in Thailand, non-bank finance companies were the source of trouble, in an echo of the 1982 Chilean story: 58 out of 91 such firms had their operations stopped, with almost all of them scheduled for liquidation. In Thailand, Korea and Indonesia, domestic financial institutions (and, in Indonesia, non-financial firms) came to the brink of default on their external short-term obligations. For Korea and Thailand, default was prevented by an emergency rescheduling of liabilities. Indonesia had to declare an effective moratorium on debt service by its corporate sector in January 1998.

Financial collapse has been closely linked to the plunge in asset prices. Growing non-performing loans and capital losses caused by currency depreciation sharply reduced bank capital. Banks were forced to sell assets and curtail lending in order to move towards capital adequacy ratios required by regulators and the IMF.[14] In turn, the asset price plunge worsened bank capital shortages in those cases (particularly Korea) in which banks were allowed to hold some of their capital in stocks of other companies.

And financial collapse has been a prime cause of the sharp currency depreciations observed since mid-1997. Corsetti *et al.* (1998) document the paradoxical fact that several of the Asean-5 nations pursued low-interest rate policies until well into the crisis. Malaysia, for instance, waited until the ringitt had fallen by over 40 per cent vis-à-vis the dollar before tightening its monetary stance in December 1997. In addition, in some cases such as Thailand's, monetary authorities injected large amounts of resources into failing financial institutions, creating unwanted domestic currency that private agents were quick to try to turn into hard currency. Clearly, fragile and illiquid banks prevented central banks from raising interest rates sufficiently to defend their exchange rate pegs; but this could last only until international reserves were exhausted, at which point the pegs had to be abandoned and exchange rates plummeted.

In short, a main outcome of the recent Asian crisis has been a collapse of their financial systems. This observation suggests that the *explanation* of the crisis must also be financial in nature. Consequently, several 'financial' theories have been proposed to explain the Asian crash, each emphasizing a particular element of an obviously complex financial reality. In our view, both theory and evidence strongly indicate that the vulnerability of financial systems in the region resulted from their *international illiquidity*.

The concept of international illiquidity will be the key organizing principle in the remainder of our analysis. It refers to a maturity mismatch of a financial system's international assets and liabilities. More precisely, we will say that *a country's financial system is internationally illiquid if its potential short-term obligations in foreign currency exceed the amount of foreign currency it can have access to on short notice.* This concept is crucial for, as we shall discuss later (and as we have shown in Chang and Velasco 1998a, 1998b), international illiquidity involves a fragile situation: it is a necessary and sufficient condition for financial crashes and/or balance of payments crises.

Were the Asean-5 countries internationally illiquid at the time their crises erupted? Answering this question requires making the concept of 'international illiquidity' operational, which requires identifying the institutions that comprise a country's 'financial system', as well as their relevant 'short-term assets and liabilities in foreign currency'. The appropriate definitions depend on government policy.

Our definition of a financial system will naturally include domestic banks and other domestic financial entities that perform bank-like operations (such as

Thailand's finance companies). In addition, because Asian governments were committed to act as lenders of last resort of private financial institutions, the Asian central banks will be included as well. This inclusion is justified because, in the presence of such a commitment, a crisis affecting private financial institutions will force a central bank to honour it, which may pull the government itself into the crisis. Indeed, we shall argue later that a balance of payments crisis is best understood as a situation in which a central bank runs out of international liquidity in an attempt to fight a financial crisis.

Accordingly, an ideal definition of the liquid international assets of the financial system would include not only the short-term external assets of private financial institutions, but also the amount of foreign currency available to the central bank for last resort lending in the event of a crisis. (Notice that the latter should, in principle, exclude the amount of reserves that have already been committed, implicitly or explicitly, to other uses in a crisis, such as the repayment of *Tesobonos* in Mexico 1994.) The definition would also include the amount of international loans that the financial system can have access to in the short run as well as the liquidation value of fixed assets. While a measure of short-term international liquid assets embodying these desiderata can perhaps be constructed, because of data constraints we use the stock of international reserves of the monetary authorities to proxy such an ideal measure.

Similarly, an ideal definition of the short-term international liabilities of the financial system would include its short-term foreign debt as well as demandable deposits denominated in foreign currency; the only difference, from the viewpoint of international illiquidity, is that the former are obligations against foreigners while the latter are obligations with domestic residents. In addition, if there is a fixed exchange rate, demandable deposits in domestic currency should also be included, since fixed rates imply that such deposits are effectively obligations in foreign currency. The relevant data on deposits in the consolidated financial system are available from International Finance Statistics (IFS), but the situation for international debt is less satisfactory. As discussed by Corsetti *et al.* (1998), the most useful source of evidence on short-term external debt is published by the Bank for International Settlements. One observation about BIS data is that they are restricted to indebtedness of a country's residents against foreign banks. More importantly for our purposes, available BIS tables are not broken down sufficiently to identify the short-term external debt of the financial system. However, they do contain data on the short-term external debt (against BIS reporting banks) of a country as a whole, as well as on the amount of external debt (including debt of longer maturity) contracted by domestic banks. These aspects of the data force us to treat domestic deposits and external debt separately.

In spite of the data limitations just noted, the evidence on the Asean-5 countries does suggest that the international liquidity position of their financial systems deteriorated before the crisis. This can be seen most clearly from the BIS data on foreign bank lending. Table 2.13 describes the behaviour of the ratio of short-term loans from international banks to reserves; obviously, an increase in the ratio implies a higher likelihood of international illiquidity. The table shows that the ratio increased between mid-1994 and mid-1997 in every case except for Indonesia, where the ratio was stable. (In Korea, Malaysia and Thailand, the ratio had also increased between 1990 and 1994. It had fallen in Indonesia but not by much. It had fallen sharply in the Philippines, but this was probably an anomaly following the Philippine Brady debt restructuring of 1991.)

Table 2.13   Short-term debt v. reserves

Short-term debt (mn US$)					
	Indonesia	Korea	Malaysia	Philippines	Thailand	Total
June 90	10 360	15 528	1 761	3 019	7 026	37 694
June 94	18 882	34 908	8 203	2 646	27 151	91 790
June 97	34 661	70 182	16 268	8 293	45 567	174 971

International reserves (mn US$)					
	Indonesia	Korea	Malaysia	Philippines	Thailand	Total
June 90	4 693	14 642	8 114	948	11 882	40 279
June 94	10 915	21 684	32 608	6 527	27 375	99 109
June 97	20 336	34 069	26 586	9 781	31 361	122 133

Debt to reserves ratio					
	Indonesia	Korea	Malaysia	Philippines	Thailand	Total
June 90	2.208	1.061	0.217	3.185	0.591	0.936
June 94	1.730	1.610	0.252	0.405	0.992	0.926
June 97	1.704	2.060	0.612	0.848	1.453	1.433

Sources: BIS, IMF.

It is also notable that the levels of the short-term debt to reserves ratio at the end of 1996 were substantially over one in Korea, Indonesia and Thailand. This suggests a financially fragile situation, in the sense that international reserves would not have been sufficient to repay the short-term debt had foreign banks decided not to roll it over. While the level of the short-term debt to reserves ratio was below one in Malaysia and the Philippines (the two countries among the Asean-5 least affected by the crisis), it doubled between mid-1994 and mid-1997. A comparison with Latin American countries is also telling. The short-term debt–reserves ratio was stable and below one in Brazil, Chile, Colombia and Peru; in Argentina and Mexico, it was 1.2 in mid-1997, thus exceeding one but not by much, and had been falling.

The BIS tables suggest, in addition, that the proportion of foreign bank lending intermediated by the domestic banking sector was stable in each case except Thailand. In the latter case, the decline in the share of the domestic banking sector in foreign borrowing is attributable, by and large, to the increased importance of finance companies. Finance companies seem to have emerged in response to regulatory distortions, but performed bank-like functions. In fact, they are included in the International Finance Statistics as part of the group, 'Other Banking Institutions'; the IFS notes that, although finance companies were 'not licensed to accept deposits from the public', they 'issued promissory notes at terms comparable to the time deposits at commercial banks'.[15] The importance of Thailand's finance companies in the financial systems was also underscored by the fact that the Bank of Thailand was committed to supporting them as a lender of last resort.[16]

The evidence thus strongly indicates that the short-term external liabilities of the financial system were growing faster than its liquid international assets. In our interpretation, this trend deteriorated the international liquidity position of the Asean-5 countries to the point where a loss of confidence from foreign creditors could bring the financial system to a crisis.

The behaviour of *domestic* deposits vis-à-vis international reserves suggests a similar picture. Table 2.14 shows the evolution of the ratio of M2 to foreign reserves for the Asean-5 economies before their crises. The high level of the M2–reserves ratio seems consistent with the hypothesis of international illiquidity. At the end of 1996, this ratio was almost 7 in Korea and Indonesia, and 4.5 in the Philippines. At the same time, the same ratio was only about 3.4 in Argentina and Brazil, and less than two in Chile and Peru. It was higher in Mexico (4.65), but there it had been falling; it is notable (and maybe more than a coincidence) that the M2–reserves ratio had been over 7 in Mexico in June 1994, just before its own crisis! The ratio in Malaysia was 3.3 at the end of 1994, and hence comparable to that of Argentina and Brazil; however, the ratio had been increasing.

The M2–reserves ratio was stable or increasing in each of the Asean-5 countries, except in Thailand, where it was falling. The behaviour of the Thai ratio most likely reflects, as we discussed above, the fact that the relevant measure of the liabilities of Thailand's financial system vis-à-vis domestic residents should include the promissory notes of the finance companies, which are not included in M2 but became increasingly important. In short, the ratio of M2 to reserves in the Asean-5 countries had been either high or increasing in each case but Thailand, whose behaviour likely reflects the accounting of finance companies. By contrast, in comparable Latin American countries the M2–reserves ratio was relatively high only in Mexico, where it had been falling drastically. This evidence, which proxies the trends and levels of the short-term asset/liability positions of the Asian financial systems vis-à-vis domestic depositors, also strongly favours the view that the Asean-5 countries had a problem of international illiquidity when the crisis started. It should be repeated that, because the Asean-5 countries had effectively fixed exchange rates, our accounting includes domestic currency deposits as obligations in international currency. The relative magnitudes of deposits to international reserves implies that the latter would not have been sufficient to honour the outstanding stock of deposits at the fixed exchange rate. Given this condition, a run by domestic depositors was bound to result in either the bankruptcy of the financial system or the forced abandonment of the fixed exchange rate system.

Table 2.14   M2 as a multiple of international reserves

	Indonesia	Korea	Malaysia	Philippines	Thailand
1990	6.16	6.48	2.91	16.33	4.49
1991	5.51	8.33	2.99	4.82	4.10
1992	5.61	7.20	2.64	4.35	4.10
1993	6.09	6.91	2.09	4.90	4.05
1994	6.55	6.45	2.47	4.86	3.84
1995	7.09	6.11	3.33	5.86	3.69
1996	6.50	6.51	3.34	4.50	3.90

Source: IMF.

FACTORS BEHIND ASIAN FINANCIAL VULNERABILITY

We have so far argued that the Asean-5 countries were in a state of international illiquidity, which made them vulnerable to financial crises. An obvious question is: how did they arrive at such a precarious position – what caused their international liquidity positions to deteriorate? We believe that three factors were crucial.

Financial Liberalization Prior to the Crisis

In the late 1980s and the 1990s, the governments of the Asean-5 countries implemented policies designed to move away from 'financial repression' and towards a freer, more market-oriented financial system. This trend included the deregulation of interest rates and the easing of reserve requirements on banks; in Korea, for instance, lending interest rates were liberalized between 1991 and 1993, and marginal reserve requirements, which had been as high as 30 per cent around 1990, were reduced to 7 per cent in 1996. In addition, policies oriented towards the promotion of competition and entry of financial institutions were enacted: requirements on the opening and branching of banks were relaxed in Indonesia and Malaysia in 1988–9; restrictions on activities of foreign banks were eased in Korea and Thailand in 1991 and 1993, respectively.[17]

From our perspective, the crucial implication of liberalization was its effect on the international liquidity position of the financial system. Existing economic theory suggests that such effect is detrimental. Clearly, lower reserve requirements allow the banking industry to maintain a lower degree of liquidity, but as we have argued elsewhere (Chang and Velasco, 1998a, 1998b), while this may be desirable on efficiency grounds, it directly exacerbates international illiquidity and increases the possibility of financial runs. Likewise, the fostering of competition in the financial industry may deliver institutions that, while leaner and meaner, are less liquid. In Chang and Velasco (1998b) we have discussed how this may happen in the banking industry. Increased competition typically forces banks to offer more attractive terms (higher interest rates) to depositors. This improves social welfare in the absence of bank runs, but it also implies that the short-term liabilities of the banking system, in this case the face value of demand deposits, must increase, impairing international liquidity.

Evidence supporting the view that financial liberalization lowers international liquidity has been provided recently by Demirguc-Kent and Detragiache (1998). Their analysis of banking industry data in eight countries between 1988 and 1995 shows that financial liberalization (understood as the deregulation of interest rates) is strongly correlated with a fall in the bank's liquidity (measured by the ratio of liquid to total assets). While more empirical work is clearly needed, our assessment of existing theory and evidence is consistent with the view that financial liberalization in Asia increased the possibility of a financial crash through its effect on international illiquidity.[18]

An Unprecedented Increase in Short-term Foreign Liabilities

Our concept of international illiquidity focuses on the difference between short-term international assets and liabilities. It was the explosive growth of the latter, in particular of short-term international debt, that accounted for the change in the international liquidity position of the Asean-5 countries.

As emphasized by Radelet and Sachs (1998), a notable feature of the Asian crisis was the extent to which foreign investors, especially foreign commercial banks, increased their loans to the Asean-5 economies up to the onset of the crisis. BIS data show that international bank lending to Asia increased from less than US$150 billion at the end of 1990 to about US$390 billion in mid-1997; in contrast, foreign bank lending to Latin America only increased from about US$180 billion to about US$250 billion over the same period. The bulk of new lending to Asia was directed to the Asean-5 countries (although the Philippines received a relatively small share).

In addition, BIS data show that most of the loans by foreign banks were short-term ones. For Asia, the share of loans with maturity over a year fell from about 38 per cent in 1990 to less than 30 per cent in mid-1997; the corresponding figure for Latin America stood at 40 per cent in mid-1997. Table 2.15 shows that, for the Asean-5 countries, short-term debt was a larger share of total debt in mid-1997 than in mid-1990, although its importance was somewhat smaller than in 1994. At the time of the crisis, short-term loans as a share of total obligations to the international banking community were 68 per cent in Korea, 66 per cent in Thailand, 59 per cent in Indonesia, 56 per cent in Malaysia and 59 per cent in the Philippines.

Table 2.15   Short-term debt and total debt

| Total debt (mn US$) | | | | | |
	Indonesia	Korea	Malaysia	Philippines	Thailand	Total
June 90	20 076	23 369	6 864	9 055	11 675	71 039
June 94	30 902	48 132	13 874	5 990	36 545	135 443
June 97	58 726	103 432	28 820	14 115	69 382	274 475

| Short-term debt (mn US$) | | | | | |
	Indonesia	Korea	Malaysia	Philippines	Thailand	Total
June 90	10 360	15 528	1 761	3 019	7 026	37 694
June 94	18 882	34 908	8 203	2 646	27 151	91 790
June 97	34 661	70 182	16 268	8 293	45 567	174 971

| Short-term as % of total debt | | | | | |
	Indonesia	Korea	Malaysia	Philippines	Thailand	Total
June 90	51.60	66.45	25.66	33.34	60.18	53.06
June 94	61.10	72.53	59.12	44.17	74.29	67.77
June 97	59.02	67.85	56.45	58.75	65.68	63.75

Source: Bank of International Settlements.

Hence the data show not only that an unprecedented increase in capital flows towards the Asean-5 countries had taken place since 1990, but also that a growing proportion of those flows were short-term ones. As shown by the behaviour of the short-term debt to international reserves ratio, these short-term capital inflows were not matched by a comparable increase in international liquid assets, implying that international illiquidity became a more serious problem. A key question naturally suggests itself: how did the financial system in the Asean-5 countries end up with so much short-term debt? Although a definitive answer remains to be found, we believe that the following hypotheses are plausible.

- Financial liberalization may once again carry part of the blame. As part of the deregulation and capital account liberalization that took place in the Asean-5 countries, obstacles to capital inflows were reduced, a change which clearly encouraged total inflows. The remaining question, then, is why short-term debt became relatively more important. One possibility is that, if before the liberalization governments wanted to encourage foreign direct investment, the barriers that were reduced basically affected short-term flows. In that case, financial liberalization clearly would have led to a rising share of short-term debt.
- Economic fundamentals may imply that increases in total capital inflows must be associated with a rising share of short-term debt. In our theoretical work (Chang and Velasco, 1998a, 1998b) we have shown that this may be the case in an economy that needs to obtain short-term loans to provide for today's consumption, and long-term loans to finance investment projects that mature later. In such a case, an increase in total capital inflows will then be distributed between short- and long-term debt, in proportions that depend on specific properties of preferences and technology.
- Miscalculation and wishful thinking on the part of Asian borrowers may also be to blame. As the effect of external shocks (dollar appreciation, Chinese devaluation, stagnation in Japan) made itself felt and macro-economic fundamentals deteriorated, firms and banks may have conjectured that the shocks were temporary, and that relatively inexpensive short-term borrowing was called for to get over the hump. The Mexican government did something similar in the course of 1994, attempting to get through a period of domestic political instability and higher world interest rates by playing on the yield curve and borrowing short to minimize interest expense. In both cases the period of turbulence was deeper and longer than had been anticipated, and ex post the decision to borrow short seems unsound.

- Finally, supply-side factors may have been at work. A larger share of short-term debt among the Asean-5 countries reflects a *worldwide* trend towards shorter debt maturities. The data from the BIS show that the short-term loans as a share of international bank loans fell from almost 40 per cent in mid-1994 to less than 35 per cent in mid-1997. This fall reflects similar trends in both developed and developing countries (although, as discussed earlier, the share of short-term debt of the Asean-5 countries has consistently been well above the world average). It is conceivable, then, that the shortening of international debt maturities reflects the relative world supply of short- versus long-term funds.

All of the above hypotheses are theoretically sound and ring true. However, more detailed work is needed to establish their role in generating the Asian crisis. More generally, this question remains a key issue for research.

An Increase in Foreign Currency Debt

In the 1990s, not only the maturity but also the currency composition of the liabilities of the financial system of the Asean-5 countries was conducive to financial fragility. As we saw above, there was a sharp increase in borrowing abroad which, Table 2.16 reveals, was overwhelmingly done in foreign currency. Since the currency composition of the financial system's domestic liabilities did not change much (dollarization of deposits has been limited in Asia, in contrast to Latin America), the increase in foreign loans also implied a sharp rise in the volume of total obligations denominated in foreign currency.

Why whould domestic financial institutions choose dollar or yen debt over domestic currency debt? Two explanations stand out. The first is a bias towards foreign borrowing implicit in the regulatory environment. In the Philippines, for instance, banks are subject to a 10 per cent tax rate on income from foreign currency loans, while other income is taxed at the regular corporate income rate of 35 per cent. Philippine banks face reserve requirements of 13 per cent for peso deposits (down from 16 per cent in 1996) and zero for foreign currency deposits.[19] Offshore or special financial centres, which dealt exclusively in foreign currency, also distorted incentives faced by borrowers. Banks operating in the Bangkok International Banking Facility were eligible for special tax breaks. The phenomenon was also present elsewhere: 'Malaysia promoted Labuan as a financial center, the Philippines developed an off-shore Euro-peso market, and Singapore and Hong Kong further developed their roles as regional financial centers. These markets were often given regulatory and tax advantages ... and much external financing was channeled through these offshore markets'.[20]

Table 2.16   External debt denominated in local currency

Total debt (mn US$)						
	Indonesia	Korea	Malaysia	Philippines	Thailand	Total
June 90	20 076	23 369	6 864	9 055	11 675	71 039
June 94	30 902	48 132	13 874	5 990	36 545	135 443
June 97	58 726	103 432	28 820	14 115	69 382	274 475

Currency positions (claims – liabilities)						
	Indonesia	Korea	Malaysia	Philippines	Thailand	Total
June 90	468	2 685	212	430	679	4 474
June 94	843	3 182	1 513	323	2 145	8 006
June 97	1 262	6 152	2 977	2 239	3 906	16 536

Local currency as % of total debt						
	Indonesia	Korea	Malaysia	Philippines	Thailand	Total
June 90	2.33	11.49	3.09	4.75	5.82	6.30
June 94	2.73	6.61	10.91	5.39	5.87	5.91
June 97	2.15	5.95	10.33	15.86	5.63	6.02

Source: Bank of International Settlements.

A second commonly mentioned culprit is the combination of high domestic interest rates (often caused by sterilization of capital inflows) plus commitment to a fixed exchange rate. The Asian Development Bank (1998) documents the large spreads between domestic and foreign borrowing costs that prompted banks and firms to seek financing abroad. The next question is why such liabilities were mostly unhedged. Radelet and Sachs (1998) write: 'Nominal exchange rates were effectively pegged to the US dollar, with either limited variation (Thailand, Malaysia, Korea and the Philippines) or very predictable change (Indonesia). Predictable exchange rates reduced perceived risks for investors, further encouraging capital inflows'. In other words, there was, as we know ex post, a non-trivial risk of nominal and real devaluations, but government words and deeds led investors to underestimate such a risk. Economists often fret about exchange rate pegs that lack credibility; by contrast, Asian pegs seem to have enjoyed too much credibility.

Since the run on Mexico's dollar-denominated *Tesobonos* in December 1994, it has become fashionable to blame foreign currency-denominated debt for a host of ills, sometimes with less than full justification. As we stressed above, it is not the case that the ratio of foreign currency-denominated liquid liabilities to foreign currency-denominated liquid assets is the proper measure of a financial system's international illiquidity. Under a fixed exchange rate, domestic currency deposits are no different from dollar or yen liabilities: a depositor withdrawing pesos or baht or Won from a bank should be able to convert them into dollars at the announced parity, and a liquid system (that is, one in which the fixed parity can be maintained) must have enough dollars or yen to meet that demand.

But there are differences between foreign and domestic currency liquid obligations. The first is that, if the exchange rate is not fixed but flexible, the central bank is able to serve as a lender of last resort in domestic currency, and this added degree of freedom may help forestall panic by depositors or creditors. In our theoretical work (Chang and Velasco, 1998a) we study this point at length. There we show that self-fulfilling bank runs can be ruled out if three factors (domestic currency liabilities, a central bank willing to serve as lender of last resort in domestic currency, and a flexible exchange rate) are present simultaneously. Conversely, the combination of foreign currency liabilities, a fixed exchange rate and insufficient international reserves, precisely the situation that prevailed in most Asian countries, leaves financial systems illiquid and vulnerable to shifts in investor sentiment.

The other channel through which foreign currency liabilities can be destabilizing comes into being after (and if) a crisis erupts and the exchange rate is devalued. If banks had borrowed in foreign currency and lent in domestic currency, the devaluation imposes a capital levy. But harmful effects can be felt even if domestic banks were not directly exposed to exchange risk: if they lent domestically in foreign currency, exchange risk was simply transferred to the borrowing firms. To the extent that these firms' revenue is not in foreign currency, a devaluation sharply reduces their profitability and cuts their debt service capacity. According to many accounts, this mechanism has been at work in the Asian episode, affecting in turn the health of domestic banks.[21]

FROM ILLIQUIDITY TO FINANCIAL PANIC

Financial systems that are internationally illiquid live at the mercy of exogenous economic conditions and the moods of depositors and creditors. As we show in Chang and Velasco (1998a, 1998b), if initial liquid liabilities are large relative to liquid assets, an exogenous shock (such as an increase in the world interest rate) or a sudden loss of confidence may prompt holders of the system's liabilities to attempt to liquidate them. But they cannot all be successful, since international illiquidity means, precisely, that the foreign currency value of their holdings cannot be covered by the amount of international liquidity available to the system. Hence a financial crisis may occur even if things would have been normal had confidence stayed high. If a crisis does take place, financial institutions may be forced to call in loans, interrupting productive projects, and sell fixed assets such as land, causing real estate and stock prices to plunge. The government may try to help, but the crisis is one of excess demand for foreign currency, and hence the government may see its own international reserves plunge in the struggle.

Acute illiquidity left Asia vulnerable to a sharp reversal in the direction of capital flows, and that is exactly what happened in the second half of 1997. Available information suggests that short-term inflows suddenly reversed themselves during 1997. Data from the Institute of International Finance show, in particular, that net international inflows of capital to the Asean-5 countries fell dramatically, to –US$12 billion in 1997, from US$93 billion in 1996. This fall in inflows is accounted for, by and large, by the behaviour of foreign banks, whose positions in the Asean-5 countries dropped by US$ 21.3 billion in 1997 after increasing by US$55.5 billion in 1996. Combining this information with BIS data, which show that foreign banks increased their lending to the Asean-5 countries by US$13 billion in the first half of 1997, Radelet and Sachs (1998) conclude that there must have been a capital outflow of about US$34 billion in the second half of 1997, equivalent to a negative shock of 3.6 per cent of GDP.

This suggests that, when potatoes became hot in mid-1997, international bankers panicked and decided to close their exposure to the more troubled Asian countries. They were able to pull out simply by refusing to roll over their loans, given the prevalence of short-term borrowing. The run by international creditors may, in addition, have not only been possible but also self- fulfilling. As discussed by Calvo (1995) and Chang and Velasco (1998b), when domestic financial entities contract short-term debt abroad to finance less liquid investments, a coordination failure becomes possible. No individual creditor will find it profitable to roll over his loan if he believes that the others will not either and that, as a consequence, domestic borrowers will be forced into bankruptcy. In turn, the sudden increase in the need for liquidity may in fact crush the financial system, confirming creditors' expectations.

The magnitude of the crisis may be a reflection that the creditors' run interacted with a domestic run on deposits. As discussed in Chang and Velasco (1998b), foreign lenders may panic and refuse to roll over short-term loans if they believe that there will be a run on domestic deposits. In turn, domestic depositors may run because they believe that financial institutions will be forced into bankruptcy, given that they cannot service their short-term obligations. But the latter could have been prevented if the financial system had had access to the necessary financing. In other words, in economies as open as the Asean-5, the distinction between a foreign lender's panic and a domestic financial run is blurred: they may happen at the same time and reinforce each other. Such a self-fulfilling panic seems to have been present in several instances of the Asian episode. It was panic dumping of Korean assets, for instance, that brought Korea to the verge of default in December 1997.[22] Such a reaction by investors seems to have been present in Thailand and Indonesia, at the very least.

Does this mean that we simply view the Asian crisis as a jump to a bad equilibrium, unrelated to fundamentals? Not quite. Much ink has been spilt on the question of whether weak fundamentals caused the Asian crisis, but answers to this question are seldom very revealing. Most sensible observers agree that there was a deterioration of macroeconomic performance in the Asean-5 countries; many sensible observers also recognize that, as we have argued above, the picture was a mixed one, and the Asean-5 did not fit the pattern of policy-induced instability that one often saw in the crashes experienced by some populist government in Latin American crashes of the 1980s. The debate stops there, for empirical observation fails to provide a clear guide as to when fundamentals are weak enough to guarantee a collapse. Most studies until now have not been able to detect a clear pattern of behaviour for macroeconomic variables in anticipation of a crisis.[23] Neither a current account gap nor a fiscal deficit nor a growth slowdown seem necessary or sufficient to trigger a crash.

Theory can help clarify matters somewhat. Recent models of crises (Obstfeld, 1994; Cole and Kehoe, 1996; Velasco, 1997) show that there is a 'middle region' for fundamentals (debt, overvaluation, unemployment and so on) that are neither 'too good' nor 'too bad', where crises can occur if and only if contagion sets in or expectations turn pessimistic. Our emphasis on illiquidity complements this perspective, and underscores the fact that financial factors are at least as important as real ones in trying to determine where that middle region lies in which self-fulfilling crashes can take place. While the behaviour of real macroeconomic fundamentals was quite varied accross Asian countries, illiquidity was a feature common to all of the ones that eventually found themselves in a crisis. In this the troubled Asian crisis differed from 1990s' Latin America, which also suffered from large real appreciation and current account deficits, but where financial systems were a great deal more liquid, and banking sectors more solid. Paradoxically, this incipient solidity was the result of the clean-up following earlier debt and/or banking crises in Argentina, Brazil, Chile, Mexico and Venezuela.

Our interpretation also helps account for some noteworthy features of the Asian episode. One, stressed forcefully by Radelet and Sachs (1998), is that the crash seems to have been largely unanticipated. They base their claim on several observations. First, interest rate spreads did not rise in the run-up to the crisis. Second, capital inflows were large even in the first half of 1997. Third, neither the credit rating agencies nor the IMF reports managed to predict what was to happen. Of these three, the first two are most striking (credit agencies have a notoriously bad forecasting record[24] and the IMF is understandably very tight-lipped in its public pronouncements) and also match the experience of Chile in 1982 and Mexico in 1994. In both cases capital inflows continued even after real fundamentals had deteriorated. In Mexico, interest rate spreads remained practically constant between the time of the assassination of presidential candidate Donaldo Colosio in March and the abandonment of the peg in December 1994.[25]

An emphasis on financial collapse also helps explain the apparent lack of proportionality between the size of the sin (deteriorating fundamentals caused in part by external shocks such as dollar appreciation and Japanese stagnation) and that of the punishment (plunging asset prices and a sharp fall in growth rates relative to trend). In our theoretical work (Chang and Velasco, 1998b) we show how, if initially financial systems are relatively illiquid, a 'small' real shock can push the economy into a region where a financial crisis is either possible (contingent on expectations) or outright inevitable. If a financial crash does occur, bankruptcies and early liquidation of investments have real consequences that 'multiply' the harmful effect of the initial shock. The process is likely to be costly and disruptive.

Finally, financial collapse – partially caused by contagion from neighbouring countries – helps explain the depth of the Indonesian troubles. As Radelet and Sachs (1998) stress, 'Indonesia's extensive meltdown is far more severe than can be accounted for by flaws in economic fundamentals, since those were not especially poor'. Indeed, Indonesia had the smallest current account deficit among the Asean-5 (3.5 per cent of GDP in 1996), enjoyed fast export growth, before the crisis the budget had been in surplus by an average of more than 1 per cent of GDP for four years, and the stock market continued to rise strongly in 1997 – until the Thai crisis erupted. But where Indonesia's fundamentals were weaker, as we have seen, was in the relative illiquidity of its economy. Its short-term external debt was large although, admittedly, the borrowers were primarily non-financial firms rather than banks. And at the end of 1996, the M2–reserves ratio was almost 7 in Indonesia – along with Korea, the highest among the Asean-5. It is not surprising that Indonesia was vulnerable to contagion.

SPECIAL ISSUES AND CONCLUSIONS

We conclude by considering what light the Asian episode sheds on some hotly contested policy issues.

Financial Liberalization and Fragility

In their (1996) paper on the 'twin crises', Kaminsky and Reinhart found that (a) of the 26 banking crises they studied, 18 are preceded by financial sector liberalization within a five-year interval, and (b) financial liberalizations accurately signal 71 per cent of all balance of payments crises and 67 per cent of all banking crises. The experiences of Chile and Mexico, and now East Asia, strongly confirm this general tendency. Freeing interest rates, lowering reserve requirements and enhancing competition in the banking sector are sound policies on many grounds – and, indeed, countries in which they are applied often experience an expansion in financial intermediation. But they can also sharply reduce the liquidity of the financial sector, and hence set the stage for a potential crisis.

While we have focused on the effects of liberalization on liquidity, a host of other potential ills have been mentioned in the literature. In particular, deregulation coupled with explicit or implicit guarantees on banks and inadequate oversight can generate a serious moral hazard problem. Overlending and excessive risk taking are likely results, as argued by Velasco (1990) for the case of Chile and by Krugman (1998) for the recent Asian apisode. A lending boom and growing share of risky or bad loans often result. As Gavin and Hausmann (1995) persuasively argue, the empirical link between lending booms and financial crises is very strong. Rapid growth in the ratio of bank credit to GDP preceded financial troubles not just in Chile and Mexico, but also in Argentina (1981), Colombia (1982–3), Uruguay (1982), Norway (1987), Finland (1991–2), Japan (1992–3) and Sweden (1991).[26]

The moral of the story is the same in both cases. Financial liberalization should be undertaken cautiously. Reserve requirements can be a useful tool in stabilizing a banking system, as the experience of Argentina in 1995 showed. Lowering them to zero, as Mexico did in the run-up to the 1994 crash, smacks of imprudence.

Dealing with Troubled Banks at a Time of Crisis

The Asian troubles have ignited a lively debate on the wisdom of closing wobbly banks. The IMF has pursued that policy vigorously, making bank interventions and closures part of its conditionality in the affected countries. Fierce critics like Jeff Sachs have charged the policy with inviting runs on healthy banks and inducing an unecessarily large credit crunch.

The proper policy prescription clearly depends on one's assessment of the crisis. If the problem is primarily one of moral hazard and overlending (as Krugman, 1998, has claimed for Asia) or of outright fraud (as Akerlof and Romer, 1993, argued for the US S&L crisis), banks are insolvent and they should be either closed or forced to recapitalize. But if the problem is one of illiquidity made acute by panicked behaviour by depositors and creditors (as we have argued), liquidity should be injected into banks, not withdrawn from them, in order to avoid costly asset liquidation.

Non-performing loans typically shoot up at times of trouble, often reaching up to a quarter of bank assets. This would seem to confirm the insolvency-cum-closure view. The problem is that it is not clear whether bad loans are causing the crisis or being caused by it. Clearly, the combination of smaller bank credit, high real interest rates and sharp real devaluations can render many loans bad that would have performed adequately had no liquidity crisis occurred. In Chile in 1982 and Mexico in 1994, many investment projects were left for dead. But, as anyone who bought a half-built shopping centre in Santiago at that time knows, those investments turned out to be perfectly sound once the economy returned to normality, and their value in dollars has risen several times in the intervening 15 years. This suggests that the liquidity problem may well be the more serious one, and that authorities should think twice before they engage in policies of wholesale bank closures.

Capital Inflows and Short-term Debt

Short-term government debt proved to be dangerous in the case of Mexico; short-term external debt has proved to be risky in the case of Asia. What can be done about it?

Restraining short-term borrowing involves no free lunch, for both governments and banks have perfectly sound reasons for wanting to make at least some of their liabilities short-term. At the same time, it is not clear that decentralized decision making delivers the optimal debt maturity structure: governments may rely too much on short-term debt if they suffer from time inconsistency or high discounting; foreign creditors may only be willing to lend short because of imperfect information or monitoring, or because of coordination failure with other creditors (if each creditor expects the others will only lend short, thus making a crisis possible, his best response is also to lend short in order to have a chance to get out if the crisis comes). These conjectures suggest that there may be a case for a policy discouraging short-term debt.

What policy, exactly, is a tricky matter. High required reserves on liquid bank liabilities (whether in domestic or foreign currency, and whether owed to locals or foreigners) is an obvious choice. It may be sound policy even if it has some efficiency costs or if it causes some disintermediation. An obvious caveat is that if banks are constrained firms will do their own short-term borrowing, as happened on a massive scale in Indonesia.

Taxes on capital inflows where the tax rate is in inverse proportion to the maturity of the inflow (and where long-term flows such as FDI go untaxed at the border) have been used by Colombia and Chile in the 1990s. They are often justified in terms of findings such as those of Sachs *et al.* (1996c), who found that a shorter maturity of capital inflows was a helpful predictor of vulnerability to the Tequila effect in 1995, while the size of those inflows was not. Empirical studies by Valdés-Prieto and Soto (1996) and Cárdenas and Barrera (1997) find that such taxes (actually, non-interest bearing reserve requirements) in Colombia and Chile lengthen average maturity while leaving loan volumes unaffected. If this is so, they may also be effective in reducing vulnerability.

Fixed versus Flexible Exchange Rates

The combination of an illiquid financial system and fixed exchange rates can be lethal. If the central bank commits itself not to serve as a lender of last resort, bank runs can occur; if it acts as a lender of last resort in domestic currency, bank runs are eliminated at the cost of causing currency runs. Hence, under fixed exchange rates plus insufficient reserves (that is, illiquidity), a crisis is unavoidable if investor sentiment turns negative; the only choice authorities face is what kind of crisis to have.

A regime in which bank deposits are denominated in domestic currency, the central bank stands ready to act as a lender of last resort and exchange rates are flexible, may help forestall some types of self-fulfilling bank crises. The intuition for this is simple. An equilibrium bank run occurs if each bank depositor expects others will run and exhaust the available resources. Under a fixed rates regime, those who run to the bank withdraw domestic currency, which in turn they use to buy hard currency at the central bank. If depositors expect this sequence of actions to cause the central bank to run out of dollars or yen, a best response is for them to run as well, and the pessimistic expectations become self-fulfilling. On the other hand, under a flexible rates regime plus a lender of last resort there is always enough domestic currency at the commercial bank to satisfy those who run. But since the central bank is no longer compelled to sell all the available reserves, those who run face a depreciation, while those who do not run know that there will still be dollars available when they desire to withdraw them at a later date. Hence running to the bank is no longer a best response, pessimistic expectations are not self-fulfilling and a depreciation need not happen in equilibrium.

In our view this represents a strong case in favour of flexible exchange rates. But there are caveats. One is that such a mechanism can protect banks against self-fulfilling pessimism on the part of domestic depositors (whose claims are in local currency), not against panic by external creditors who hold short-term IOUs denominated in dollars. To the extent that this was the case in Asia, a flexible exchange rate system would have provided only limited protection.[27]

Proper implementation is subtle. If they are to be stabilizing, flexible rates must be part of a regime, whose operation agents take into account when forming expectations. Suddenly adopting a float because reserves are dwindling, as Mexico did in 1994, or several Asian countries have done recently, may have the opposite effect by further frightening concerned investors. In fact, the case has been made that it was precisely the sudden (but late) abandonment of the peg that pushed Mexico to a 'bad equilibrium'.[28]

The Case for an International Lender of Last Resort

If financial crises such as those in East Asia were at least partially caused by self-fulfilling liquidity squeezes on banks, there is a role for an international lender of last resort that can help overcome a financial system's international illiquidity. Funds from above to prevent unnecessary credit crunches and avoid costly liquidation of investment can increase welfare.

The usual (and valid) objection is moral hazard. But this need not be a rationale for policy paralysis. Fire insurance and bank deposit guarantees also risk inducing moral hazard, but the risk can be minimized by proper contract design and appropiate monitoring. No one advocates banning fire insurance simply because it leads some homeowners to be careless with their fireplaces. The same is true of an international lender of last resort.

NOTES

1. Our view of crises has been heavily influenced by the previous work of Guillermo Calvo; in particular, see Calvo (1995, 1996). A partial and chronological list of other papers discussing aspects of this view includes Díaz-Alejandro (1985), Velasco (1987), Dornbusch *et al.* (1995), Calvo and Mendoza (1996), Frankel and Rose (1996), Kaminsky and Reinhart (1996), Sachs *et al.* (1996a, 1996b, 1996c), Sachs (1997), Goldfajn and Valdés (1997), Corsetti *et al.* (1998) and Radelet and Sachs (1998).
2. This section draws on Velasco (1987, 1991), Sachs *et al.* (1996b) and Velasco and Cabezas (1998).
3. The operational balance is the public sector borrowing requirement minus the inflationary component of debt payments. There was some debate in 1995 about whether the actual Mexican deficit was higher in 1994, if lending by state development banks was added. We do not believe so: since this lending was on commercial terms and often against collateral, it does not belong in an economic measure of the deficit. For a more detailed discussion, see Sachs *et al.* (1996b).
4. See Sachs *et al.* (1996b) for more details.
5. See Sachs *et al.* (1996b) for more details.
6. See Velasco (1991) for details.
7. See, for instance, Corbo and Hernández (1994).
8. See Obstfeld (1994).
9. Notice that, in addition, average current account deficits in Indonesia hardly changed from the 1980s to the 1990s.

10. Current account sustainability is a notion that is conceptually unimpeachable but practically of little use, for it requires that one calculate present values of sequences of unknown future flows. Observed ratios of total debt to GDP provide a very imperfect measure of sustainability.
11. The data in this table are from J.P. Morgan. Radelet and Sachs (1998) compute larger real appreciations.
12. In particular, Chinn (1998) estimates a structural model of real exchange rate determination and finds that, once one corrects for underlying structural change, the extent of misalignment is quite limited, and smaller than the real appreciation numbers in Table 2.12 suggest.
13. A Goldman Sachs report issued in December 1997 ranked and quantified the fragility of financial systems in the region. An index of of 12 factors of fragility – including destabilizing financial liberalization, rapidly rising credit-to-GDP ratio, high foreign currency liabilities, weak capital or loan reserve levels, and underregulated non-bank financial institutions – gave a score of 22 (against a worst possible score of 24) to Thailand and Korea, and 20 to Indonesia, 15 to Malaysia and 14 to the Philippines.
14. See Radelet and Sachs (1998) for a detailed description of this process.
15. IFS, January 1998, p. 679.
16. See Corsetti *et al.* (1998), section 3.2.
17. This information is taken from Asian Development Bank (1998), which includes a fairly detailed discussion of financial liberalization in the Asean-5 countries.
18. It must be noted that this view on how liberalization contributed to the Asian crisis differs from other ones that have been proposed. In particular, an alternative mechanism, suggested by Caprio and Summers (1993) and Hellman *et al.* (1994), is that financial liberalization may have reduced the 'franchise value' of banks and induced them to take on more risk. While this mechanism may have been at work, it is unclear that its effects are strong enough to explain the Asian crisis. Also the evidence about the 'franchise value' story is mixed: as discussed by Demirguc-Kent and Detragiache (1998), the fall in the banking system liquidity associated with financial liberalization suggests that its franchise value increases, instead of falling, with liberalization.
19. IMF, 'Philippines – Recent Economic Developments', April 1997, cited by Radelet and Sachs (1998).
20. Asian Development Bank (1998).
21. See Corsetti *et al.* (1998), Radelet and Sachs (1998), Asian Development Bank (1998).
22. Even Corsetti *et al.* (1998), who are notoriously sceptical of such lines of explanation, recognize as much. See Corsetti *et al.* (1998, p. 44).
23. See, among many others, the papers by Frankel and Rose (1996), Kaminsky and Reinhart (1996) and Sachs *et al.* (1996).
24. See Kaminsky and Reinhart (1997).
25. Both spreads between peso and dollar Mexican assets and between US and Mexican dollar assets were stable. See Sachs *et al.* (1996b) for details.
26. In Mexico and Chile, as in the case of some Asian countries more recently, the perception of government guarantees may have created a moral hazard problem and led banks to take on excessive risk. Velasco (1991) discusses evidence for this in the case of Chile. Krugman (1998) stresses the role of moral hazard and overinvestment in Asia.
27. Floating is not totally useless in this case, for panic by foreign creditors could perfectly well be triggered by a run by domestic depositors, with the outcome being self-fulfilling. For details on this line of argument, see Chang and Velasco (1998b).
28. See Calvo (1994) and Sachs *et al.* (1996a).

REFERENCES

Akerlof, G. and P. Romer (1993), 'Looting: The Economic Underworld of Bankruptcy for Profit', *Brookings Papers on Economic Activity*, **2**, 1–60.

Calvo, G. (1995), 'Varieties of Capital Market Crises', Working Paper 15, Center for International Economics, University of Maryland.

Calvo, G.(1996), 'Comment on Sachs, Tornell and Velasco', *Brookings Papers on Economic Activity*, **1**.

Calvo, G. and E. Mendoza (1996), 'Reflections on Mexico's Balance of Payments Crisis: A Chronicle of a Death Foretold', *Journal of International Economics*.

Caprio, G., and D. Klingebiel (1993), 'Dealing With Bank Insolvencies: Cross Country Experience', World Bank.

Chang, R. and A. Velasco (1998a), 'Financial Fragility and the Exchange Rate Regime', RR #98-05, C.V. Starr Center for Applied Economics, NYU, February; also NBER WP 6469.

Chang, R. and A. Velasco (1998b), 'Financial Crises in Emerging Markets: A Canonical Model', Working Paper, Federal Reserve Bank of Atlanta, March.

Corbo, V. and L. Hernández (1994), 'Macroeconomic Adjustment to Capital Inflows. Latin American Style versus East Asian Style', The World Bank Policy Research Working Paper No. 1377.

Corsetti, G., P. Pesenti and N. Roubini (1998), 'What Caused the Asian Currency and Financial Crises?', mimeo, NYU, March.

Demirguc-Kent, A. and E. Detragiache (1998), 'Financial Liberalization and Financial Fragility', Working Paper, IMF and World Bank.

Diamond, D. (1997), 'Liquidity, Banks and Markets', *Journal of Political Economy*, **105**, 928–56.

Diamond, D. and P. Dybvig (1983), 'Bank Runs, Deposit Insurance and Liquidity', *Journal of Political Economy*, **91** (3), 401–19.

Díaz-Alejandro, C.F. (1985), 'Good-bye Financial Repression, Hello Financial Crash', *Journal of Development Economics*, **19**.

Dornbusch, R., I. Goldfajn and R. Valdés (1995), 'Currency Crises and Collapses', *Brookings Papers on Economic Activity*, **2**, 219–95.

Frankel, J. and Andrew K. Rose (1996), 'Currency Crashes in Emerging Markets: An Empirical Treatment', *Journal of International Economics*, **41**, 351–68.

Gavin, Michael and Ricardo Hausmann (1995), 'The Roots of Banking Crises: The Macroeconomic Context', mimeo, Inter-American Development Bank.

Goldfajn, I. and R. Valdés (1997), 'Capital Flows and the Twin Crises: The Role of Liquidity', Working Paper 97-87, International Monetary Fund, July.

Hellman, T., Murdoch, K. and J.E. Stiglitz (1994), 'Addressing Moral Hazard in Banking: Deposit Rate Controls vs. Capital Requirements', unpublished manuscript.

Kaminsky, G. and C. Reinhart (1996), 'The Twin Crises: The Causes of Banking and Balance of Payments Problems', International Finance Discussion Paper No. 544, Board of Governors of the Federal Reserve System, March.

Krugman, P. (1979), 'A Model of Balance of Payments Crises', *Journal of Money, Credit and Banking*.

Krugman, P. (1998), 'What Happened in Asia?', mimeo, MIT.

Obstfeld, M. (1994), 'The Logic of Currency Crises', *Cahiers Economiques et Monétaires*, **34**.

Radelet, S., and J. Sachs (1998), 'The Onset of the Asian Financial Crisis', mimeo, Harvard Institute for International Development, March.

Sachs, J. (1997), 'Alternative Approaches to Financial Crises in Emerging Markets', Development Discussion Paper No. 568, Harvard Institute for International Development, January.

Sachs, J., A. Tornell and A. Velasco (1996a), 'The Collapse of the Mexican Peso: What Have We Learned?', **22**.

Sachs, J., A. Tornell and A. Velasco (1996b), 'The Mexican Peso Crisis: Sudden Death or Death Foretold?', *Journal of International Economics*.

Sachs, J., A. Tornell and A. Velasco (1996c), 'Financial Crises in Emerging Markets: The Lessons from 1995', *Brookings Papers on Economic Activity*, **1**.

Velasco, A. (1987), 'Financial and Balance of Payments Crises', *Journal of Development Economics*, **27**, 263–83.

Velasco, A. (1991), 'Liberalization, Crisis, Intervention: The Chilean Financial System 1975–1985', in T. Balino and V. Sundarajan (eds) *Banking Crises*, International Monetary Fund.

Velasco, A. and P. Cabezas (1998), 'A Tale of Two Countries: Alternative Responses to Capital Inflows', in M. Kahler (ed.), *Capital Flows and Financial Crises*, Ithaca: Cornell University Press for the Council on Foreign Relations.

3. The East Asian financial crisis: regional and global responses

Ross Garnaut and Dominic Wilson

When Western policy makers met at Bretton Woods in 1944 to redesign the international monetary system, they were spurred by recent memories of the Great Depression and the turbulence of the inter-war years. Like the Great Depression in the West, the financial crisis of 1997 is a defining event in East Asia, with the capacity to change thought about appropriate policies and institutions throughout and beyond the region (Garnaut, 1998a). It comes as no surprise that East Asia's problems have prompted calls for reforms to the international financial architecture. Important questions are being asked in East Asia about the appropriate balance between global and regional cooperation in the resolution of financial crises.

A precondition for sound judgments on these issues is diagnosis of the crisis. What went wrong in East Asia? In what ways did policy contribute to the crisis? What has policy contributed and what more can it contribute to recovery?

The role of global institutions, and in particular the IMF, in the response to the East Asian crisis has been pervasive. But regional institutions and players have also been significantly involved. The Asian Development Bank made major contributions to the three major IMF-led packages, while Japan, Singapore and Australia also played leading parts in the assistance packages. Less visible, but just as important, were the processes of semi-formal cooperation between regional central banks, which facilitated a swift response to the Thai crisis when it broke in July 1997.

In examining the role of regional cooperation in avoiding and managing financial crisis, two realities become clear. The first is that sensible national policy making and sound domestic institutions are the first line of defence. The second is that global and regional arrangements must be complementary, not competitive. Policy makers should avoid the temptation to invent new arrangements without a strong case not only that the old ones have been less than perfect, but also that proposed new arrangements would work.

THE MAKINGS OF THE CRISIS

The 1997 financial crisis was the result of the interaction of a number of problems. Its origins lay in the mismanagement of macroeconomic policy. The challenges to policy were increased by the removal of barriers to international capital and by a long boom which in its late stages encouraged unrealistic views about the variance of economic growth in the region.

Flawed exchange rate regimes were an important part of the problem. The majority of exchange rate regimes in the region were hybrids, neither rigidly fixed, as in the currency board system, nor freely floating. Instead, these currencies were more or less firmly pegged to baskets of currencies dominated by the US dollar. As the dollar's value rose from 1995, these currencies experienced nominal appreciations against the currencies of other trading partners, hurting competitiveness, particularly in the important Japanese market.

At the same time, high domestic demand kept inflation above the levels of major trading partners, adding to the upward pressure on real exchange rates. In 1996, consumer price index (CPI) inflation stood at 6.5 per cent for Indonesia, 3.5 per cent for Malaysia and 5.8 per cent for Thailand (Table 3.1). A slump in the international electronics market aggravated the export slowdown, inducing sharp falls in terms of trade and sales growth, particularly in Thailand, Malaysia and Korea, where the industry had been important to the economies' stellar export performance.

Table 3.1   Inflation for selected East Asian economies (consumer price, annual %)

	1990	1991	1992	1993	1994	1995	1996	1997
Australia	7.3	3.0	1.0	1.9	1.9	4.6	2.6	0.3
China	3.1	4.0	5.8	14.5	24.6	16.6	8.3	2.8
Hong Kong	9.8	11.0	9.9	8.2	9.1	9.0	6.0	6.8
India	8.9	14.0	11.4	6.3	10.4	10.1	9.4	7.0
Indonesia	7.8	9.0	8.3	9.3	8.5	9.3	6.5	11.6
Japan	3.1	3.0	1.9	1.0	0.9	0.0	0.1	1.8
Korea, Rep.	8.6	9.0	6.4	5.2	5.7	4.7	4.5	4.7
Malaysia	2.7	4.0	4.8	3.7	3.5	6.0	3.5	2.6
Philippines	14.2	19.0	8.4	7.8	9.4	7.9	8.4	5.1
Singapore	3.4	3.0	2.9	1.9	3.7	0.9	1.4	2.0
Sri Lanka	21.5	12.0	11.6	12.0	7.9	7.9	15.9	11.6
Thailand	5.9	6.0	3.8	3.6	5.3	5.0	5.8	5.6
Vietnam	60.0	67.5	17.6	5.2	14.4	12.7	4.5	4.0
Taiwan	4.2	3.6	4.5	2.9	4.1	4.7	3.1	1.1

Source: Asia Pacific Economics Group (1998), reproduced from Garnaut (1998a).

Current account deficits expanded sharply in several economies in 1995 and became a focus for concern, particularly in Thailand, where the deficit reached 7.9 per cent of GDP in 1996. In Malaysia, the deficit reached its peak at over 10 per cent in 1995 but eased back to 5 per cent in 1996. In South Korea, the deficit started lower but increased rapidly in 1996 (Table 3.2). Deteriorating current account positions increased the risks of a change in sentiment in foreign exchange and capital markets.

The counterpart of the deteriorating current account positions across the region was large inflows of foreign capital. The increases in capital flows took place in the broader context of greatly increased international capital mobility. Enhanced communications technology and policy reforms to remove official controls had reduced barriers to cross-border capital movements, most importantly in the 1980s for developed economies and in the 1990s for East Asian developing countries. Developed country investment funds, operating in an environment of greatly increased domestic competition, grew rapidly and these countries became major investors in emerging markets in the 1990s for the first time.

Table 3.2   Current account for selected East Asian economies (% of GDP)

	1990	1991	1992	1993	1994	1995	1996	1997
Australia	−5.4	−3.8	−3.9	−3.6	−5.2	−5.5	−4.0	−3.4
China	3.1	3.3	1.3	−1.9	1.4	0.2	0.9	2.1
Hong Kong	4.7	2.9	5.8	7.2	2.3	−2.6	−2.5	−6.8
India	−3.4	−0.7	−1.8	−0.8	−1.1	−1.8	−1.0	−1.2
Indonesia	−2.6	−3.3	−2.0	−1.3	−1.6	−3.5	−3.4	−3.6
Japan	1.2	2.0	3.0	3.1	2.8	2.2	1.4	2.0
Korea, Rep.	−0.7	−2.8	−1.3	0.3	−1.0	−1.8	−4.8	−3.2
Malaysia	−2.0	−8.9	−3.8	−4.5	−5.9	−10.2	−4.9	−4.7
Philippines	−6.1	−2.3	−1.9	−5.5	−4.6	−2.7	−4.7	−4.0
Singapore	8.5	11.6	11.3	7.3	16.2	18.0	15.0	15.2
Sri Lanka	−3.7	−6.6	−4.6	−3.7	−4.7	−4.0	n.a.	n.a.
Thailand	−8.5	−7.7	−5.7	−5.1	−5.7	−8.1	−7.9	−2.2
Vietnam	−5.6	−1.9	−0.7	−8.3	−6.9	−9.8	−16.2	−8.6
Taiwan	6.7	6.7	3.8	3.0	2.5	1.8	4.0	1.8

Source: Asia Pacific Economics Group (1998), reproduced from Garnaut (1998a).

Capital inflows to the region were not a new phenomenon. Many economies had long been recipients of substantial foreign direct investment. The new development was an increase in the scale of flows, including a large inflow in portfolio capital as foreigners purchased securities on more active domestic stock markets and lent directly to the private sector and indirectly through domestic banks. The change in the composition of capital flows was compounded by declining export competitiveness, which reduced the incentives for export-oriented direct investment, particularly from Japan. A deceleration of growth and in some cases a slowdown in capital inflow increased the challenges of external finance for countries running current account deficits.

Apart from the increase in portfolio capital, inflows took on other worrying characteristics in the context of stable exchange rates and financial sector weaknesses. Attempts to sterilize capital inflows generally kept interest rates across the region above their levels in the United States. The resulting interest rate differentials encouraged domestic institutions to borrow in dollars and relend. Authorities did not seek to moderate this and in some cases, as with the Bangkok International Banking Facility, took measures that positively encouraged it.

Much of the rapid build-up in external debt was dollar-denominated and short-term. By 1996, the ratio of short-term external liabilities to foreign reserves stood at 213 per cent in South Korea, 181 per cent in Indonesia and 169 per cent in Thailand. Since exchange rate stability was often taken for granted, foreign currency debt was generally unhedged.

In an environment of easy credit, investor optimism and poor risk management, lending soared and was increasingly directed to more speculation-prone activities, particularly in the property sector. The region's unbroken record of high growth from 1987 dimmed memories of recession. Talk of 'new paradigms' and an 'Asian way' emerged, lulling financial institutions into unrealistic assessments of future prospects. For a while, the process was self-sustaining. Rising asset prices made the balance sheets of corporations and banks appear healthier than they were. Institutions which gambled on increases in asset values were consistently rewarded, and the borrowing and investment capacities of the gamblers were enhanced (Garnaut, 1998a). By late 1996, stock market and real estate values in several economies contained significant elements of speculative excess. Well before the crisis broke, rates of non-performing loans were disturbingly high in Thailand, South Korea and Indonesia.

BURSTING THE BUBBLE

In Thailand, concern about the current account, slow export growth and over-borrowing became more prominent throughout 1996 and early 1997 (Warr, 1997). Thai stock and property markets moved downwards from mid-1996

(Table 3.3). Falls in property and stock market values in turn revealed weaknesses in the balance sheets of some Thai companies, particularly in the financial sector. In late May, the largest Thai finance company collapsed, and the authorities embarked upon vigorous exchange rate intervention. When shudders on Wall Street in late June encouraged a general withdrawal from equities, speculation against the baht quickly swallowed a large share of Thai reserves, forcing a float in early July (McKibbin, 1998).

This was the trigger for the spread of financial problems across the region: the phenomenon that came to be known as 'contagion'. The Thai experience caused investors to question the reliability of presumed government guarantees in other countries in East Asia, particularly in relation to exchange rates but also, in some countries, to asset values. Risk premia rose for investment in East Asian developing economies.

Table 3.3   Stock market price index for selected countries: 1/1/96 = 100 (local currency)

	1/1/96	28/6/96	1/1/97	30/6/97	1/1/98	30/3/98	6/1/98
China	100	145	166	226	216	226	257
India	NA	100	82	104	86	89	81
Japan	100	104	84	90	59	63	58
Singapore	100	104	98	88	64	68	51
Taiwan	100	125	131	160	121	124	100
Sri Lanka	100	86	86	104	97	93	NA
Philippines	100	127	122	108	46	62	52
Australia	100	108	117	126	104	111	103
Indonesia	100	114	120	133	30	28	17
Hong Kong	100	109	133	151	106	114	85
Thailand	100	97	64	42	15	24	15
Malaysia	100	116	125	109	38	51	35
Korea	100	89	68	74	19	31	21

Source: Datastream.

There was also justifiable concern that problems in one regional economy would affect the opportunities for trade and investment in others. In some cases, real depreciation in some East Asian economies implied greater competition in export markets. In others, falling growth and reduced domestic demand in the economies of important trading partners pointed directly to deteriorating prospects for trade and growth, particularly since a large part of export growth had been driven by intraregional trade (Figure 3.1). The depreciations that followed were exceptionally widespread and large (Figure 3.2).

FINANCIAL PRESSURES

Plummeting exchange rates and asset prices placed enormous pressure on financial institutions. Even in countries with sound financial systems, recessions are accompanied by rises in non-performing loans. At the same time, large falls in asset values increase the losses from bad loans by reducing the value of collateral. In economies with weak financial systems, the rise in non-performing loans and fall in asset values have a much larger effect.

The widespread unhedged exchange risk greatly aggravated these financial sector weaknesses. Banks in Thailand, Indonesia and Korea faced a situation where the domestic currency equivalent of dollar-denominated short-term debt rose sharply, with creditors now refusing to roll debt over. Even where

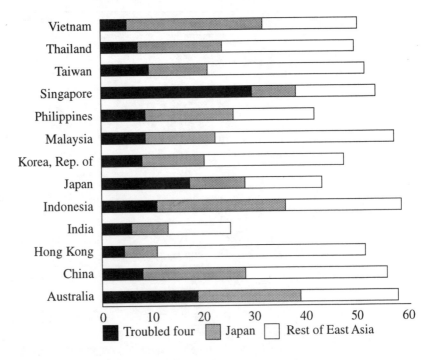

Source: Direction of trade, IMF, IEDB, ANU, reproduced from Garnaut (1988a).

Figure 3.1   Export destination shares, selected economies, 1996 (%)

domestic banks themselves had lent in dollars, credit risk increased dramatically, since many corporate borrowers faced difficulties in honouring their loans at the new exchange rates. Widespread threats of insolvency were the result, encouraging further investor withdrawal and loss of confidence.

The effectiveness of the government response played an important role in determining how the crisis developed. Political changes in Korea and Thailand were conducive to decisive adoption of new policies and firm commitment to their implementation. In Indonesia, by contrast, incoherence in the domestic policy response and its interaction with international institutions compounded and sustained the economy's problems.

Some countries have had superficially similar experiences, with either the bursting of asset bubbles or the falling exchange rate, without similarly severe consequences. The presence of large quantities of unhedged foreign borrowing linked the two parts of the crisis together. The simultaneous collapse of asset prices and exchange rates weakened the balance sheets of domestic banks and

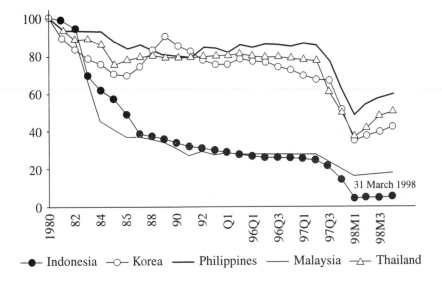

Note: Data are period averages except for the last point, which is that of 31 March 1998. The exchange rate is expressed as US$ per Japanese Yen.

Source: Asia Pacific Economics Group (1998), reproduced from Garnaut (1998a).

Figure 3.2 Nominal exchange rate against US$ for troubled countries (1980 = 100)

companies, increased the risk of bad debt and induced further falls in the value of assets and foreign exchange as a downward spiral took hold.

The key to recovery in the region lies to a large extent in the response of the tradables sector. As long as financial systems can be repaired sufficiently to allow the restoration of balance sheet stability in otherwise profitable enterprises producing tradable goods and services, large increases in competitiveness should allow increases in net exports to lead the restoration of growth.

In mid-1998, the outlook on net exports is mixed. There has been a large increase in net exports, but so far mainly through reduction in imports. The pick-up in exports across the region appears to be slower than it was in Mexico in 1995, although the picture is complicated by the difficulties of accurately separating price and volume effects. There is anecdotal evidence that, in all of the troubled East Asian economies, financing problems are hampering the ability of some exporters to reap the benefits from devaluation. The recession in Japan and the continued weakness in the yen also pose problems for a more rapid export-led recovery across the region.

CHOOSING EXCHANGE RATE REGIMES

Even at this early stage, a number of lessons are clearly visible in recent events. One relates to the choice of exchange rate regimes. Fixed exchange rates have some advantages. Stability in the exchange rate with respect to major trading partners may reduce the transactions costs of international trade and investment. A firm commitment to a fixed rate may also provide a stable anchor for macroeconomic stability, assisting the maintenance of fiscal and monetary discipline. Problems with fixed rate systems emerge when domestic policy is not managed in a way that validates the rate or where rigidities prevent downward movement in costs when the exchange rate becomes overvalued. Floating rates are not as vulnerable to large sustained misalignments, but short-term misalignments may occur. Volatility in floating rates is the rule, rather than the exception.

In East Asia, exchange rate pegs have encouraged unhedged borrowing, a feature that has come to notice in the recent crisis. Where this occurs, a subsequent depreciation is disruptive in ways that seriously damage the financial system and economic performance. Misalignments in a pegged rate create one-way bets for speculators, which themselves are seriously destabilizing. Greater international capital mobility has increased the difficulties of maintaining fixed rates. The much larger flows in private capital that are now common raise the chances that speculation will convert misalignments into crises and that private capital will be able to overwhelm official attempts to maintain a given rate.

There is growing support for the view that it is hard to fix exchange rates, short of extreme systems, along the lines of currency boards (Walters, 1998). Systems of this sort cannot be ruled out on a priori grounds. When economic conditions have settled from the crisis, they should and will be seriously considered in some additional East Asian economies. A high degree of wage and price flexibility in the economy is needed for a firmly fixed system to survive. Even where there is sufficient flexibility, short-term adjustment costs can be severe and an economy that adopts such a system must be prepared to live with them.

The choice of exchange rate regime requires special attention when an economy chooses to liberalize its capital account. Reductions in barriers to foreign capital often induce large capital inflows, putting upward pressure on nominal exchange rates that is frequently reversed at a later stage. This was part of the story in Mexico in 1995, as it was in the lead-up to the recent crises in Thailand and Korea. The strong lesson of the recent experience is that the traditional adjustable pegs are highly vulnerable to the conditions that generated the current crisis, and which may recur in East Asia and elsewhere.

IMPLICATIONS FOR THE FINANCIAL SECTOR

A second general lesson of the crisis is to underline the importance of a robust financial sector to economic stability. A largely undifferentiated shock in the region has had very different effects, depending on the strength of the financial sector. Countries with strong financial systems have so far proved relatively robust in face of the crisis: Taiwan has proved to be reasonably well insulated from the crisis. Hong Kong's economy has held up reasonably well to an attack on its currency peg and dramatic falls in asset values, and Singapore's to a huge decline in the imports of major trading partners, although short-term declines in output are considerable.

This contrasts with the situation in countries where financial insitutions were weak, prudential supervision inadequate and risk management poor. Weak corporate bankruptcy laws have also prevented swift closures of insolvent companies, notably in Indonesia and Thailand, increasing the difficulty of collecting debts and further weakening the banking system.

Financial liberalization complicated the tasks of regulators, as it has in a large number of economies as far apart as Australia and Sweden. Successful financial liberalization cannot be viewed simply as a process of deregulation. If anything, the regulatory framework becomes more important in a liberal environment. In this context, insufficient focus was given to the task of strengthening supervisory and regulatory capacity. In particular, there was too little focus on the big prudential issues: capital adequacy, transparency in financial reporting and avoidance of related party transactions. Complex and diffuse prudential rules tended not to be enforced.

Asset price bubbles likewise present dilemmas for regulatory authorities. The message reinforced by events in Thailand, Indonesia and Korea is that asset price booms and busts and exchange rate volatility are an unavoidable part of economic life in market economies. Domestic policy settings and financial institutions must be capable of withstanding them. The ability of the financial sector to survive shocks is crucial to recovery. Inability to raise finance limits the ability of exporters to exploit depreciated exchange rates, a problem that has so far made its strongest appearance in Indonesia.

PREDICTING AND MANAGING CRISES

Assessments of the health of the region's economies, by private and public and by domestic and international institutions in the lead-up to the crisis, were inadequate. Poor information, particularly about the state of the corporate and banking sectors, hindered the monitoring of the crisis and raised investment risk. Transparency, particularly in finance, is an important way of generating confidence about assets and institutions that are fundamentally sound. Uncertainty about the true state of balance sheets and mistrust of official data encouraged more indiscriminate withdrawal from companies and banks than the underlying realities warranted.

The crisis also indicates that economic monitoring must pay attention to a broader range of indicators, including financial sector data, than is implied by the conventional focus on macroeconomic imbalances. A broader list of potential warning signs should include rapid credit growth, increases in corporate gearing, property and equity price rises, high levels of bad debts, a rising proportion of lending to the property sector and qualitative measures of the extent of unhedged debt. Sharp rises in the ratio of short-term external liabilities to foreign reserves should also be interpreted as an indicator of possible problems.

It can be argued that the need for transparency applies, not only to domestic institutions, but also to the IMF. Uncertainty generated by conflicts between Fund advice and the views of governments and commentators was enhanced by the lack of transparency surrounding the IMF's early recommendations, particularly in negotiations with Indonesia. This was corrected in later agreements.

A third general lesson of the crisis relates to the role of good governance in general to economic stability. The crises in East Asia drew attention to the problems of collusion and corruption in relations between business and government. Problems of directed lending to organizations favoured by the authorities exacerbated the build-up of risk and encouraged moral hazard.

Recent events have also thrown light on the advantages of political systems that allow swift and smooth political transitions and rapid policy responses. Thailand and Korea, for instance, were able to convince markets relatively quickly of their commitment to necessary reforms. Indonesia's experience lies at the opposite end of the spectrum. The chain of political unrest that culminated in the resignation of President Suharto has greatly increased risk premia, probably for a long time. Erratic policy responses have added to investor perceptions of risk, creating further pressure for currency falls. The economic policy agenda has been extended, and in the process has become vastly more complicated, and international involvement in it more sensitive.

COPING WITH CAPITAL FLOWS

In addition to the three broad lessons above, another half lesson can be drawn, relating to the challenges of coping with capital movements. The last few months have seen renewed discussion of capital controls, particularly on short-term flows (Jomo, 1998; Montes, 1998). The reintroduction of capital controls is not a long-term solution to the region's problems, largely for practical reasons. For very open economies, manipulation of the invoicing of payments can in any case create large effective capital flows, whatever the formal arrangements.

In the context of the crisis, Malaysia and Thailand both tried to impose short-term capital controls in attempts to defend their currencies. The effect was at best negligible and at worst positively harmful, since risk premia were arguably raised in response. China and Vietnam, which retained heavy capital controls, were relatively insulated from the crisis, but in China's case a strong current account, large foreign exchange reserves and massive foreign direct investment were probably a more important part of the story. A strong argument can also be made that, by maintaining capital controls, Vietnam, with its huge current account deficit, is simply postponing an inevitable and painful adjustment.

Although arguments that countries with open capital accounts should reimpose controls ought to be viewed with caution, greater attention should be focused on the problems of managing financial and capital account liberalization. The crisis reveals that more careful thought needs to be given to the sequencing of reforms for countries which are yet to liberalize their capital account, including China and Vietnam. Developing a sound domestic financial system must precede the realization of the benefits of an open capital account.

IMPLICATIONS FOR POLICY

Good domestic policy and sound institutions are still the best insurance against crisis. Countries that had sound, well-managed financial systems were not pushed into crisis, though they may face a year or two of low or negative growth. Differences in the quality of political systems, financial institutions and policy responses lie at the heart of the different outcomes in Singapore and Taiwan, on the one hand, and Thailand, Indonesia and Korea, on the other. Some degree of instability is an inevitable part of economic life, particularly in asset markets. Economies that have so far weathered the storm have done so because they have proved robust in a hostile environment.

The crisis underlines the importance of old macroeconomic policy virtues. It has increased awareness of the importance of financial sector institutional arrangements and of good governance more broadly. The old global institutions were geared to provide support for the old policy agenda, but what about the new?

DETERMINING THE OPTIMAL DIVISION OF LABOUR

Recent events demonstrate that what started out as national problems can have large regional and global ramifications. What is the appropriate sphere of responsibility, respectively, of national, regional and global institutions? A number of criteria are useful in defining the optimal division of labour. One is that the costs of providing help must be distributed in a manner that generates an efficient level of assistance. We can take some guidance from the theory of public goods. Efficient provision is more likely to occur if all those who benefit from assistance contribute to the cost, and if those who benefit more contribute more.

A financial crisis of the kind that has been experienced recently in parts of East Asia does great economic damage in each economy which succumbs to crisis, considerable damage to neighbouring economies that are linked to the crisis economy by intense trade and investment, and some damage to the global economy. The efficient internalization of external costs suggests the need for international support at a global level, with the support coming disproportionately from the economy's own region. Not all types of external costs are spread in the same way. The concentration of international banking strength amongst a small number of genuinely multinational players means that global banks will be well represented as creditors in a banking crisis anywhere in the world. Banks from the crisis economy's immediate region might not be especially well represented. The predominance of global externalities in a banking crisis suggests that global institutions should continue to play the main part in the working through, and especially in the funding, of the banking dimension of financial crises.

A second criterion is that the provision of assistance should involve efficient use of the expertise and information necessary to resolve the problem. In the

East Asian crisis, the prominence of weakness of financial institutions and regulatory systems in the problem, and their reform in the solution, raise the value of international support from economies with close knowledge of the financial problems and institutions of the troubled economies. Support will be most valuable if some economies with strong financial systems fall into this category. This second criterion for identifying the optimal sources of international support in financial crisis will point disproportionately to economies in a troubled country's own region.

A third criterion for identifying the optimal source of international support is institutional capacity, including leadership, in the provision of assistance. Here the global system, through the IMF, has had large advantages in the provision of support in the East Asian crisis. Regional institutions within the Western Pacific, or across the Pacific including North America, do not have well established traditions of cooperation in financial crisis.

Asian Pacific Economic Cooperation (APEC) has shown some promise, being able to draw on US leadership capacity in the absence of willingness in Japan or other large states in the Western Pacific to take political risks to lead. There is now some tradition of consultation amongst APEC finance ministers on international financial issues, which is likely to grow into institutional capacity to cooperate in a crisis. But cooperation at this level is still in its early stages.

We can illustrate how these criteria can be applied to the East Asian situation by considering the issue of funding arrangements in financial crises. With international banks heavily exposed in most financial crises, the efficient allocation of costs suggests that global institutions should play a major role in the resolution and funding of financial crises. The efficient use of information and expertise indicates that regional economies may have a comparative advantage in providing assistance. And the issue of institutional capacity implies that any package is likely to require strong involvement from the IMF, although assistance from regional networks may also be valuable.

The suggested division of labour (extensive involvement from global institutions with a strong supporting regional role) roughly corresponds to the actual response in East Asia. And, in fact, the existing arrangments for securing funding commitments worked reasonably well in the recent crisis. While the IMF took the formal lead in the assistance packages, in reality some division of labour between global and regional institutions already operated. Western Pacific central bankers met in July 1997 as part of the Executive Meeting of East Asia and Pacific Central Banks (EMEAP) process and agreed to examine a new Asian facility to supplement the IMF's funding. This established process of cooperation allowed the region's central banks to craft a quick response to the crisis and to organize the provision of emergency credit in the Thai crisis.

Over US$10 billion was quickly committed by EMEAP finance ministries in August. It was an advantage that the financial reach of the IMF could be extended in the East Asian crisis through the use of regional networks, particularly since, in the case of Thailand, the United States did not participate. Asia–Pacific finance ministers agreed under the Manila Framework, in November 1997, to formalize the EMEAP arrangements that enabled a swift regional commitment. In the circumstances so far, the commitments to the international funding packages for the four countries where the IMF was involved have been adequate. Actual disbursements have been slow and small in Indonesia. In the difficult Indonesian case, it may be that a larger regional input into the policy content of the packages could have improved the result. It is a weakness of the regional input that this was not forthcoming.

STRENGTHENING REGIONAL INVOLVEMENT

The extent to which the costs of crisis in one economy have been transmitted throughout the international economy has been a distinguishing feature of the East Asian crisis and one that the international community has only gradually come to recognize. International transmission has operated most powerfully through trade and investment linkages. As a result, the costs of the crisis have been concentrated amongst the troubled economies' major trade and investment partners, strengthening the case for a greater regional role in supporting the recovery. There are three broad areas where regional initiatives can enhance and complement the role of the global institutions. The first area lies in strengthening regional cooperation on monetary issues. Significant cooperation already takes place, not only through EMEAP, but also through a network of bilateral dollar repurchase agreements between regional central banks. The Manila Framework has endorsed further action. On top of the decision to formalize the cooperative financing arrangements that emerged during the Thai crisis, participating finance ministers agreed in November 1997 to enhance technical cooperation and to create a mechanism for regional surveillance.

The Asian Surveillance Group established in November 1997, as a result of commitments made under the Manila Framework, is made up of deputy central bank governors and Finance Ministry secretaries from the Manila Framework countries. It gathered for the first time in Tokyo in March 1998 and plans to meet every six months to discuss and monitor regional developments. The new grouping will operate as a complement to the current EMEAP process, which can retain its focus on technical issues. Unlike EMEAP, it includes Finance Ministry officials and so has clearer links to the political level. Its small size and common focus should give it a flexibility not possible at the global level, allowing it to take on a wider range of tasks. A forum of this kind could, for instance, be used to develop programmes of technical cooperation and assistance that enable economies with more sophisticated financial systems to contribute to the development of improved legal and institutional infrastructure in financial sectors elsewhere.

This last point touches on a second main area, financial sector reform, where regional initiatives can also help. The recent crisis has raised concerns over the quality of information and supervision in financial sectors throughout the region. Restoring investor confidence in the safety and transparency of financial systems will be a central part of the recovery process.

An agreement by APEC members to adhere to a set of mutually agreed minimium financial standards could be a useful addition to the institutional architecture. A set of minimum requirements for financial sector regulation could be designed and endorsed by APEC finance ministers. These might include the BIS's Basle Committee's Core Principles for Effective Banking Supervision, the IMF's Special Data Dissemination Standards for the publication of economic and financial information, and an agreement on common definitions for non-performing loans. Progress on these measures could then form part of APEC members' individual action plans.

An agreement along these lines would have two main advantages. One is that it would reduce the perception within the region that reforms are being imposed from outside. The other is that it could move ahead of parallel developments at a global level, allowing swifter action to restore confidence in the region's commitment to the necessary reforms. The APEC finance ministers' meeting at the end of May 1998 endorsed the Basle Core Principles on banking supervision but stopped short of concrete measures to ensure their adoption.

Although regional initiatives may provide a framework for financial sector reform, many of the largest obstacles to reform are technical. Thailand, for instance, needs support in drafting legislation, constructing institutions and technical expertise. Central bank or government cooperation on these issues will be an important channel of support. APEC finance ministers have already agreed to expand existing training programmes and staff exchanges for bank and securities regulators. In many cases, the process of transferring expertise has already begun through the private sector. Foreign banks, for instance, are already beginning the task of developing hedging instruments in some of the troubled economies, a move that may prevent a repeat of the massive exchange risk exposure that underlay the recent crisis.

There are potentially large benefits from reducing the transaction costs of these kinds of transfer through the private sector, smoothing the path for financial institutions from more advanced economies in the region to provide support and expertise for the private sector in economies where financial weakness has caused problems. Regional governments can play an important role in this process, by accelerating the work already undertaken in APEC and the WTO to reduce the barriers to cross-border flows in financial services and the obstacles to foreign investment in financial sectors. Provisions in the IMF packages have pushed governments towards some further liberalization in this area, but IMF-imposed proposals alone risk provoking a backlash once crisis has given way to recovery.

The transfer of ownership of regional companies to foreign investors has made governments understandably nervous, particularly given the perception that enterprises are changing hands at 'firesale' prices. But the case for broader foreign involvement in financial services, bringing greater expertise and more robust institutions, is much stronger than in many other sectors. This is especially true given recent evidence of the costs of weaknesses in these areas.

In the light of the current crisis, there are additional arguments for increasing the access of international banks to domestic financial markets in the region. One is that foreign equity can play a major part in recapitalizing financial systems in the area, a process that is already under way. Another advantage is that increasing foreign bank access would reduce the vulnerability of the financial sector to economy-wide shocks (Fane, 1998). Major foreign banks have globally diversified portfolios. A fall in the real exchange rate would have been less catastrophic for domestic financial systems if a large proportion of banks' loans had not been concentrated in the local economy.

The final area where a regional response has an important role to play relates more directly to recovery from the current crisis. As already mentioned, the process of recovery will depend on the ability of economies in the region to exploit their improved competitiveness to generate rapid export growth. The combination of enhanced competitiveness and weak domestic demand in East Asia, and continued expansion and a strong dollar in the United States, will inevitably lead to large changes in net exports on both sides of the Pacific. In particular, the US current account deficit will expand significantly. There is a danger that these growing imbalances will generate protectionist political responses in the United States, as they did in the mid-1980s. APEC's traditional role as a forum for maintaining support for open trade relations is more important than ever in this context.

CREATING INSTITUTIONAL CAPACITY

The issue of institutional capacity is an important one. In each of the three areas identified above, the appropriate institutional arrangements are likely to be different. APEC appears to be the obvious forum for encouraging cross-border flows in financial services and maintaining the openness of the regional trading system.

Enhanced cooperation on monetary issues may be better tackled in a smaller grouping. APEC is likely to be too unwieldy, and in any case would be in danger of being overloaded, if too much were added to its trade and investment focus. APEC has the advantage that it includes as a full partner Taiwan, with its considerable financial strength and relevant institutional experience. But the inclusion of Latin American states, and now Russia, in APEC, with fewer shared interests in regional financial cooperation than the original Western Pacific members, make it likely that a subset of APEC members would be a more relevant grouping for any substantive support in a crisis.

The crisis has imposed some logic of its own on the possible membership of such a grouping. The economies of the Western Pacific suffered direct contagion effects from regional problems, facing currency speculation and often depreciation, and are thus identifiable members of a regional financial network. These countries have the greatest incentives to improve financial systems throughout the region, since they appear to suffer most from failures within any regional economy.

This grouping, which roughly overlaps with the membership of EMEAP, has the advantage of being small and is already partly institutionalized. It also includes countries with well-developed financial systems that will be able to transfer expertise and advice. An important extension would be to develop this grouping under APEC's umbrella, which might allow the inclusion of Taiwan (a considerable advantage).

Recent events have highlighted the weakness of existing regional institutions for monetary cooperation. In June 1998, following a stock market correction in the United States that some attributed to concern about the Japanese economy, and warnings from the Chinese authorities that they might be forced to devalue if the yen continued to fall, the US Treasury engaged in joint foreign exchange intervention with the Japanese Ministry of Finance, and pushed for changes in domestic economic policy.

Table 3.4   External debt for selected East Asian economies (% of GDP)

	1990	1991	1992	1993	1994	1995	1996	1997
Australia	42.2	44.9	46.3	50.3	45.9	46.8	—	—
China	12.9	12.3	14.7	13.5	17.5	15.3	15.0	14.0
India	23.7	29.2	32.1	32.8	29.6	29.2	24.5	22.7
Indonesia	50.9	50.9	50.5	45.3	45.2	43.4	38.9	—
Korea, Rep.	9.5	9.7	10.5	10.5	10.7	9.4	11.2	15.0
Malaysia	33.2	33.4	29.0	32.1	31.9	32.2	28.8	29.1
Philippines	57.1	58.2	50.3	54.6	50.7	50.9	—	—
Thailand	23.2	23.8	22.4	20.9	22.2	20.1	19.8	25.0
Vietnam	237.3	224.6	159.4	178.8	138.3	122.5	—	—
Taiwan	0.5	0.5	0.3	0.3	0.2	0.2	0.1	0.1

Source: Asia Pacific Economics Group (1998), reproduced from Garnaut (1998a).

The Treasury's intervention starkly illustrated the extent to which major regional initiatives still depend on the leadership of the United States. The problem with dependence on US leadership is that its concern for East Asian stability is diluted by western hemisphere and global interests and responsibilities, and by domestic political distractions. The development of Western Pacific capacity for international economic policy leadership would allow more adequate embodiment of regional interests in the cooperation agenda. For example, only with Western Pacific and, especially, Japanese leadership is it likely that Indonesian stabilization will attract the financial and other support that is warranted by the dimensions of the problems and the regional interest in their solution.

REFERENCES

Asia Pacific Economic Group (1998), *Asia Pacific Profiles*, Canberra: ANU.
Asian Development Bank, 1988.
Banco de Mexico, 1995.
Fane, G. (1998), 'Prudential Regulation of Financial Institutions in the 1997–98 Crises in Southeast Asia', in *The East Asian Crisis: From Being a Miracle to Needing One?*, London and New York: Routledge.
Feldstein, M. (1998), 'Refocusing the IMF', *Foreign Affairs*, **77** (2), 20–33.
Garnaut, R.G. (1998a), 'The East Asian Financial Crisis: An Overview', in *The East Asian Crisis: From Being a Miracle to Needing One?*, London and New York: Routledge.
Garnaut, R.G. (1998b), 'The Financial Crisis: A Watershed in Economic Thought about East Asia', *Asian–Pacific Economic Literature*, May.
Jomo, K.S. (1998), 'Financial Liberalization, Crises and Malaysian Policy Responses', mimeo, Economics Department, University of Malaya.
McKibbin, W. (1998), 'The Crisis in East Asia: An Empirical Assessment', Brookings Discussion Paper in International Economics.
Montes, M.F. (1998), 'The Currency Crisis in Southeast Asia: Updated Edition', Singapore: ISEAS.
Walters, A. (1998), 'Exchange Rate and Monetary Regimes' in *The East Asian Crisis: From Being a Miracle to Needing One?*, London and New York: Routledge.
Warr, P. (1997), 'Thailand', *Asia Pacific Profiles*, Canberra: ANU.

4. Latin America confronting the Asian crisis

Gerardo Esquivel and Felipe Larraín B.*

INTRODUCTION

The recent crisis in several Asian countries has raised serious concerns in Latin America about the possibility of a 'contagion' effect that could trigger a full-blown crisis in the region. This concern is partly based on a simple extrapolation of the so-called 'tequila effect' of 1995 that negatively affected, at least temporarily, several emerging market economies, including some with presumably strong economic fundamentals. To date, the crisis scenario has not materialized in Latin America, but markets in the region remain unstable. After the collapse of the Russian ruble in late August, some Latin American markets deteriorated even further.

Indeed, there at least two good reasons for Latin American countries to be worried about the possibility of a further spreading of the Asian crisis. First, it is not only the currencies of emerging-market economies such as Thailand, Malaysia and Indonesia that have fallen. More stable and respected currencies such as the South Korean Won and the Japanese yen depreciated sharply against the US dollar between mid-1997 and mid-1998. Other Asian economies such as China and, especially, Hong Kong have also been affected by the crisis. This indicates the magnitude of the current crisis and its repercussions around the world. Second, some Latin American countries have important economic problems of their own. In some cases, these problems have been further aggravated by the first impacts of the Asian crisis on worldwide capital flows and commodity prices. Consequently, some countries in the region are significantly vulnerable to additional external shocks. In fact, starting in October 1997, Latin American stock markets and exchange rates were severely hit by a wave of financial panic whose origins can be traced to Asia.

The purpose of this chapter is to evaluate the likely implications of the Asian crisis for Latin America and to discuss some of the policy options that Latin

* The authors would like to express their thanks for the valuable comments of Rodrigo Vergara and the able assistance of Alexandra Lomakin.

American countries have in order to confront successfully the repercussions of the crisis. We first review the contributions of several theoretical models to our understanding of what causes a crisis. Next, we discuss some of the lessons that can be drawn from previous experiences of crises. Finally, we evaluate the current situation of four major Latin American countries and discuss their prospects for the immediate future.

WHAT DO WE KNOW ABOUT THE DETERMINANTS OF CURRENCY CRISES?

First-generation Models

Paul Krugman developed the first analytical model of balance of payments crises in 1979. He argued that crises occur when a continuous deterioration in the economic fundamentals becomes inconsistent with an attempt to fix the exchange rate. Krugman's model identifies excessive domestic credit creation either to finance fiscal deficits or to provide assistance to a weak banking system as the original problem. More specifically, his model assumes that the government does not have access to capital markets and therefore has to monetize its expenditures. This increase in the quantity of money in the economy tends to reduce domestic interest rates. Since world interest rates have not changed, this induces capital outflows and a gradual loss of foreign exchange reserves. Further down the road, the economy eventually becomes the victim of a speculative attack that triggers the abandonment of the fixed exchange rate system. In the model, the timing of the attack is determined by a critical level in the amount of reserves. The fall of reserves to this threshold induces speculators to exhaust the remaining reserves in a short period of time to avoid capital losses.

The Krugman model and its extensions represent what has become known as *first-generation* models of balance of payments crises.[1] The main insight of these models is that crises arise as a result of an inconsistency between domestic policies (that is, excessive public spending that becomes monetized) and a fixed exchange rate. In this sense, a crisis is both unavoidable and predictable in an economy with a constant deterioration of its economic fundamentals.

Second-generation Models

More recently, a number of authors have focused on the possibility of having currency crises even in the absence of a continuous deterioration in economic fundamentals. Models built along this line are known as *second-generation* models of balance of payments crises. A key aspect of these is the existence of a circular process that leads to the existence of more than one equilibrium (Obstfeld, 1994, 1996). Since pure expectations may lead to one or another equilibrium position, many of the second-generation models implicitly or explicitly accept the possibility of *self-fulfilling crises*.[2] This type of crisis occurs, for example, when the sheer pessimism of a significant group of investors provokes a capital outflow that leads to the eventual collapse of the exchange rate system, thus validating the negative expectations. In this sense, second-generation models tend to emphasize the reinforcing effects of the actions of economic agents in determining the movements from one equilibrium position to another.

In a typical second-generation model there is no obvious and predictable situation leading to the collapse of the exchange rate. Most models assume a government with explicit incentives either to defend or to abandon the exchange rate system. Consequently, many second-generation models underscore the interactions between government policies and the perceptions of economic agents, such as when private agents perceive that the government of a slowly growing economy may pursue expansionary fiscal policies. In this case, economic agents may anticipate such a policy and react by attacking the domestic currency, thus accelerating the collapse of the exchange rate system. Since the change in policy does not necessarily occur,[3] a crisis in these models tends to have a highly unpredictable component.

Although second-generation models have several features in common, they also differ in crucial respects. In some models, economic fundamentals play a key role in determining when a crisis may occur. In particular, they identify an intermediate range of economic fundamentals for which a crisis may or may not occur. Thus a country with relatively 'good' fundamentals will never experience a currency crisis.[4] Although it is not possible to predict when a currency crisis will occur in these models, at least one can infer which countries are more vulnerable.

In other second-generation models, crises are not affected by the position of the fundamentals and may simply be the result of pure speculation against a currency. There are at least two types of analysis along these lines. Models of *herding behaviour* stress that costs of information may lead foreign investors to take decisions based on limited information and this, in turn, leaves the economy more sensitive to rumours (Calvo and Mendoza, 1997). *Contagion effects*, on the other hand, emphasize that groups of countries belonging to the same region may be perceived as sharing common policy characteristics or objectives (Drazen, 1998). When one country falls into crisis, investors may perceive a higher risk of a crisis in neighbouring countries. Foreign capital will then flee the neighbouring countries, thus provoking the collapse of their exchange rate, thereby materializing the pessimistic prediction of investors.

LESSONS FROM THE PAST: THE LATIN AMERICAN CRISES OF THE EARLY 1980s

In this section, we briefly review some crucial aspects of the Latin American crises of the early 1980s, as they provide important lessons and contrasts for the current episode. In another publication we identified a group of economic variables that are crucial to understanding the conditions that may lead to a currency crisis, and measured econometrically the effects of these variables in explaining the probability of crisis (Esquivel and Larraín, 1998). In this section we focus on some of these key indicators.

During the early 1980s, several Latin American countries sharply devalued their currencies. At first, the simultaneous occurrence of many currency crises in the region seemed to point towards a purely external shock, for example a terms of trade collapse or a jump in foreign interest rates. A more detailed analysis, however, promptly made clear an internal cause. Most countries affected by the crisis had been running large fiscal deficits for prolonged periods.

Table 4.1 shows five key economic indicators for five of the largest Latin American economies affected by currency crises in the early 1980s: Argentina, Brazil, Chile, Mexico and Peru. These data clearly reveal the potentially explosive economic situation in these countries on the eve of the crisis. The first row in Table 4.1 is the average public sector deficit from 1979 to 1981.[5] The situation was dramatic: most countries were running very large fiscal deficits during the pre-crisis years, at an average rate ranging from almost 5 per cent of GDP in Peru to over 9 per cent in both Brazil and Mexico. The notable exception was Chile, which had a substantial fiscal surplus in the order of 4 per cent of GDP over the same period. In spite of this, Chile developed a major balance of payments crisis as well.

The next three variables in Table 4.1 show the existence of close similarities across these Latin American countries. Seigniorage (measured as the increase in the monetary aggregate M1 as a percentage of GDP) shows that the governments of these countries, especially Mexico and Peru, were substantially monetizing the deficit. Although Chile had a fiscal surplus, its average annual inflation rate was close to 30 per cent between 1979 and 1981; thus the Chilean public sector was collecting seigniorage even if it did not have a clear need for it. The currencies of all five countries experienced a sharp real appreciation during the 24 months previous to their respective crisis. As measured by an index of the multilateral real effective exchange rate, real appreciations ranged from 20 per cent to 36 per cent between 1979 and mid-1981. Appreciations of such magnitude normally go together with an aggregate expenditure boom that leads to a sharp drop in the relative price of tradables to non-tradables, encouraging imports and discouraging exports. Such a pattern is reflected in the fourth variable in Table 4.1 (the current account balance).

The current account balance as a percentage of GDP shows that all these countries had large deficits in their external accounts right before the crisis. Chile provides the most extreme example, with an average annual deficit of almost 11 per cent of GDP between 1979 and 1981. This is all the more striking if we consider that the Chilean government was running a massive fiscal surplus at the time. As documented by Larraín (1991), this pattern is explained by an unsustainable private consumption boom.

Table 4.1   Selected macroeconomic indicators for some Latin American countries

	Argentina	Brazil	Chile	Mexico	Peru
Public sector balance (% of GDP) Average 1979–81	–6.0	–9.8	3.7	–9.1	–4.7
Seigniorage (% of GDP) Average 1979–81	3.2	2.5	2.0	4.7	5.3
Real exchange rate appreciation within the 24 months previous to each country's crisis	36	29	20	20	22
Current account balance (% of GDP) Average 1980–81	–6.2	–5.0	–10.8	–5.9	–3.7
Credit to the private sector as % of GDP (growth rate between 1977 and 1981, %)	43.1	–28.2	155.3	24.1	22.1

Sources: Larraín and Selowsky (1991), The World Bank, IMF and JP Morgan.

The last variable in Table 4.1, the expansion of commercial bank credit to the private sector as a percentage of GDP, is one of the most interesting and has usually been overlooked in discussions of currency crises.[6] Sharp increases in bank credit indicate the existence of a lending boom. As Table 4.1 shows, there is clear evidence of a 'lending boom' in Chile at the time. The ratio of commercial bank credit to GDP in Chile increased by 155 per cent between December 1977 and December 1981. This credit surge in Chile followed the deregulation of its financial sector and the opening of its capital account and helped to finance the private consumption boom. This variable then helps to explain why the Chilean economy was vulnerable to a currency crisis in spite of having a very strong fiscal position. Credit increases were significant but much lower in Argentina, and more modest in Mexico and Peru during this same four-year period, while Brazil alone suffered a credit contraction.

In conclusion, most episodes of crises in Latin America during the 1980s fit well the logic of first-generation models of balance of payments crises. Crises in the 1980s were normally the result of excessive government expenditure that continuously eroded the external position of the economies and that eventually broke down the exchange rate regime. The main exception in this respect was Chile, where the crisis came, not from a high public sector deficit, but as the natural consequence of an unsustainable private consumption boom financed through the banking system.

THE CRISES OF THE 1990S: MEXICO (1994) AND ASIA (1997)

On 19 December 1994, the Government of Mexico announced the widening of the peso's exchange rate band. Two days later, after the Central Bank had lost several billions of dollars in foreign exchange reserves, the Government floated the peso. By then, rumours about the probability of an eventual suspension of payments on dollar-denominated bonds (the infamous *Tesobonos*) had spread and prompted a run on Mexican bonds. Interest rates soared and the exchange rate collapsed. By the end of December, the Mexican currency was being traded at a rate of 5 pesos per dollar, up from 3.5 in mid-December; by mid-March the exchange rate reached 7.4 pesos per dollar, a depreciation of more than 100 per cent from its pre-crisis value.

The period immediately following the Mexican crisis was one of confusion and financial panic. Many other currencies in Latin America came under severe pressure and the stock markets in many emerging economies suffered sharp contractions between January and March of 1995. Most of these effects, however, were short-lived.[7] Only Mexico and Argentina endured economic decline in 1995, and both rebounded strongly in 1996–7.

The Asian crisis, however, has proved considerably more durable. In July 1997, the Thai currency was devalued despite repeated statements by government officials that such a measure would not be taken. In a matter of days, the currencies of Indonesia, the Philippines and Malaysia came under heavy attack and started to plunge. By the end of October, the South Korean Won was battered and threats of a generalized crisis across Asia increased.

The two crises just sketched, Mexico in 1994 and Asia in 1997, share two particularly intriguing features: first, only a few months before the crises these economies were widely regarded as solid and stable, with very good economic prospects;[8] second, even days before the crises, financial and economic analysts seemed to be completely unaware of what was coming.[9] That both economies were among the most closely watched by the financial community makes these two characteristics even more intriguing.

One possible explanation for these 'surprise crises' is that, unlike Latin America in the 1980s, Mexico in 1994 and Thailand in 1997 had demonstrated no evidence of recent fiscal or monetary expansionary policies. Table 4.2 shows the same five key indicators used in Table 4.1 to discuss the Latin American crisis of the 1980s, but with data for Mexico, Thailand, Indonesia, Malaysia, the Philippines and Korea. The first two variables in Table 4.2, fiscal balance and seigniorage, show a completely different pattern from that observed in Latin America in the 1980s. Mexico, Thailand and Indonesia ran, on average, a fiscal surplus in the years preceding the financial crises. The other countries in Table 4.2, Malaysia, Korea and the Philippines, were in equilibrium or ran relatively small fiscal deficits. The seigniorage variable also shows a very different pattern from that of Latin American countries in the 1980s: there is no evidence of a substantial process of monetization before the crisis occurred, with the exception of Malaysia.

The last three variables in Table 4.2, however, do resemble more the Latin American situation in the 1980s. Table 4.2 shows that most countries that suffered a crisis in the 1990s had been running large current account deficits in the pre-crisis period. Mexico, Thailand and Malaysia carried a deficit above 6 per cent of GDP per year. Indonesia, Korea and the Philippines carried slightly more moderate deficits, between 3.3 and 4.6 per cent. More importantly, in all of the Table 4.2 countries except Korea, there was a relative large real exchange rate appreciation before the crises. Finally, in three of the six countries, Mexico, Thailand and the Philippines, the crises were preceded by a lending boom.

These variables combined clearly show that, excepting Korea, all countries considered had shown some signs of vulnerability well before the actual crises occurred. These signs, however, were not the typical ones observed in the past; that is, there was no direct evidence of fiscal relaxation or sharp increases in the quantity of money. Instead, the symptoms of the crisis were mainly rooted in the financial sector of the economy. Thus the crises of the 1990s have more elements in common with the Chilean crisis of 1982 than with the other crises of the 1980s in the region.

Table 4.2   Selected macroeconomic indicators for Mexico and some Asian countries

	Mexico	Thailand	Indonesia	Malaysia	Philippines	South Korea
Fiscal balance (% of GDP)						
Average 1992–4						
Average 1994–6	0.5	2.2	0.7	2.4	–0.2	0.3
Seigniorage (% of GDP)						
Average 1992–4						
Average 1994–6	1.1	1.0	1.3	3.8	1.4	1.0
Current account balance (% of GDP)						
Average 1993–4						
Average 1995–6	–6.4	–7.9	–3.3	–7.4	–4.6	–3.4
Real exchange rate appreciation within the 24 months previous to each country's crisis	13.1	15.5	12.1	12.8	17.7	4.4
Credit to the private sector as a % of GDP						
(% increase between 1990 and 1994)						
(% increase between 1992 and 1996)	103.2	37.8	12.1	13.4	104.6	15.6

Sources: The World Bank, IMF and JP Morgan.

In summary, there are two aspects that are common to almost every crisis discussed above: a substantial real exchange rate appreciation and a relatively large current account deficit. Interestingly, most crises have been preceded by large spending booms that lead to significant current account deficits. Whether the cause of the external deficit is the result of an excess of public spending (as in the case of most Latin American countries in the 1980s), an excess of private consumption (as in Mexico in the 1990s) or a boom in private investment (as in most Asian countries in the 1990s), it appears to have had second-order importance. Therefore a large current account deficit and an overvalued real exchange rate may be interpreted as summary variables indicating that a crisis is coming. Indeed, in related work we have found econometric evidence that these two variables are highly significant in explaining exchange rate crises in a broad sample of middle- and high-income countries (Esquivel and Larraín, 1998).

Perhaps one of the most important lessons about the recent crises reviewed in this section is that, contrary to popular belief, there have usually been clear signals that something is fundamentally wrong in the economy before a currency crisis. This does not mean, however, that a crisis or its timing is totally predictable. Rather, it only means that it is possible to identify a set of conditions that make an economy prone to suffering a crisis. In the next section we use this conclusion to assess the situation of some Latin American economies in the aftermath of the Asian crisis.

LATIN AMERICA'S PROSPECTS IN THE AFTERMATH OF THE ASIAN CRISIS

With good reason, there is serious concern in the region about the contagion of the Asian crisis. In October 1997, a strong speculative wave negatively affected most stock markets and currencies in Latin America. In this section we address Latin America's prospects on the basis of our discussion above. We briefly review key macroeconomic and vulnerability indicators in four of the largest economies of the region: Argentina, Brazil, Chile and Mexico. In the following section we evaluate and discuss the policy options that these countries have in order to confront the Asian crisis successfully.

Macroeconomic Indicators

Looking at key macroeconomic variables is a good starting point for assessing the current conditions in a country and for identifying its potential vulnerabilities. Figure 4.1 shows the evolution of the current account as a percentage of

GDP for Argentina, Brazil, Chile and Mexico between 1992 and 1997. The data show a clear pattern: countries that were running large current account deficits in the first part of the 1990s, that is, Argentina and Mexico, experienced sharp corrections in their current accounts as a result of the Mexican crisis of 1994–5. Since then, the external accounts of these countries have deteriorated somewhat. Argentina and Mexico, however, still exhibit a relatively small current account deficit. Brazil, which had a more balanced external situation at the onset of the Mexican crisis, suffered a continuous deterioration of its external accounts: it moved from a current account surplus of 1.5 per cent of GDP in 1992 to a deficit in excess of 4 per cent in 1997. Chile, affected by a large terms-of-trade deterioration since 1996, exhibits the largest external deficit among the four countries.

Figure 4.2 shows the fiscal balance as a percentage of GDP for the same group of countries, with more heterogeneous results. The fiscal position looks

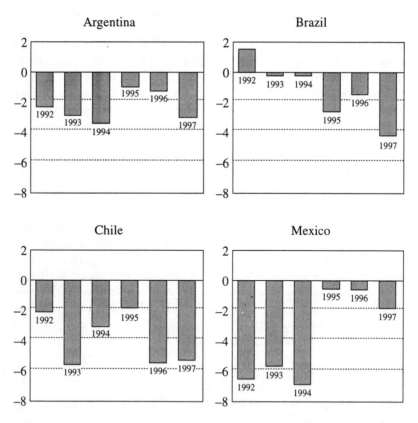

Figure 4.1   Current account balance, 1992–7 (% of GDP)

relatively healthy for three of the four countries: Chile had fiscal surpluses throughout the 1990s, though the surplus declined after 1995; Mexico's fiscal situation has been close to balanced between 1992 and 1997; Argentina's fiscal balance has deteriorated slightly since 1993, when it ran a surplus, but the magnitude of the deficit is relatively small.

On the other hand, Brazil has been running large fiscal deficits, in excess of 5 per cent of GDP per year, during the past three years. Two comments are worth making about the fiscal situation of Brazil. First, although the magnitude of Brazil's fiscal imbalance seems small when compared to the two-digit deficits of some Latin American countries in the 1980s, it is undoubtedly high when compared to the current fiscal situation of the rest of the region, and to recent international standards. Moreover, Brazil's fiscal deficit has been *increasing* during the last three years, and in 1998 will exceed 7 per cent of GDP. Second, as Figures 4.1 and 4.2 clearly show, Brazil's current account

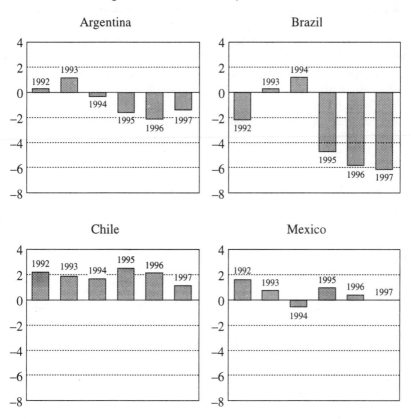

Figure 4.2   Fiscal balance, 1992–7 (% of GDP)

deficit closely mirrors its fiscal deficit, although it is smaller in magnitude. This combination of twin deficits has proved explosive many times in emerging markets. It is therefore imperative for Brazil to cut its fiscal deficit. This is Brazil's most important current macroeconomic challenge.

Figure 4.3 charts the pattern of the real exchange rate index in the region from 1992 to April 1998. The data show that Brazil and Chile have had the sharpest appreciations in the last years, around 20 per cent compared to 1990–92. In Brazil, the appreciation accelerated after the Real Plan was implemented in July 1994. In Chile, the domestic currency had accumulated an appreciation of more than 30 per cent between 1990 and September 1997. Thus the depreciation of the Chilean currency in late 1997 and early 1998 took some pressure off the exchange rate, as reflected in the slight rise in the Chilean real exchange rate between September 1997 and April 1998.

In Mexico, the appreciation of its currency in 1996 and 1997 led to a complete loss of the competitiveness gains obtained with the devaluations of 1994 and 1995. This trend, however, has been partially reversed with the nominal exchange rate adjustments of mid-1998. On the other hand, Argentina's peso also appreciated sharply in the 1990s; even in recent years, when Argentina's inflation has fallen below international levels, the fixed parity of the peso to the strong US dollar has led to a continuous appreciation of the Argentinean currency. As of April 1998, as Figure 4.3 shows, Chile was the only country in this group that had experienced a slight currency depreciation since the beginning of the Asian crisis. Recently, however, following the

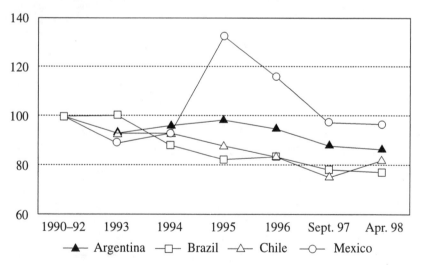

Figure 4.3   Real exchange rate (1990–2 = 100)

collapse of the Russian ruble and as a result of the increased instability in world markets, Mexico's currency has also depreciated significantly.

Finally, Figure 4.4 shows domestic credit to the private sector as a percentage of GDP in Argentina, Brazil, Chile and Mexico. The data clearly show that there was not a credit boom in the region between 1992 and 1996. On the contrary, Brazil and Mexico had a significant credit reduction, while domestic credit in Chile and Argentina showed a moderate upward trend. Credit expansion has not been significant in these economies in the past several years, and this factor does not seem to be an important destabilizing factor for the near future.

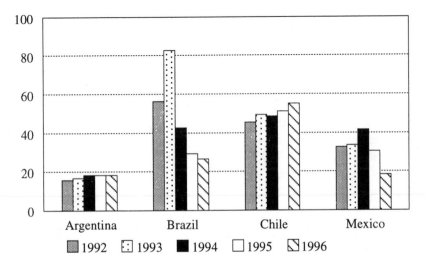

Figure 4.4   Commercial bank credit to the private sector (% of GDP)

External Vulnerability

To assess the prospects of the Latin American economies in an unstable external environment, it is crucial to evaluate the vulnerability of these countries to a reduction in world demand resulting from Asia's financial and economic turmoil. In this regard, two indicators are important: exports to Asia as a percentage of total exports and the share of primary products in total exports. The former measures the direct trade exposure of Latin American countries to Asia; the latter shows the exposure of Latin American countries to reductions in commodity prices, a phenomenon which is often observed during periods of global recession.

Figure 4.5 presents these two variables. The figure clearly shows that Argentina, Brazil and Mexico have relatively low levels of exposure to Asia: 14 per cent, 12 per cent and 3 per cent, respectively. Among the four countries examined, Chile is the most exposed to the Asian crisis, as 32 per cent of Chile's exports go to Asia.

Regarding primary exports, all four Latin American countries in Figure 4.5 show relatively large shares of these goods in their total exports. This characteristic leaves all these countries in a highly vulnerable position before sudden changes in world demand. This degree of vulnerability is, however, very differentiated across the countries in our sample. Among these four Latin American countries, Mexico has the lowest share of primary exports, with 22 per cent, while Brazil and Argentina's primary exports represent around one-third of their total exports. On the other hand, Chile's primary exports represent 62 per cent of its total exports, the largest share in the group.

Chile is thus the Latin American country most exposed to the 'Asian flu' on the trade front. It has the largest exposure to the Asian markets and its exports depend heavily on primary products. Argentina and Brazil, on the other hand, have intermediate dependence levels on both primary product's exports and the Asian markets. Mexico, with its strong ties to the US market, seems to be relatively safe as long as the US economy continues growing solidly. The main channel, however, through which the Asian crisis has affected Mexico is through its effect on the price of oil.

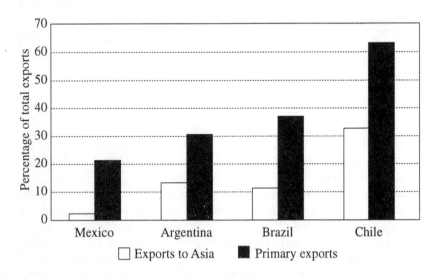

Figure 4.5   External vulnerability (% of total exports)

Latin America's Prospects: an Assessment

Overall, Brazil appears as the most vulnerable economy among these four Latin American countries. It has large fiscal and current account deficits, and presents the sharpest currency appreciation. Given the economic importance of Brazil in the Southern Cone, however, and its close commercial ties with Argentina (and also, though less significantly, with Chile), the whole region would be affected if Brazil succumbed to a currency crisis.

Chile, though more vulnerable in a narrow trade sense, has much stronger fundamentals, as indicated by a solid credit rating. In fact, despite its terms-of-trade deterioration and its heavy exports dependence on Asia, Chile's credit rating is still the best in Latin America.

The occurrence of a crisis in one country, however, may seriously undermine the economic conditions of the other countries in the region. There is clear evidence of the existence of a regional 'contagion' effect that may propagate a crisis. A simple exercise may illustrate this point. Using the results from a previous work (Esquivel and Larraín, 1998), we can calculate the probability of a currency crisis in a country with the economic conditions that Chile currently has. We estimate the probability of crisis for Chile to be about 16 per cent. If a neighbouring country falls into a currency crisis, however, the probability of a crisis in Chile rises to 26 per cent. Thus the pure contagion effect in this case is about 10 percentage points. To illustrate the importance of this effect, consider that, out of 111 crises studied in a sample of 30 countries, we found that about half of the countries whose estimated probability was greater than 25 per cent experienced a currency crisis the next year. This result may illustrate the importance of the contagion effect as well as the relevance of keeping the economic stability in the region as a whole.

On the surface, Mexico appears to have a relatively less uncomfortable position from which to confront the Asian crisis. In a sense, the country has benefited from the substantial and painful process of adjustment that followed the crisis of 1994. One point of concern, however, is the rapid real exchange rate appreciation that took place between 1995 and 1997, which eroded most of the competitiveness gain obtained with the exchange rate adjustments of 1994–5. This trend has been partially reversed during 1998 owing to a change in the exchange rate policy that allows the Mexican peso to float more freely. The new policy has reduced the risks of an exchange rate crisis, facilitating a rapid and substantial depreciation of the Mexican currency in the second semester of 1998.

A common point of concern for both Chile and Mexico is the deterioration in the price of their main export commodity. Copper prices have plummeted from levels of US$1.20 per pound before the Asian crisis, to around 75 cents per pound since the crisis. Copper accounts for more than 40 per cent of

Chilean exports and the effect on the copper price by itself amounts to an income loss of almost two percentage points of GDP for Chile in 1998.

Likewise, Mexico has suffered from a sharp decline (about 30 per cent) in the price of oil, one of its main export products. Mexico, however, has two strengths to confront this event. First, Mexico depends on the US market for 85 per cent of its exports and the US economy is relatively well positioned to confront the Asian crisis. Second, thanks to the structural reform process that began in 1985, Mexico depends much less on oil exports, which currently represent only about 12 per cent of total exports, down from 70 per cent in 1981. Nonetheless, Mexico's government revenues still depend heavily on oil.[10] This explains the large reduction in expected revenues of the Mexican government in 1998, which has been met adequately with large cuts in public expenditure to avoid a further deterioration in the fiscal accounts.

POLICY OPTIONS IN THE FACE OF THE ASIAN CRISIS

Macroeconomic Management and Structural Reforms

The Asian crisis hit Latin America with a lag of just a few months. Starting in October 1997, stock markets fell substantially and several currencies came under severe attack. In response to this panic and to its aftermath, the Brazilian government decided to counterattack the speculation against the domestic currency by raising short-term interest rates. As a result, overnight interest rates rose from about 22 per cent to over 40 per cent at the peak of the crisis. Later, in November 1997, the Brazilian government announced an important package of measures aimed at reducing the fiscal deficit. During 1998, interest rates fell back to the levels of September 1997, around 20 per cent, and then climbed back to over 40 per cent, remaining highly volatile.

Notwithstanding the efforts of the Brazilian government in late 1997 to attack the problem at its roots, the fiscal adjustment proposed by the government has not been enough to reduce the vulnerability of the economy. The fiscal adjustment will probably have to be strengthened in order to have a lasting effect on the stability of the country. It is clear that keeping the interest rates at 30 per cent or even 20 per cent (with inflation at less than 4 per cent) cannot be sustained for long without a significant deterioration in the assets of the banking system and, thus, increased risk of financial collapse.

Brazil needs not only to implement the fiscal package presented in November 1997, but also to make progress in structural areas such as the reforms to social security, public administration and privatization. Although significant progress has occurred in some of these (including the recent successful privatization of Telebras, the domestic telecommunications company), several crucial aspects of the administrative reform are still waiting for Congress approval and their implementation will probably not occur for several months. Additionally, some reports suggest that some of the policy measures announced in 1997 have been postponed or delayed without justification. It is clear that moving in the direction of deepening structural reforms is the appropriate way for Brazil to regain the initiative and to attain the credibility necessary to reduce interest rates. A related issue is that Brazil needs to increase the flexibility of its exchange rate policy so that it can gradually move away from its current overvaluation.

As a result of the financial shock of late October 1997, the Chilean peso reversed its course of sustained appreciation in the 1990s and suffered significant pressure towards depreciation. The central bank drastically raised interest rates and spent about US$1.6 billion (or 9 per cent of its foreign exchange reserves) intervening to support the peso in the foreign exchange market. In spite of this, the Chilean peso depreciated by around 10 per cent against the US dollar between October and December 1997. Given the pressures that the economy was experiencing, particularly the collapse of copper prices, and the conditions of instability prevalent in the financial markets, the devaluation of the Chilean peso should be seen as a necessary correction in an otherwise unsustainable appreciating trend. In light of the high dependence of Chilean exports on Asian markets and on primary products, however, a prudent economic policy is strongly desirable. Appropriately, Chile's government cut fiscal spending twice in 1998, and accepted a modest devaluation of the currency.

Through most of 1998, Argentina endured high real interest rates and a significant stock market decline, but was able to maintain its fixed exchange rate to the dollar. Considering the macroeconomic indicators discussed above, however, Argentina may face serious problems if Brazil falls into crisis. In such a case, Argentina's monetary arrangement (a currency board) would become subject to severe pressures and its currency could undergo a speculative attack, as in the first months of 1995. The Argentinian authorities will likely stick to the full convertibility policy, since exchange rate stability is so much at the heart of the country's reform process. They can also take heart from the fact that the two most visible countries with currency boards (Argentina and Hong Kong) were successful in defending their currencies when neighbouring currencies fell, in 1995 and 1997, respectively.

Currency boards, however, have costs and risks. They tie the hands of the policy makers and eliminate the role of the central bank as a lender of last resort. In the event of a run on deposits in the financial system, the central bank would face a tough dilemma: it could maintain the currency board but only at the cost of a collapse in the financial system, a collapse of much greater dimensions than under alternative monetary regimes. Even if the system does not collapse, the costs of this policy in terms of output and/or employment can be very high, as evidenced by Argentina in 1995 and Hong Kong in 1998 during the Asian crisis. The best way for Argentina to confront these pressures is to deepen even further its reform programme, particularly the liberalization of its labour market. This reform, however, faces unusual complications in the current political conditions of a weakened administration.

After the 1994–5 crisis, Mexico undertook a painful adjustment in its economy that included a severe macroeconomic contraction and the introduction of corrective measures in its financial sector, yet current conditions in the banking system are far from optimal and, unless the problems in the financial system are tackled on time, they may become the Achilles heel of the Mexican economy. The recent financial pressures have also provoked a jump in the exchange rate that has helped to relieve some of the appreciation pressures accumulated in the real exchange rate between 1995 and 1997. One of the main sources of concern for Mexico now is the uncertainty associated with the political conflict over the bailout of the banking system. Resolving this problem soon will greatly help Mexico to face the Asian crisis. Otherwise, the economic situation could become extremely complex and explosive in the near future.

Dealing with Capital Flows

The Asian crisis has put the issue of how to deal with capital flows at the forefront of economic discussion. In particular, one of the most debated aspects is the role of capital controls in affecting the magnitude and composition of capital that a country may attract. Many authors have suggested that imposing some form of capital control may help a country avoid unnecessary exchange rate fluctuations and, more generally, may reduce an economy's vulnerability to external shocks. The stability of Chile after the Mexican crisis has often been quoted as a leading example of the benefits of such policies, and thus we address this case in a little more detail.[11]

In 1991, Chile implemented a 20 per cent non-remunerated reserve requirement on foreign credits that was increased to 30 per cent in 1992. Whether the reserve requirement has been an effective tool to stem the inflow of short-term capital, however, is subject to debate. Recently, Larraín *et al.* (1997) have shown that capital control measures in Chile affect the composition of capital inflows away from those flows that are subject to taxes. In the short run, though, controls appear not to have a significant effect on the overall magnitude of the flows, while some overall deterrent effect remains in the medium to long term.

Another option that has been widely used to defend the real exchange rate in the presence of large capital inflows is the relaxation of a number of restrictions on capital outflows. These policies, used in both developed and developing countries, include the reduction of restrictions for profit and capital repatriation on foreign investments, and the liberalization of investment options abroad for institutional investors. Nonetheless, as Laban and Larraín (1997) argue, the liberalization of capital outflows is more likely to induce higher capital inflows since it makes the decision to invest in domestic assets less irreversible. Thus liberalizing outflow controls may be a good measure in itself, but it is likely to provide little relief in reducing the pressures on exchange rate appreciation that arise from capital inflows.

Nonetheless, the role of capital controls is fundamentally different in normal periods, in the presence of large capital inflows (as in Latin America during most of the 1990s), than at times of potential crisis, when inflows turn into outflows (as after October 1997). In periods of crisis, inflow controls become redundant and by and large mainly increase the cost of capital for domestic companies in international markets; increased outflow controls, on the other hand, are likely to reduce net inflows.

CONCLUSIONS

Some important lessons emerge when comparing the experiences of Latin America in the 1980s, Mexico in 1994 and Asia in 1997. First, not all currency crises are alike. Most crises in Latin America during the 1980s had a strong fiscal component and, in that sense, tend to fit well with the explanations posited by traditional models of balance of payments crises. On the other hand, it is clear that crises in Chile (1982), Mexico (1994) and Asia (1997) did not have a fiscal origin and therefore the roots of the crises are located elsewhere, mainly in the financial sector. Second, contrary to popular assertions, and in spite of their different nature, most crises have been preceded by strong indications of fundamental weakness in the economy. Some of the most important signals are given by the current account deficit, the real exchange rate appreciation and a rapid expansion of credit to the private sector. In addition to these signals, standard balance of payments crises (mainly in the 1980s) were also preceded by large fiscal deficits and high rates of seigniorage.

On the basis of the analysis of this chapter, one may assess the current conditions in four economies of Latin America. Brazil, the regional giant, is the most vulnerable economy in the region and needs to take further steps to adjust its economy beyond the reduction of its twin deficits in the current account and the public budget. In particular, Brazil needs to implement a series of structural reforms in the social security scheme, in the administration of the state and in privatization. Some of these measures have already been proposed and approved by the Congress, but further efforts need to be made to ensure their implementation. Together with some liberalization in its exchange rate policy, this is probably the best option for Brazil to prevent a major recession stemming from very high interest rates.

The case of Chile provides an interesting contrast. Widely regarded as the strongest economy of the region prior to the Asian crisis for its performance after the Mexican devaluation of December 1994, Chile has seemed to lose its aura as a safe heaven. Some analysts have gone as far as to say that Chile has become the most vulnerable economy of Latin America. This assertion does not withstand scrutiny. In spite of having been hard hit by a terms of trade shock, Chile is structurally healthy, with the highest investment and saving rates in Latin America and probably the strongest banking system of the region. It faces, however, a major trade challenge coming from its heavy exposure to copper and Asia, and would certainly face tougher times were Brazil's problems to intensify.

Argentina has made important progress since 1995, especially in the consolidation of its banking system. Weaker regional demand, however, and the loss of competitiveness associated with the Asian crisis will surely take its toll in terms of higher trade deficits. Perhaps Argentina's weakest point is its high dependence on Brazil, which since the MERCOSUR agreement has come to absorb some 30 per cent of the country's exports.

Mexico has a significant advantage in its more diversified export base, its large integration with the US economy and its flexible exchange rate policy. Like Argentina, Mexico has to be careful with its external accounts, especially in light of the collapse in oil prices. The government has reacted by sharply adjusting fiscal spending in recent months, in tandem with the decline in oil prices. Mexico's Achilles heel, however, is the weak situation of its banking sector and the economic and political complications of the FOBAPROA programme.

How can countries better deal with potential currency crises? Clearly, a correction of the fundamental macroeconomic imbalances of the country, as outlined above, is an important part of the story. This is only a necessary condition, however, and may not be sufficient to avoid contagion. For countries that are in the midst of structural reforms, potential crises should be used as an opportunity to deepen the reforms, as Argentina did in 1995 and Brazil should attempt now. There are two main reasons for this: first, legislative approval for reforms is easier to obtain at times of crisis; second, a further push for reforms is a very good signal that the economic and political authorities can send to the markets. Doing everything right, however, minimizes the risk of a crisis, but is no sure guarantee against it, as the work on self-fulfilling crisis and some of the other second-generation models makes clear.

Capital controls, on the other hand, have no role at times of crises. Stepping up outflow controls may deter some outflows but, on balance, is likely to discourage net inflows. Increasing controls on inflows at a time when capital is flowing out is largely superfluous, and increases the cost for local companies looking for financing abroad.

NOTES

1. Extensions to the Krugman model have been developed by Flood and Garber (1984) and Connolly and Taylor (1984). More recently, Krugman (1991) extended the analysis to a target zone model. Flood *et al.* (1984) incorporate the role of sterilization in the analysis. For a survey of these models, see Agenor *et al.* (1992).
2. See Flood and Marion (1998) for a recent summary of this literature.
3. Output does not even have to be an objective of the government at all. It suffices that economic agents believe it is.
4. This is the case, for example, of the model discussed in Sachs *et al.* (1996).
5. Note that this indicator is a broad measure of the fiscal situation in each country. It includes the balance of both the central government and the public enterprises. See Larraín and Selowsky (1991) for a detailed description of the data and sources.
6. An exception is Sachs *et al.* (1996).
7. It is important to note, though, that 1995 was a year of strong growth for the world economy, and that terms of trade improved considerably for commodity exporters.
8. In this regard, see Radelet and Sachs (1998) for a summary of the IMF Executive Board discussions on Indonesia, Korea and Thailand that preceded the 1997 crisis.
9. See, for example, the evidence discussed in Goldfajn and Valdés (1998) and in Radelet and Sachs (1998). Although in the case of Mexico there were some early warnings about the possibility of a crisis (see, for example, Dornbusch and Werner, 1996), no one can accurately claim to have anticipated the magnitude of the crisis.
10. More than 30 per cent of Mexico's government revenue is directly tied to oil.
11. See Laban and Larraín (1998) for a detailed discussion on this issue.

REFERENCES

Agenor, Pierre-Richard, Jagdeep S. Bhandari and Robert P. Flood (1992), 'Speculative Attacks and Models of Balance of Payments Crises', *IMF Staff Papers*, **39**, 357–94.

Calvo, Guillermo and Enrique G. Mendoza (1997), 'Rational Herd Behavior and the Globalization of Securities Markets', mimeo, University of Maryland.

Connolly, Michael B. and Dean Taylor (1984), 'The Exact Timing of the Collapse of an Exchange Rate Regime and its Impact on the Relative Price of Traded Goods', *Journal of Money, Credit and Banking*, **16**, May, 194–207.

Dornbusch, Rudiger and Alejandro M. Werner (1996), 'Mexico: Stabilization, Reform and No Growth', *Brookings Papers on Economic Activity*, **1**, 253–315.

Drazen, Alan (1998), 'Political Contagion in Currency Crises', mimeo, University of Maryland.

Esquivel, Gerardo and Felipe Larraín (1998), 'Explaining Currency Crises', Faculty Research Working Paper No. R98-07, John F. Kennedy School of Government, Harvard University, June.

Flood, Robert and Peter Garber (1984), 'Collapsing Exchange Rate Regimes: Some Linear Examples', *Journal of International Economics*, **17**, 1–13.

Flood, Robert and Nacy Marion (1998), 'Perspectives on the Recent Currency Crisis Literature', NBER Working Paper No. 6380, Cambridge, Mass.

Flood, R., P. Garber and C. Kramer (1984), 'Collapsing Exchange Rate Regimes: Another Linear Example', *Journal of International Economics*, **41**, 223–34.

Goldfajn, Ilan and Rodrigo Valdés (1998); 'Are Currency Crises Predictable?,' *European Economic Review*, **42**, 873–85.

Krugman, Paul (1979), 'A Model of Balance of Payments Crises', *Journal of Money, Credit and Banking*, **11**, 311–25.

Krugman, Paul (1991), 'Speculative Attacks on Target Zones', in Paul Krugman and Marcus Miller (eds), *Target Zones and Currency Bands*, Oxford: Oxford University Press.

Laban, Raul and Felipe Larraín (1997), 'Can a Liberalization of Capital Outflows Increase Capital Inflows?', *Journal of International Money and Finance*, **16**, 415–31.

Laban, Raul and Felipe Larraín (1998), 'The Return of Private Capital to Chile in the 1990s: Causes, Effects and Policy Reactions', Faculty Research Working Paper No. R98-02, John F. Kennedy School of Government, Harvard University.

Larraín, Felipe (1991), 'Public Sector Behavior in a Highly Indebted Country: The Contrasting Chilean Experience', in F. Larraín and M. Selowsky (eds), *The Public Sector and the Latin American Crisis*, San Francisco: International Center for Economic Growth.

Larraín, F. and M. Selowsky (eds) (1991), *The Public Sector and the Latin American Crisis*, San Francisco: International Center for Economic Growth.

Larraín, Felipe, Raul Laban and Romulo Chumacero (1997), 'What Determines Capital Inflows?: An Empirical Analysis for Chile', Faculty Research Working Paper Series, John F. Kennedy School of Government, Harvard University.

Obstfeld, Maurice (1994), 'The Logic of Currency Crises', NBER Working Paper No. 4640, Cambridge, Mass.

Obstfeld, Maurice (1996), 'Models of Currency Crises with Self-fulfilling Features', *European Economic Review*, **40**, 1037–47.

Radelet, Steve and Jeffrey Sachs (1998), 'The Onset of the East Asian Financial Crisis', mimeo, Harvard Institute for International Development, March.

Sachs, J., A. Tornell and A. Velasco (1996), 'Financial Crises in Emerging Markets: The Lessons from 1995', *Brookings Papers on Economic Activity*, **1**, 147–215.

PART II

Debt Restructuring and Orderly Work-outs

5. Exorcizing Asian debt: lessons from Latin American roll-overs, work-outs and write-downs

Vinod K. Aggarwal[*]

The Asian crisis has once again raised the issue of how relations between lenders and debtors might be better managed to prevent the recurrence of such problems. In considering alternative schemes to reform international institutions, regulate financial intermediaries, improve debtor policies, and the like, scholars and policy makers have looked to the historical record to see how problems have been handled in other situations. Yet few have examined the lessons that the Latin American debt crises offer to Southeast Asia. In fact, some are sceptical about learning from earlier crises. For example, Joseph Stiglitz has recently argued that 'models about crises that developed in response to the Latin American debt crisis in the 1980s are completely inadequate for understanding the causes or solutions of the East Asian crisis'.[1] The most recent case of massive financial intervention prior to the current Asian problems was the Mexican peso crisis of 1994–5. And, before this recent crisis, the debt work-outs beginning in 1982 may provide lessons from the past.

The purpose of this chapter is to show the relevance of debt resolution efforts in other regions in earlier historical periods to current Asian problems. It will argue that the lessons of Latin American debt rescheduling efforts in the 1930s to 1940s, the 1980s and the most recent Mexican crisis are quite germane to increasing our understanding of orderly debt work-outs. In particular, it will be suggested that efforts by international institutions such as the IMF, or bargaining between lenders and debtors on their own, have often failed to generate solutions to debt problems. Instead, recent frequent intervention by the United States and other creditor governments – including less common but crucial actions by the United States and others going back to earlier in the 20th century – have been decisive in resolving debt crises. An analysis of the Latin American experience suggests that calls for leaving debtors and lenders to work

* I am grateful to Trevor Nakagawa, Paul Dosh, Kun-Chin Lin and Keith Nitta for their valuable research assistance and comments on this chapter. Moonhawk Kim and Jonathan Tsao helped to gather empirical material for this chapter.

out their own problems, or the prevalent view that the IMF has been doing an adequate job in managing debt crises, are misguided.

The first section begins with an overview of some common assessments of the management of debt crises, focusing on intervention by creditor governments. It is suggested that the common wisdom on intervention is misleading, and does not adequately reflect the more intricate and complex history of creditor government intervention and international institutional roles. This section then presents a brief schematic of debt bargaining that focuses on the key actors in negotiations. Subsequent sections then examine instances of debt bargaining going back to the 1930s and 1940s, the 1980s, the 1995 Mexican crisis and the current Asian crisis, respectively. In concluding, we consider some implications of comparative analysis for debates about the resolution of international financial crises.

VIEWS OF DEBT CRISIS MANAGEMENT

The conventional wisdom about the historical record of debt rescheduling has been summarized succinctly by Barry Eichengreen and Albert Fishlow.[2] They argue that the resolution of debt crises during the era of bond finance in the 1930s was characterized by minimal government intervention. By contrast, in the 1980s, they suggest that 'Lending and coordination of debt restructuring by the IMF arguably prevented the crisis from spreading further'. In examining the 1995 Mexican crisis, they do find that intervention took place less through 'multilaterals like the IMF as through the leadership of the United States'.[3] The underlying logic of these assessments is that, in the 1930s, bond financing did not pose a systemic risk, as compared to the 1980s. As to why the United States should play the lead role in the Mexican crisis of 1995, Eichengreen and Fishlow discuss US interests in Mexico in preventing economic collapse with consequent problems in immigration and a 'perceived failure of the U.S.-promoted model of liberalization and privatization'.[4]

Is this assessment of the history of intervention in debt rescheduling accurate? The sections that follow will show that the United States was much more involved in earlier debt resolution efforts than Eichengreen and Fishlow have indicated. For example, in the 1930s' defaults, the United States generally did not intervene directly to help bondholders. Yet neither did most Latin American rescheduling negotiations conclude in the 1930s, instead lasting well into the 1940s and 1950s. And in the case of two major debtors, Mexico and Peru, the US attitude proved critical, with differing US considerations and actions leading to a highly favourable accord for Mexico, but an equally unfavourable agreement for Peru. In the 1980s, the evidence also fails to support the view that the IMF played the highly positive role that Eichengreen and Fishlow indicate. Indeed, it was only when the United States responded to the 1987 Brazilian moratorium and the 1988 Mexican political crisis with the Brady Plan (which called for significant debt write-downs), that the crisis that affected nearly all Latin American countries in the 1980s (and many others as well) moved towards resolution.

The importance of understanding US motivations and actions, as well as the relationship of US policies to international institutions and the debtor–lender relationship, goes beyond quibbles about historical detail. How the United States has chosen to intervene, and on whose side it has done so, reveals US strategic, political and economic motivations, as well as shedding light on the path to bargaining outcomes. Moreover, understanding the motivation of the United States and creditor countries more generally helps us to consider questions of institutional designs and reform in international institutions that might facilitate the management of international debt crises.

To better understand how debt reschedulings have taken place, and the role of creditor governments, it is useful to consider the nature of the bargaining game. As has been argued elsewhere,[5] we can consider strategic interaction between lenders and debtors as involving a multiplicity of actors. Figure 5.1 illustrates 10 possible bargaining relationships. Among similar actors, we have interaction (1) among debtors, (2) among lenders, (3) among creditor governments and (4) among international organizations. In addition, we have six remaining interaction possibilities among pairs of different types of actors. Although one could analyse each of these relationships, we need not examine each in detail in order to understand the basics of debt rescheduling negotiations.

In practice, the debt rescheduling issue area initially encompasses the terms of rescheduling (which include spreads, fees and repayment arrangements),[6] the amount of new loans made available to debtors, and the type of adjustment debtors must follow (if any) as part of their arrangements with lenders. This characterization of issues involved in negotiations relies on the empirical pattern observed among bargainers: in general, they restrict their discussion to these financial matters and to concerns about future relationships with their counterparts. As long as actors involved in negotiations accept the bounds of the issue area, negotiations will revolve around the resolution of such issues, while the types and numbers of actors involved in negotiations should remain the same.[7]

Empirically, most private debt rescheduling discussions have initially involved individual debtor countries on one side, and bondholders or bankers on the other. Banks and bondholders have generally succeeded in forming coalitions (of varying cohesion) to bolster their position. By contrast, debtors have historically failed to unite in a common negotiating front, although they made several efforts to do so in the 1980s.[8]

   By linking debt to security or trade issues, debtors and lenders have often attempted to involve creditor governments (CG) in negotiations. When debtors have succeeded in linking debt to a CG's national interest, these governments have at times provided financial aid and also pressured private lenders to make concessions to debtors. Yet CGs have also faced appeals from their bankers (or bondholders) to become involved as their allies in debt negotiations.[9] Private lenders have often called on their governments to enforce contractual

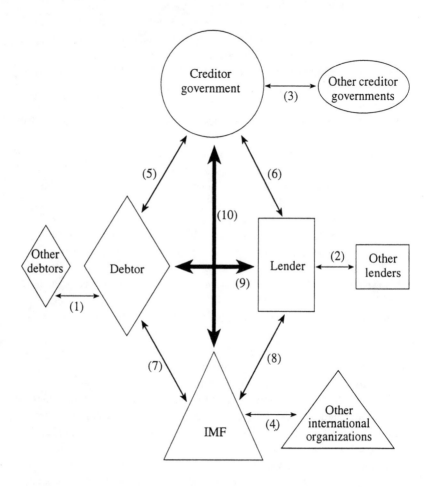

Source: Aggarwal (1996, ch. 2).

Figure 5.1   The actors and potential bargaining relationships in debt rescheduling

provisions of their loans, cloaking their pleas for creditor state intervention by invoking the 'national interest'. At times, of course, creditor governments have become involved in debt negotiations of their own volition to meet their own strategic, political or economic objectives.[10]

How do CGs make their intervention decisions? It is argued that three considerations are important: strategic security concerns, financial concerns and political concerns.[11] With respect to security interests, these depend on factors such as the types of political alliances CGs have with other major powers, the number of competing major powers in the system, the importance of international financial institutions and the nature of economic competition with other CGs. The outcome of debt rescheduling on lenders can affect CG security interests in several ways. For example, decisions by a debtor and its lenders to engage in equity swaps, whereby lenders receive assets in debtor countries, will influence the terms of competition among creditor governments. Also active intervention by one creditor government to aid its banks can put the banks in non-intervening countries at a considerable financial disadvantage. The decision by Japanese banks in the late 1980s to pool their developing country loans under the guidance of the Japanese government for rescheduling purposes has had strategic implications for US interests in its own banks.

With respect to financial concerns in their lenders, the primary factors are (1) the amount of money loaned by banks domiciled in the CG to the particular debtor as compared to the total amount of loans made by the CG's lenders to all debtors, and (2) the amount of the CG's lenders' loans to the debtor in proportion to the total amount of loans made by all lenders. The first factor is an indicator of the vulnerability of the lenders located in the CG; the second influences the CG's level of interest in taking the lead in rescheduling matters as the primary government actor.

Finally, with respect to political issues and their relationship with debtors, CGs are concerned with the impact of debt rescheduling on their trade relations, political alliances, ideological concerns and possible spillovers to areas such as immigration. Severe economic adjustment programmes generally lead to sharp cuts in imports and to increased efforts by debtors to promote their exports, both of which are likely to strain trade and other relations between the CG and the debtor. For example, increased immigration pressure from Mexico, resulting in part from its economic problems, has led some analysts to call for a more active role by the US government to aid Mexico. A similar argument has been made with respect to the fragility of democracies in Latin America and the deleterious effects of continued adjustment programmes on governmental stability.

Lastly, in times of perceived threat to the international financial system, international institutions such as the IMF, the World Bank or the League of Nations have become actively involved in the debt rescheduling process. In particular, these institutions have often responded to pressures from creditor countries that wished to encourage specific policies in debtor countries without being directly associated with their promotion.

To simplify, we can consider the debt bargaining game as one between a group of lenders (with varying degrees of unity), facing a single debtor, with the possibility of intervention by creditor governments and/or international organizations. In the next four sections, we examine the negotiations that took place in several historical cases, with an eye to better understanding the involvement of the United States and other creditor governments.

DEBT BARGAINING IN THE 1930s AND 1940s

The United States, predominant creditor of the 1920s, sent abroad nearly US$9 billion from 1919 to 1929, accounting for about two-thirds of all investment.[12] Lending fluctuated considerably during this period, with major declines in 1921, 1923, 1926 and 1928. Some observers remained optimistic about continued lending, but by 1929 borrowers paid over a billion dollars more in interest, dividends and amortization than they received in new loans and investments. The last severe drop in 1928 (due to the diversion of funds to the US stock market) crushed the servicing prospects of both European and Latin American borrowers. Lending picked up in 1930 and 1931, but was too little too late. The deflationary shock to the world economy had taken its toll: depression had set in. By 1933, 12 Latin American countries and 10 European countries suspended at least part of their debt servicing.[13] Although some Latin American countries restored partial servicing in the mid-1930s, by 1937, 85 per cent of these bonds were in default.[14] In 1935, slightly over US$1.5 billion of a total US$1.88 billion in outstanding bonds were in default. The amount in default declined to US$750.5 million by 1945, before falling to US$127 million by 1952.[15]

Following the default of large numbers of countries, debt negotiations between bondholder groups and debtors began almost immediately, yet resolution of these debt problems would come only in the 1940s and 1950s.[16] The cases of Mexico and Peru, both heavily indebted countries with a long history of debt rescheduling going back into the early part of the 19th century, are particularly illuminating in examining the debt rescheduling effort and the role played by the United States.

Mexico

Whereas most countries went into default in the 1930s, Mexico had been in default since 1913, following the severe chaotic conditions after the departure of Porfirio Díaz.[17] Various efforts to come to an agreement with bondholders failed prior to the 1920s. In the first half of 1922, negotiations between Mexican Finance Minister Adolfo de la Huerta and the International Committee of Bankers of Mexico (ICBM) (formed in 1919) resumed. A number of issues hampered these negotiations. The Mexican government insisted that any debt settlement include a new loan. President Alvaro Obregón argued that without new funds, Mexico would probably be unable to live up to any agreement. Members of the ICBM stipulated, however, that no new loan would be granted without a debt agreement and official US recognition of the Obregón government.

The State Department's continued concern over Article 27 of the new Mexican Constitution, which asserted control over land and subsoil rights, lessened the likelihood of US recognition. Following complex negotiations, Huerta signed a new debt accord in June 1922, consolidating Mexico's foreign and railway debts, and certain internal obligations held by foreigners. This tentative accord awaited ratification from Obregón. Despite the lack of a new loan in the accord, de la Huerta assured Obregón that obtaining new loans would be simple after the agreement's ratification, judging from his previous negotiations with the bankers. In addition, the preamble of the accord stated that the ICBM recognized the 'difficulties with which Mexico has had to contend and the limitations upon her capacity for the immediate payment'. It desired to cooperate 'with the Mexican government in the solution of its problems and in the upbuilding of its credit'.[18]

Obregón, however, refused to ratify the agreement, stating that he was sceptical of the 'good faith and sincerity' of the committee.[19] Instead, he directed de la Huerta to immediately open negotiations for a new loan. But Thomas Lamont of the ICBM reminded de la Huerta that no loan was possible until the United States recognized the Obregón government, stating that 'the American government during the past year often explained that it did not encourage its citizens to make loans to governments not recognized by the White House'.[20] Realizing that recognition from the United States would not be forthcoming without a debt agreement,[21] Obregón reluctantly signed the de la Huerta–Lamont debt accord in August 1922; the Mexican Congress ratified it in September. Following this accord and the Bucareli Conference that led to additional treaties of interest to the United States, Washington extended formal recognition to Obregón's government in August 1923.

Despite this new agreement, by 1924 Mexico was once again in default. At this point, the United States demonstrated little interest in the bondholders' problems because it had resolved some of its other key objectives with the Bucareli agreement. Additional agreements in 1925 and 1930 failed to generate significant debt repayments and Mexico once again defaulted on these agreements soon after they were concluded. Efforts to resolve the default

continued throughout the 1930s, but, for the most part, the United States
showed little interest in the debt negotiations.

This aloof attitude changed dramatically with the onset of the Second World
War. Following preliminary feelers in early 1940, the United States began to
negotiate a settlement of outstanding issues with Mexico. By late 1940, the
United States had proposed a draft agreement addressing outstanding claims
involving agricultural and oil claims. Mexico–United States government-level
relations fundamentally improved with the signing of an agreement in 1941.[22]
The accords included a promise by Mexico to pay US$40 million in compen-
sation for agrarian claims and the establishment of a joint commission to
determine the amount of compensation owed to the oil companies. The United
States also agreed to a trade treaty and to commitments to purchase silver to
back the Mexican peso, and to make loans to Mexico through the
Export–Import Bank. US's interest in deferring to Mexico because of its
broader objectives is reflected in the pressure it put on the oil companies to
take the US$23 million settlement offered for the Mexican oil expropriation of
1938. When the companies objected, the State Department told them either to
take it or to accept nothing; the oil companies relented.[23] With these arrangements in the works, the US government had no interest in helping the lenders
in their negotiations with Mexico over its debt.

The US's interest in a quick resolution of the debt problems at this point was
not lost on the ICBM. After proposals and counterproposals, a new agreement
was reached on Mexico's direct foreign debt in November 1942. Overall, the
Mexican government would pay 23.7 cents on every dollar of secured debt
bonds, and only 14.2 cents on every dollar of unsecured debt bonds. Over
US$500 million in direct government debt (principal and interest) would be
paid by US$50 million in debt service.[24]

Peru

After the 1929 stock market crash, Peru's financial difficulties multiplied. The
drastic decline in the value of Peru's leading exports cut the nation's purchasing
power, limiting its ability to import, and shrinking government revenues from
import taxes.[25] Between 1929 and 1932, the value of Peru's exports fell from
335 million soles to less than 180 million soles, decreasing the government's
income by 45 per cent.[26] In May 1931, the government issued a decree
suspending payment on the interest until December, and diverting funds due on
the national loan for the 'purpose of paying off all arrears of salaries and pay
of all Government employees and forces'.[27] In January 1932, the Peruvian
government passed a law indefinitely extending the moratorium on the entire
external debt service.

At this stage of the negotiations, the United States showed a great deal of sympathy for the Peruvians, especially because they had cooperated with a mission by Edwin W. Kemmerer, a US economics professor who had been recommended as an impartial advisor for Peru. Throughout the 1930s, negotiations dragged on between the bondholders and Peru without a sign of resolution. With the onset of the Second World War, as in the Mexican case, the US government began to take a more active interest. With an eye on security concerns, the United States was reluctant to push the Peruvians very hard, despite significant pressure from bondholders. In fact, the Export–Import Bank agreed to a loan of US$10 million for Peruvian purchases from the United States. Shortly thereafter, Peru expropriated planes from the German airline Lufthansa; shortly after that, in March 1941, it closed Transocean, a German shipping group.[28] The US government continued to encourage negotiations between the bondholders and Peru, but its primary motivation for involvement was clear.

In November 1942, Nelson Rockefeller suggested that the US government buy Peruvian bonds and convert the total amount to Peruvian soles, which Peru would pay on low interest.[29] Such an action, however, would have antagonized the Peruvian Bondholders Council and other financial groups, and thus was rejected by the State Department. Efforts to resolve the debt came to naught, despite continued negotiations between Peru and the Council. By the early 1950s, however, the Council had convinced the World Bank to help it block loans to Peru. In July 1951, Peru began to make overtures to the Council for a settlement of its outstanding debt. As expected, the Council's block of its credit strongly encouraged Peru to be more forthcoming. In April, when Peru had sought a World Bank loan to develop its Port of Callao facilities, it asked if the World Bank 'would be willing to make such a loan without waiting for a final settlement of Peru's eternal debt'. In response, World Bank President, Eugene Black, wrote back:

> if [Peru's] President would indicate to the Bank that Peru was prepared to negotiate with the Bondholders' representatives, and, if a reasonable settlement could be negotiated, to recommend its approval by Congress, the Bank would consider making such a loan before final settlement had been reached.[30]

In response to this direct linkage, Peru moved quickly to accommodate the Council's demands. By July, President Black announced that the World Bank would be willing to negotiate with Peru to conclude the Callao Port loan, but still insisted: 'Before concluding the negotiations, however, I would expect to receive confirmation that the President is prepared to make a recommendation to Congress'.[31]

In discussions with US government officials, Peruvian Ambassador Fernando Berckemeyer clearly recognized the direct linkage of successfully signing an accord to receiving a fresh supply of World Bank loans. After discussing the various projects for which Peru sought financing from the World Bank, the US embassy acknowledged Berckemeyer's perspective: 'the only hindrance to the immediate establishment of these credits is the lack of a satisfactory settlement for the Peruvian foreign debt ... and he feels optimistic that with the proposed offer for settlement that he hopes to get from his Government, this hindrance will be eliminated'.[32]

By August, Peru was willing to address the objections the Council had raised with regard to Peru's 1947 offer. Peru offered to pay back interest on the bonds, and the principal in full.[33] As some disagreements continued on the date from which back interest would be calculated, the British government increased their pressure. When the World Bank appeared to consider making Peru a small loan, the British took 'violent exception to the loan', warning that '"the city" [London financial interests] will have nothing further to do with the Bank if the Bank pursues such a course'.[34]

Although some minor obstacles involving the question of succession of rights on the new bonds (whether payment of arrears went to present owners or to owners who did the exchange) and the base for revision of the 1947 offer,[35] the Peruvians essentially acquiesced to the bulk of the Council's demands. In short, with strong pressure from the British government and international institutions, the Peruvians had little choice but to agree to considerably more onerous terms than Mexico had negotiated in 1942.

In summary, both the Mexican and Peruvian cases illustrate a rather more complex history than a simple 'hands off' policy by the United States on debt rescheduling. While the lack of a systemic threat kept the United States from dramatically intervening in Mexican debt negotiations, a host of other concerns often became linked to the debt issue and affected their resolution. And when strategic US interests became involved with the onset of the Second World War, the United States clearly leaned in Mexico's direction against the bondholders. In the case of Peru, while the United States was reluctant to press Peru during the war, it had little trouble in going along with the bondholders' use of the World Bank to secure their objectives. Nor, it might be added, did the World Bank resist this linkage to private debt negotiations. Moreover, it is worth keeping in mind that the long-standing lack of Mexican and Peruvian access to sources of lending as a result of their default and inability to come to a resolution with bondholders demonstrates that lack of intervention was hardly propitious for a quick resolution of debt problems.

THE DEBT CRISIS OF THE 1980s

The Organization of Petroleum Exporting Countries' (OPEC) successful manipulation of oil prices in 1973–4 has been seen, justifiably, as one of the most significant events in political relations between developed and less developed countries (LDCs).[36] The impact of this price increase on the international financial system has been equally striking. In 1973, the medium- and long-term debt of LDCs (over one year in maturity) was US$97.3 billion; by the end of 1981, it had soared to US$425.2 billion. By 1981, the crisis began to take shape. Faced with strong inflationary pressures, the United States pursued tight monetary policies that both drove up interest rates on existing loans (which had been made at floating rates) and induced a recession in the developed countries, thus hurting export prospects for the debtors. In addition, capital flight from many debtor countries exacerbated the crisis, as did worsening terms of trade for debtors. For non-oil-producing debtors, these shocks, combined with steep oil prices before 1981, were threatening. For oil exporters such as Mexico, the effect of an oil price plunge in 1981, higher interest rates and worsening export prospects proved lethal. Although Mexico was not the first to seek bank rescheduling (Poland and Argentina needed to reschedule as early as 1981), its massive debts of over US$80 billion proved too much for the existing rescheduling mechanisms to handle. By August 1982, Mexico neared complete default. As banks continued to retrench, Brazil, Argentina and other major debtors found themselves in similar crises. By 1983, over 25 countries were in arrears, initiating more than a decade of rescheduling efforts that only drew to a close in the mid-1990s.

Although the IMF was an active participant throughout the debt rescheduling efforts, the United States and other creditor governments led the process through bridge loans in the first instance, and later through the Brady Plan debt write-down. Indeed, the IMF strategy of continuous roll-overs and jumbo loans, while initially shared by the United States, merely prolonged the resolution of the debt crisis and ensured that Latin America would lose a decade of growth.

To examine the active role of the United States during this period, we can consider the case of Mexican debt rescheduling. It is worth noting that the United States also undertook very similar actions in other Latin American countries. As we shall see, the United States was an active participant from the start, and enlisted the IMF to help in debt rescheduling. The effect of initial US policy was to prolong the debt crisis. Only in the late 1980s, when faced with growing political and strategic concerns, did the United States take decisive action to end the debt problem.

On 13 August 1982, Mexican Finance Minister Silva Herzog met US Deputy Treasury Secretary R.T. McNamara, a managing director of the IMF, Jacques de Larosière, Chairman of the Federal Reserve, Paul Volcker and then Secretary of the Treasury Donald Regan in quick succession. His message was that Mexico could no longer meet its obligations and needed immediate help.[37] Although sympathetic, de Larosière insisted that Mexico would have to acknowledge any help provided by the IMF, and insisted that Silva immediately begin work towards developing an economic adjustment programme.[38] For his part, Volcker telephoned the major central banks about an impending US$1.5 billion loan, of which the Fed had agreed to provide half. Meanwhile, the Mexicans called the heads of Chase, Citibank, Morgan and Bank of America to arrange a meeting for the following week.[39]

Silva then turned to Regan directly to solve the cash flow problem. After tough negotiations, the US Treasury agreed to provide US$2 billion in cash: US$1 billion as prepayment for Mexican oil and US$1 billion in credit towards US food exports to Mexico.[40] Taking advantage of Mexico's vulnerability, the US government secured a US$50 million negotiation fee and a 20 per cent discount on the oil.[41]

On 18 August the Federal Reserve called a group of central bank deputies to an emergency meeting at the Bank for International Settlements (BIS) in Basle. The central bankers decided to give Mexico a US$1.85 billion credit, of which the United States agreed to contribute US$925 million. The bridge loan was to be released in three tranches with disbursement of the first third hingeing on the negotiation results between Mexico and the IMF over austerity measures.[42]

The US government and the IMF also pressured commercial banks to participate in a loan to Mexico. On 20 August, Silva Herzog met an advisory committee of Mexico's bankers and then over 800 bankers in New York, requesting a 90-day moratorium on principal repayments; Anthony Solomon, head of the New York Fed, pressured the banks to cooperate with the Mexican financing programme.[43]

Following an intense period of complicated negotiations during which the money centre banks and creditor governments pressured smaller banks to participate in the loan, the advisory committee and Mexico agreed to a new package on 8 December. It called for a new US$5 billion jumbo loan, to be repaid in six years, with a three-year grace period, at an interest rate of 2.125 per cent over the US prime rate or 2.25 per cent over London interbank offered rate (LIBOR), topped by a 1.25 per cent fee.[44] Some US$20 billion of debt owed by Mexico from August 1982 to the end of 1984 would be rescheduled and repaid in eight years with a grace period of four years at an interest rate of 1.875 per cent over LIBOR and a fee of 1 per cent.[45] Despite problems with recalcitrant banks, prospects for an agreement improved following a bridge loan of US$433 million by the large banks in February 1983. The final agreement, signed on 3 March 1983, involved 530 banks.

Over the next couple of years, the main effort on the part of the IMF and bankers was to roll over loans and ensure that Mexico continued to service its debt fully. The Baker Plan, promoted by the United States in 1985, failed to alter the basic course of debt negotiations. Thus, despite US government concern for Mexico's stability and its implications for trade, immigration and drug trafficking, little changed in the pattern of debt negotiations. Domestic pressure to do more came from outside the Bush administration. For example, the Governor of Arizona, Bruce Babbitt, was an advocate of giving Mexico greater support, warning that Mexico was 'the ultimate domino'. He went on to complain that the administration was placing too much pressure on Mexico and that Republican assistance to the PAN could endanger the PRI's willingness to promote a more open Mexican political system.[46] Others argued for more active US government intervention to ensure that the banks made additional concessions to Mexico to tackle the problems created by the earthquake in Mexico city in the 1990s. On the whole, the United States appeared willing to nudge the banks and Mexico towards continued cooperation, but remained unwilling to actively promote major reduction in debt. Despite growing political problems in Mexico, the IMF continued to insist on Mexican adherence to an adjustment programme. It still saw itself as the stabilizer of the international financial system and the arbiter of debt negotiations between banks and debtor countries.

Signs of a new US attitude came in October 1988, following the Brazilian debt moratorium of 1987 and serious political instability in Mexico following the 1988 elections. As oil prices fell, and concern grew about Mexico's political and financial problems, the United States cobbled together a US$3.5 billion bridge loan to Mexico in the hope that this offer would give President-elect Carlos Salinas some breathing space.[47] Still Mexico's problems continued to worsen.

Following discussions of debt reduction schemes in the latter part of 1988, US Treasury Secretary Nicholas Brady proposed a new approach in March 1989 to handle the debt crisis, based in part on a plan proposed by Japan and France in 1988.[48] This action placed the United States firmly behind the process of debt reduction. Brady proposed that debt reduction and/or debt service reduction be combined with increased lending and continuation of growth-oriented economic adjustment. The United States endorsed debt reduction as necessary to help reforming countries break out of the debt cycle, viewing excess debt and net transfer of resources as stifling economic recovery in countries that could otherwise serve as important export markets. IMF managing director Michel Camdessus also endorsed Brady's proposal. Camdessus stressed that countries willing to enact domestic reforms 'need to be able, from the outset, to count on a more adequate alleviation of the present drag of debt-service payments on their adjustment efforts'.[49]

Following Brady's speech, Mexico's Finance Minister Pedro Aspe met US officials.[50] Mexico submitted a letter of intent to the IMF, requesting US$3.6 billion through the Extended Fund Facility (EFF). The request also included specific proposals for debt and debt-service reduction on its US$57 billion commercial debt. The Fund concurred with the Mexican proposal, and in May 1989 the two parties agreed to a three-year extended arrangement including an immediate disbursement of funds from the Compensatory and Contingency Financing Facility (CCFF).[51] Most importantly, this unprecedented arrangement included debt reduction: 30 per cent of each purchase under the EFF was to be set aside for debt and debt-service reduction, and, pending agreement with its creditor banks, Mexico would be allocated up to 40 per cent of its quota to support reduction. The Fund displayed its support of debt reduction by disbursing the cash to Mexico before the debtor had reached an agreement with its creditors.[52]

Despite US endorsement of debt reduction, the banks were reluctant to make concessions to Mexico. By late July 1989, however, the stalemate was finally broken. That month Secretary Brady was scheduled to accompany President Bush to the G-7's annual economic summit in Paris. French President Mitterrand, who had proposed alternative strategies for resolving the debt crisis and consistently clashed with the United States over the proper handling of the situation, was to be the host of the summit. Bush administration officials worried that Mitterrand would attempt to embarrass the United States over the debt issue.[53] Earlier, with an eye towards the summit, Secretary Brady personally telephoned the chairmen of the largest New York banks, urging them towards settlement. The US government thus accelerated its efforts to produce an agreement prior to the Paris summit to deflect criticism of its new approach.[54]

Strong intervention by the US Treasury Department finally brought results. After four months of talks between Mexico and the 15-bank steering committee, Brady convened a meeting with both sides in Washington, and produced an agreement.[55] The July package presented Mexico's creditors with three options. The first was to reduce the principal of the debt by 35 per cent. This entailed exchanging loans for 30-year bonds at 65 per cent of the face value of the loans. These bonds would pay interest at 13/16 per cent over LIBOR (the same rate as before the discount). The second option was interest rate reduction. Here banks would exchange their loans for 30-year government bonds with the same face value, but with a fixed interest rate of 6.25 per cent. The final option on the menu was the extension of new loans in proportion to outstanding exposure. Except for the amount reduced, banks were to offer new loans worth 25 per cent of their outstanding exposure, with a 15-year payback period (beginning after a seven-year grace period), at an interest rate of seven-eighths over LIBOR.

Of the US$48.5 billion of medium- and long-term debt covered by participating banks, 41 per cent chose the principal reduction option. This cut the face value of US$20 billion worth of loans by 35 per cent, yielding a saving of US$625 million annually, assuming then current interest rates of 9 per cent. A further 49 per cent of the banks chose interest reduction, meaning that nearly US$24 billion of the debt would pay 6.25 per cent interest, yielding an annual saving of approximately US$700 million for Mexico. However, to purchase the US zero-coupon bonds used to guarantee the exit bonds, Mexico borrowed US$5.8 billion from the World Bank, the Japanese Export–Import Bank and the IMF.

The negotiations in the 1980s indicate that the United States and other creditor countries, rather than the IMF, proved to be the decisive actor. Creditor governments initially supported the roll-over and jumbo loan approach to debt rescheduling (which ultimately proved futile) as well as promoting a new approach to debt rescheduling. The original effort to simply roll over debt and insist on full payment with drastic Mexican adjustment clearly favoured the banks. Only as dissent increased in Latin America, posing strategic concerns as well as domestic criticisms in the United States, did the US government pursue debt reduction. While this action was ultimately endorsed by the IMF, it did not take any initiative during the 1980s to alter fundamentally the course of debt negotiations that strongly favoured the banks. As we shall see, the underlying pattern of the US role would be repeated in the 1995 peso crisis, to which we now turn.

THE 1995 MEXICAN CRISIS

In March 1994, when Mexican PRI Presidential candidate Luis Donaldo Colosio was shot on the hustings in Tijuana, a financial crisis was averted by timely and effective policy management.[56] The crisis was managed by officials from the Finance Ministry, in particular José Angel Gurria. Gurria was an experienced negotiator who had participated in Mexico's debt negotiations as well as the financial services negotiations in the North American Free Trade Agreement (NAFTA). In March 1994, he was the head of Nacional Financiera, one of Mexico's most powerful development banks. Gurria understood that a major run on the peso could occur.

In an effort to head off a speculative attack, officials at Finance activated a US$6 billion swap facility that had been negotiated between Hacienda and the US Treasury (the leading Mexican official responsible was Guillermo Ortiz). Although negotiated 'secretly' around the time of the debate between US Vice President Al Gore and NAFTA critic H. Ross Perot, the swap facility had been known to insiders for months. To gain time in order to get approval from the US government to activate this Fund, Aspe, Ortiz, Gurria, Miguel Mancera (the head of the central bank) and other finance officials, with the agreement of the President, decided to shut down the Mexican stock market (Bolsa de Valores) for a day. Ortiz called Lawrence Summers, Undersecretary for International Affairs at the US Treasury, who activated the Exchange Swap Fund. Then the Mexican finance officials 'began trying to win back investor confidence by calling everyone they could think of around the world from traders to chief executives'.[57] The management of the crisis caused by the assassination of

Colosio demonstrated how growing economic integration required the construction and maintenance of increasingly complex domestic and international coalitions. Although the bargaining around the assassination led to a positive payoff for Mexico and foreign firms, it did not address the roots of the balance of payments problems, which continued to grow. In particular, it did not reduce the government's reliance on foreign savings, which left it little room for policy mistakes.

The growing strength of foreign investors was demonstrated in the aftermath of the Colosio assassination, when a group of mutual funds sent the Mexican government a list of suggestions to bolster the currency. According to *The Wall Street Journal*, 'To lend weight to their advice, the funds said they were willing to pour an additional $17 billion into Mexico this year if the government enacted reforms'.[58]

The second crisis began shortly after Ernesto Zedillo met Carlos Salinas in the presence of Pedro Aspe in November, less than two weeks before the transfer of government, and discussed a devaluation of the peso. Aspe opposed the measure, in spite of declining reserves, and Zedillo and Salinas accepted Aspe's position. A similar meeting had been held in September 1994, in which Guillermo Ortiz favoured a devaluation, and no action was taken. Not only had Rudiger Dornbusch, Aspe's former teacher at MIT, insisted on the need for a devaluation; so too had Lloyd Bentsen, US Secretary of the Treasury.

On 8 December, Minister of Finance Jaime Serra outlined his 'Economic Criteria for 1995'. The document was prepared in consultation with members of the outgoing administration (including former Finance Minister Pedro Aspe, former President Carlos Salinas and former Undersecretary of Finance, Guillermo Ortiz). Business analysts judged the document insufficient and called for a correction of the current account deficit. Luis Germán Carcoba of the Business Coordinating Council called for a meeting with Serra, which was scheduled for 15 December. Although capital flight had already begun and the peso had risen to the top of the band (3.46 pesos to the dollar), Serra remained optimistic.

The next day Serra gave an interview to *The Wall Street Journal* in which he denied the possibility of a devaluation. The following Monday the peso broke through the official band and the stock market fell by 4 per cent. In the evening, an emergency meeting was held between Serra, Miguel Mancera (of the Bank of Mexico) and members of Mexico's business elite. Although an agreement to widen the band rather than let the peso float was reached, comments by Mancera hinted that Mexico did not have the reserves to defend the peso against another serious attack. The meeting gave the bankers the opportunity to buy dollars prior to Serra's announcement of the devaluation, and billions of dollars fled the country in a matter of hours. 'It's the first time in history that a devaluation was consulted on', commented former finance official Jesús Silva Herzog.[59]

The outcome of the bargaining in December 1994 was sub-optimal for all major players. As a result, a new bargaining game was initiated, with the United States taking the lead role, and more concern for the linkages between financial solvency, NAFTA and political stability. Although the economic costs of the devaluation were sufficient to suggest that the crisis was a significant event for a large number of powerful private actors, they do not capture the fears among policy makers of linkages between economic disruption, immigration, political unrest and the spillover effects on other emerging markets. The US administration, in particular, expressed concern that the crisis in Mexico could result in political instability in Mexico, and ultimately lead to an increase in immigration pressures. Moreover, the so-called 'Tequila effect' began to spread throughout 'emerging markets', depressing stocks, weakening currencies and prompting other Latin nations to reconsider the pace of economic liberalization.

Even the US and Canadian dollars came under pressure in the aftermath of the bailout. The market for Brady bonds fell on average by about 2.5 per cent, thus adding to the debt problems of other debtor nations. In short, the grave implications of the Mexican crisis compelled policy makers to take drastic action to avert a more serious disruption of global finance. The extraordinary measures required to confront the crisis exceeded the capacity of existing institutions and eventually led to a new bargaining game with new actors and issue linkages.

The devaluation of the Mexican peso in December 1994 triggered a financial panic that required massive intervention. By the end of January 1995, President Bill Clinton had cobbled together a package of loan guarantees in excess of US$50 billion. Massive state intervention was required to launch NAFTA, the centrepiece of market-led economic integration in Latin America.

It might be argued that the Mexican financial crisis threatened the stability of the global economy, especially emerging markets. However, the threat of a generalized systemic collapse was less significant than during the debt crisis that began in 1982. In spite of this, a far more costly bailout of the Mexican economy was engineered by the international financial community, led by the United States. The reason lies in the crucial importance of Mexico to the United States in the context of NAFTA, and the extent to which US business interests were affected by the devaluation.[60]

The bailout revealed cracks in the international financial system: six European members of the IMF – Britain, Germany, Denmark, the Netherlands, Belgium and Switzerland – abstained on the vote to provide US$17 billion in loans to Mexico. They said the plan was pushed through too hastily (documents were received only an hour before the meeting to vote on the package) and without regard for the IMF's other obligations or problems of moral hazard.[61]

US officials noted that the speed of the markets had outstripped the ability of bureaucratic agencies like the Fund to respond.

The emergency bailout, combined with Mexico's domestic adjustment measures, only addressed part of the problem. Under the terms of the bailout package assembled by the United States, Mexico will receive US$20 billion in loans with up to 10-year maturities through the Treasury's Exchange Stabilization Fund. The Federal Reserve agreed to provide short-term bridge financing of up to US$6 billion. The other industrialized nations would provide an additional US$10 billion in credit through the Bank for International Settlements (BIS).

President Clinton's pressure on the BIS to contribute to the Mexican bailout was not openly resisted, but the enthusiasm of European central bankers was minimal. The IMF extended US$17.8 billion in credit. Of this, US$7.8 billion (300 per cent of Mexico's IMF quota) were made immediately available. The remaining US$10 billion were set aside to be provided to the extent that the government central banks in the BIS fell short of their US$10 billion target. Overall, the IMF provided 688 per cent of the quota for which Mexico was eligible, the largest ever financing package approved by the Fund. In fact, the total bailout package includes money that is far from secure. Most of the real, hard money is from the United States, which is why it can set the lending conditions. It is unlikely that any further money could come from outside the NAFTA partners.[62]

Clinton's bailout was unpopular domestically and would not pass the Republicans and Democrats in Congress, some of whom wondered why similar steps were not taken to bail out Orange County or US workers in distress. The measure had to be taken using executive powers to spend through the exchange stabilization funds of the US Treasury and by strong-arming the IMF. Clinton was able to achieve this by linking the crisis to US security and leadership in the global economy.

US Secretary of the Treasury Robert Rubin said that the release of fresh funds demonstrated that Mexico was fully complying with the conditions of the bailout. The first US$10 billion would come from the United States between February and June 1995, as long as Mexico complied with targets. The remainder would be made available as necessary. By August 1995, Mexico's reserves had climbed back to US$15.7 billion; US$26 billion in *Tesobonos* had been paid off, leaving only US$3.1 billion due; and the Mexican government had shifted back to issuing peso-denominated bonds.

The bailout package imposed strict conditionality measures on monetary and fiscal policy as well as foreign borrowing. Loan guarantees were backed by oil revenues held as collateral by the Federal Reserve Bank of New York. Mexico has to buy back the pesos it has exchanged for dollars with the United States at 2.25 per cent or more over Treasury bill rates of varying maturities.[63] The terms included the unusual accounting practice that every withdrawal of funds would have to be approved in advance by the US Treasury, which would oversee how all the money was spent. The Mexican government also set up a fund, backed by the World Bank, to ensure that local banks met the minimum capitalization levels required by regulators – again, a form of socialized risk. The US executive arranged the financial package for Mexico because it believed that Mexican financial stability was in the interests of the US economy. A financial meltdown in Mexico could have repercussions throughout the 'emerging markets' of Latin America and Eastern Europe and could ultimately result in a loss of jobs at home. Nevertheless, the idea of bailing out a foreign country was unacceptable to members of the Congress, many of whom accused the President of being too concerned for wealthy investors and speculators.

In short, as in the previous cases we have examined, the United States took the lead in coping with the debt problem in Mexico. In this case, it did so without much support from Europeans and others who saw the problem as one that did not threaten the international financial system and thus one that they could ignore.

THE 1997–8 ASIAN CRISIS

The recent Asian crisis once again demonstrates the crucial role of the United States in international debt negotiations. In the following three cases, the United States played quite distinct roles commensurate with its strategic, political and economic objectives. In Thailand, it was noticeable by its absence; in Korea and Indonesia, it played a very active role. Once again, the efforts of the IMF, while initially supported by the United States, proved to be inadequate or inappropriate for the task at hand.

Thailand

Before the Thai baht began to falter in June 1997, few analysts foresaw its financial crisis. In December 1996, the IMF's report, *Thailand: The Road to Sustained Growth*, raised no concerns. As late as April 1997, Thailand's sovereign risk rating was a straight A. Although Thailand did have a relatively high current account deficit of about 8 per cent of GDP, most saw this as benign. After June 1997, however, analysts rushed to explain Thailand's vulnerability. Morris Goldstein of the Institute for International Economics, for example, pointed to financial-sector weaknesses in Thailand as the cause of its currency crisis. Specifically, he argued that the Thai economy had experienced a credit boom stoked by large net capital inflows, most of it directed to real estate and equities. 'This overextension and concentration of credit left the ASEAN-4 [Thailand, Indonesia, Malaysia and the Philippines] vulnerable to a shift in credit conditions'.[64]

In Thailand, that vulnerability was heightened because of the Thai Central Bank's policy of pegging the baht to the US dollar, which encouraged Thai banks and firms to borrow in foreign currency at short maturities for often imprudent ventures. As a result, after the baht came under attack, US Deputy Treasury Secretary Lawrence Summers estimated that 'nonperforming loans in the Thai banking sector may be around twenty percent of GDP'.[65] *The Economist* estimated that, by July, the central Thai bank was spending US$2.6 billion a month to keep the financial system going.[66]

By April 1997, when speculative pressures against the baht began building up, the IMF and the US government were openly urging the Thai government to force banks to declare their bad debts and begin to clean the financial system up. Even after it was forced to announce a managed float of the baht in early July, which devalued the baht by about 20 per cent, Thailand refused to apply new economic measures or to openly seek IMF assistance. For their part, however, the IMF and the United States did not treat Thailand's currency crisis as a serious problem. In July, when the baht lost 20 per cent of its value, Daniel Tarullo, the US administration's top international economic advisor, recalled that 'there were no crisis meetings and certainly no sense that this was the start of an economic crisis that might roll around the world'.[67] As a result, although the IMF urged action on Thailand, it did not press Thailand strongly enough to produce change. Fred Bergsten, director of the Institute for International Economics, argues that the international monetary regime's early warning system failed to prevent exactly the kind of crisis it was created to prevent: 'The IMF and the Group of Seven countries should have really put the heat on the Thais'.[68]

Thailand finally requested IMF assistance in August 1997, and on 20 August it signed a letter of intent with the IMF in Tokyo. The IMF authorized US$17 billion to rescue the Thai economy. The IMF itself contributed US$4 billion, the Asian Development Bank US$2.7 billion, Southeast Asian countries US$3.5 billion and Japan US$4 billion. In keeping with the IMF's mission, Thailand agreed to a series of reforms, economic and financial, in return for funds. These can broadly be grouped into six policies areas:[69] (1) fiscal policy contraction, (2) bank closures, with the IMF immediately identifying 58 out of 91 Thai finance institutions to be suspended and, subsequently ordering 56 of these to be liquidated, (3) enforcement of capital adequacy standards, (4) tight domestic credit to defend the exchange rate, (5) agreement to fully repay debt, and (6) liberalization reforms including tariff reduction, reducing barriers for foreign investment and reducing monopoly powers.

In contrast to other Asian nations in crisis, however, after the ineffective Chavalit government gave way, Thailand eagerly enacted IMF reforms. IMF officials quickly and repeatedly praised Thailand for enacting reforms and closely following the fund's programme, holding it up as a model for other countries. Yet the IMF's medicine only exacerbated financial troubles, and businessmen in Thailand, including a former foreign minister, only saw a gloomy future. 'We're going down and we don't know when we'll reach the bottom'.[70] The abrupt announcements of bank closures only served to inflame the panic instead of instilling confidence and added to the current liquidity squeeze, making it more difficult for existing banks to continue normal lending operations.[71] Credit all but dried up. As a result, private investment had fallen by 11.9 per cent from March 1997.

While official currency reserves are slowly recovering, at close to US$27 billion, the country still has a limited ability to service creditors. Bankers predict that a sudden call on loans will precipitate the financial system's collapse. Thailand remains mired in a deep recession that most analysts predict will last through 1999. In its fourth letter of intent with the IMF, the Thai government predicted that the economy will shrink by 5.5 per cent in 1998, with investment falling 24 per cent.[72] National unemployment has doubled, to 2 million people, and the government expects 800 000 more people will lose their jobs by the end of the year. Manufacturing production has fallen by 21 per cent since June 1997. As of June 1998, the stock index continues to flounder at an 11-year low, and the baht has lost 37 per cent of its value since June 1997. The Thai consumer price index rose by 10.7 per cent and the wholesale price index jumped 20.7 per cent in June 1998, the biggest increase in a decade.

IMF officials have acknowledged their error and, in November, officials restructured the loan agreement with Thailand, offering more comprehensive financial restructuring plans to go along with bank closures in an attempt to restore confidence in the financial sector and increase financial solvency.[73] The IMF has also eased requirements to allow for a 1999 budget deficit of 3 per cent of GDP.

In early 1997, US officials had joined the IMF in urging the Thai government to clean up its financial system, particularly its non-peforming loans. By August, however, the United States had dropped out of the process, and during the loan negotiations was conspicuous by its absence. In stark contrast to Japan, the United States directly contributed no funds to the bailout, and US administration officials remained silent on developments in Thailand. The US inaction was widely criticized in Asia, and the Thais themselves were shocked and angered at what they saw as the failure of a long-time ally to come to their aid.

The US decision not to participate in the original IMF bailout was motivated by several factors: (1) US officials were angry that Thailand had defied earlier US and IMF advice to reform its economic and financial practices; (2) the

United States may not have fully realized the gravity of the situation since the official IMF assessment was still that Thailand was fundamentally strong economically. As late as the November Asia-Pacific Economic Cooperation (APEC) summit meeting, President Clinton was describing the Thai and Malaysian currency crises as 'a few small glitches in the road';[74] (3) there was no shortage of available financing since Japan, whose banks were the most exposed by the currency meltdown, was very willing to provide funds; (4) the post-Cold War context has meant the United States is less concerned about communist threats in Asia and thus less willing to help strategic allies such as Thailand. Furthermore, 'The Vietnam-era military alliance of the United States with Thailand had been substantially attenuated by Thailand's failure to agree to the pre-positioning of military materiel off-shore in Thai waters in support of U.S. forces in the Persian Gulf';[75] and (5) the Clinton administration feared a domestic political backlash from key isolationist members of Congress already aroused by perceived waste in UN peacekeeping costs, and so did not want to fight for funding.

The US strategy appeared to backfire almost immediately, as the currency crisis continued to spread beyond Thailand, quickly moving to the larger economies of Indonesia and Korea. Despite the IMF's intervention, the financial crisis, largely driven by currency speculation, continued to spread to beyond Thailand to the Philippines, Malaysia, Indonesia and, most importantly, Korea. The IMF eventually promised the Philippines US$1.1 billion in aid, Indonesia up to US$40 billion and Korea up to US$60 billion. By the time Korea requested IMF assistance in December 1997, the US government had changed strategy with respect to Thailand.

As in the Cold War, the United States has now come to view Thailand as a bulwark, though this time against spreading financial problems, not communism. The United States has principally been concerned that uneven implementation of IMF conditions in Indonesia should not lead Thailand and, particularly, Korea to resist similarly. The United States began playing a direct role in the Thai economic problems in early 1998. In March 1998, President Clinton officially welcomed Thai Prime Minister Chuan to Washington. The US administration used the meeting to re-establish connections with Thailand and soothe Thai feelings over the US inaction in the summer of 1997. The United States also used the opportunity to announce US$1.7 billion of aid to Thailand, through the US Export–Import Bank, the Trade Development Agency and the Overseas Private Investment Corporation (OPIC).[76] The administration also launched a major programme to help Thai students in the United States, through the State Department, US Information Agency (USIA) and the Immigration nation service (INS) to allow Thai students to work as well as study in the United States.

The United States has given this aid as encouragement for Thailand to continue implementing IMF conditions and undertake reform, and as a tangible reminder that the United States stands alongside the IMF and its goals. In a July 1998 visit to Thailand, US Treasury Secretary Robert E. Rubin proclaimed, 'The U.S. stands with you as you face this challenge ... Though this will be a hard path to follow ... failure to implement reform would lead to far worse conditions and far longer duress'.[77] Once again, as in other cases of debt resolution, the United States has been brought into the debt rescheduling process.

South Korea

Ever since its take-off in the 1960s, the Korean economy has been displaying a remarkable macroeconomic performance. Despite the slowdown in annual GDP growth, the economy recorded 5.9 per cent growth in 1997 while keeping unemployment and inflation down to 2.6 per cent and 4.4 per cent, respectively. The 1997 economic crisis was first foreshadowed by the falling unit prices of semi-conductors, which squeezed corporate profits. The decline in export prices was then exacerbated by bankruptcies of major conglomerates, such as the default of Hanbo Steel Corporation in January 1997.

Historically, Korea had been quick to adjust to currency overvaluation, but this time, despite added pressure from the 1994 depreciation of the Chinese yuan and the 1995 depreciation of the Japanese yen, Korea failed to act.[78] As of mid-1997, Japanese banks had about US$23 billion in loans and other credits to South Korea, European banks had US$36 billion and US banks had extended US$10 billion of credit to South Korea. In October, the South Korean Won began to slump rapidly in value. Soon after, the Dow Jones plunged 554 points in response to Asian economic difficulties. In November, Korea turned to the IMF, and on 4 December 1997, the IMF approved a US$21 billion loan for South Korea, part of a bailout package that will total nearly US$60 billion. Two days later, the Central Bank of Korea announced that it had received US$5.22 billion.

By late December 1997, Korea's reserves were almost gone, shrinking at a rate of US$1 billion a day. The US government and the IMF recognized that the original strategy had failed and agreed to accelerate US$10 billion of the committed loans as a bridge to prevent a default. More important, the US Federal Reserve and other major central banks called in the leading commercial banks and urged them to create a coordinated programme of short-term loan roll-overs and longer-term debt restructuring. The banks agreed to roll over the loans coming due immediately, and the crisis was averted.[79] Despite the roll-over, Korea still had to pay off about 10 per cent of the due loans on 31 December, leaving only US$9 billion in foreign currency reserves.[80]

Despite initial resistance from smaller international lenders in a replay of the 1980s' debt crisis, global lenders agreed in January 1998 to roll over Korea's maturing obligations for 90 days, easing worries about default on some US$40 billion in debt due by 31 March.[81] This conflict between banks was most apparent among US commercial and investment bankers, who had been spearheading private sector involvement in the Korean bailout. With billions of dollars in outstanding loans to Korean banks, US banks had a large stake in the bailout's success or failure. But beyond protecting their own investments, bankers also tried to position themselves to capture a share of the profits that would accompany the management of any transactions to resolve the crisis, such as straightforward loans or bond issues, or a more complicated conversion of private bank debt into government-backed bonds.[82] These potential profits are no small matter, which perhaps in part explains the Korean government's subsequent efforts to secure independently as much as US\$35 billion in new financing. Korea's move to sell bonds on its own interfered with foreign banks' efforts to lead the repackaging of Korea's almost US\$40 billion in short-term debt.[83]

In early January, about US\$34 billion of Korea's US\$92 billion in short-term debt was owed by Korean commercial banks, with US\$25 billion of that due by the end of March.[84] On 8 January 1998, the IMF and South Korea agreed to a 90-day roll-over of short-term debt. Soon thereafter, US Treasury Secretary Robert E. Rubin urged international lenders to join the 90-day roll-over in order to facilitate the resolution of the crisis.

IMF rescheduling efforts were aimed more at debts owed by banks than at debts owed by private borrowers, in part because bank debts constituted the bulk of short-term obligations, but also because of the role bank failures can play in fuelling financial panic. Thus the failure of corporations that dwarfed many banks was still seen as preferable to the failure of any large Korean bank. As *The Wall Street Journal* noted, the IMF also sought to avoid cushioning industrial conglomerates from the consequences of their excessive borrowing.[85]

Martin Feldstein argues that the IMF may have encouraged future bad lending by taking control of the situation without waiting for lenders and borrowers to begin direct negotiations with each other.[86] Chang also criticizes the IMF's haste in deciding to accelerate financial liberalization. Given the poor state of financial regulation, it was not at all obvious that loosening the reins further would open up the market for more able financial institutions. On the contrary, the institutions ready to take advantage of such openings were in many instances the same ones that had made poor loans to badly managed Korean institutions![87]

By mid-January, the IMF had eased its macroeconomic targets for Korea: the inflation target was raised from 5 per cent to 9 per cent, the monetary growth target was raised from 9 per cent to 14 per cent, the budget surplus requirement was dropped and the capital adequacy standard was delayed, allowing Korean banks to continue to make loans.[88] Clearly, the IMF's initial conditions had been overambitious.

According to You Jong Keun, a top economic advisor to South Korean President-elect Kim Dae Jung, 'international banks 'are trying to get as much as they can in this deal, but they are also under pressure to take some kind of haircut''.[89] But given the pressure for international banks to take a loss on their loans to Korea, as well as the worldwide losses already incurred by stock investors in Korean companies, the Korean government tried to negotiate an interest rate below the market rate.[90] Lenders were asking that the new loans carry an interest rate of seven to eight percentage points over LIBOR. With over 100 creditor banks having extended loans to Korean banks, negotiating an interest rate far below the market rate presented its own problems. Since the debt swap was voluntary, the government had to pay sufficient interest to entice banks to participate in the exchange. Otherwise, the liquidity crisis would continue.[91] The banks ended up with less than three percentage points above LIBOR.[92] The Korean government publicly challenged such interest rates and has continued to fight for lower rates.[93]

On 28 January, international creditor banks and the South Korean government announced a plan to exchange US$24 billion of short-term debt for new loans maturing in one, two and three years. The agreement restructured only loans made to Korean banks, leaving billions of dollars in loans to private Korean companies not yet restructured.[94] To the extent that the debt maturities were increased, the lenders have had to wait for their money.

On 30 January, the Korean stock market reopened after a three-day holiday and stocks rose more than 7 per cent. On another positive note, Seoul's usable reserves then totalled US$12.4 billion, up from US$8.9 billion at the end of the previous year. The government said that it wanted at least US$40 billion in reserves by the end of 1998.[95] In February, the Ministry of Finance and Economy announced the closure of one-third of the country's 30 merchant banks because of their thinly capitalized condition and previous excessive borrowing. By one estimate, the 30 merchant banks lent at least six trillion Won (US$3.6 billion) to six big conglomerates that filed for court protection from creditors in 1997; shareholder equity in the banks was only two-thirds that amount. The banks also lent heavily to Indonesia, and owed foreign creditors about US$20 billion.[96] A government-backed 'bridge bank' was created to assume the failed institutions' assets and liabilities.[97]

More recently, Korea has been making considerable progress towards recovery. Capital inflow from a recent bond offering, IMF bailout funds and central bank loans to overseas branches of local banks has boosted Korea's usable foreign exchange reserves to US$30.3 billion (as of April 1998).[98] Corporate reforms by the banking sector are leading to possible elimination of large companies. [99] Furthermore, the government is steadily pursuing restructuring of the financial sector by promoting mergers, such as the one between Hana and Boram banks.[100] After providing the crucial initial momentum, the United States failed to provide significant leadership as its funding for IMF encountered protracted delays in Congress. Indeed, the rapid depletion of the regular IMF reserves resulting from the loans to Asia and Russia forced the organization to resort to its emergency reserves.[101]

Indonesia

Until recently, Indonesia had been lauded by the World Bank for avoiding the worse symptoms of the Dutch disease (excessive reliance on natural gas or raw material exports), which had sabotaged development in many other Third World countries. The charismatic–authoritarian Suharto regime governed over an ethnically and geographically fragmented society and the world's fourth largest population. Under Suharto, government–business relations became increasingly ruled by corruption and nepotism. Yet at moments of economic crisis, such as in the mid-1960s and during the oil boom–bust cycles in the 1970s and 1980s, Suharto had chosen to follow the advice of Western-trained economists. In the current Asian crisis, he has behaved otherwise.

By mid-1998, the rupiah had dropped from 2400 to the dollar a year earlier to its current level of over 14 000. Consequently, the dollar value of foreign debt has soared. Inflation and unemployment have skyrocketed, while foreign trade is at a standstill, and companies listed on the stockmarket are technically bankrupt. Economic predictions for the year 1998 are for real GDP to decline by 10 per cent, inflation to increase to 80 per cent, and the government budget deficit is estimated at 8.5 per cent for the coming year, which will be wholly financed by foreign borrowings.[102]

The respective roles of the IMF and the United States in Indonesia's macroeconomic and debt crisis can be examined in three periods, each of which is marked by a breakdown of a prior agreement, and the eventual resumption of talk between the Indonesian government and the IMF and US officials. As the economic crisis in Indonesia deepened, the United States increased its involvement, particularly in defending the IMF's policies against critics and exerting political pressure on Suharto. President Habibie and the IMF have recently entered the fourth agreement, which is best understood as a political decision by the Clinton administration to tie the rescue plan to political improvement as well as usual compliance with IMF economic targets.

The first IMF letter of intent addressed to the government of Indonesia on 31 October 1997 was not publicly disclosed. It is known that the agreement was sketchy, hastily put together, and included demands for bank closures and government budget reduction. Harvard economist Jeffrey Sachs criticized the IMF's approach, arguing that East Asian countries are quite unlike Latin America, Africa and other historical cases of countries needing IMF intervention to impose spending and credit discipline.[103] The IMF later partially accepted the criticism, and permitted the Indonesian government to run a budget deficit. In January, Suharto announced a budget without any of IMF's austerity measures. The stockmarket in Jakarta crashed, and on 27 January the government declared what amounted to a moratorium on all Indonesian corporate debt. Suharto's attitude of denying the exigencies of the crisis effectively destroyed the first agreement.

With the spectre of regional market contagion becoming a real threat after October 1997, the United States reversed its early position of non-commitment regarding Thailand and presented a 'second line of defence' of US$3 billlion in support of the IMF plan.[104] US Treasury officials were careful to portray the United States and the IMF as playing reversed roles from the Mexican case, where the United States led the rescue effort. Although at this point Indonesia was seen as fundamentally strong, the United States had got out in front of the IMF in defence of its geopolitical stake in containing the effects of the 'contagion'.

It had also become increasingly evident that the IMF programme would not work in troubled Asian economies without US participation. Economically, a large sum of money was needed. Early on in the crisis, the United States had spurned Japan's plan for an independent Asian monetary fund of US$100 billion, and consequently had to assume the burden in the Indonesian rescue. Apart from this financial commitment, US policy remained largely inchoate and indistinct from the IMF position. A summit meeting of President Clinton and President Suharto in Vancouver in November hardly dealt with the crisis, with Clinton's attention mainly lingering over issues of human rights.[105]

Under pressure from abroad, Suharto signed a new letter of intent on 15 January. The '50-point programme' was surprisingly detailed and extensive in its demands, and highly incendiary for the structural reforms that would cut down the wealth and power of the Suharto family. However, Suharto soon proved the sceptics right by indicating his desire to remain in power, picking Habibie as the vice-president, a man with no power base and a predilection for big government and expensive projects. The IMF agreement was economically sabotaged in February, when Suharto began toying with the notion of a currency board, which would fix the value of the rupiah to the dollar at a rate of 5000–5500.[106] The IMF and the United States reacted strongly. On 6 March, the IMF suspended a scheduled US$3 billion infusion. Five days later, Suharto was re-elected to a seventh five-year term, and formed a cabinet of close supporters with little competence and experience in economic reform, including his daughter Tutut as the minister of social affairs in charge of overseeing relief.[107]

The United States continued to support the IMF position. In response to Suharto's so-called 'IMF-Plus' plan with the currency board, Clinton sent former vice-president Walter Mondale to Indonesia in an effort to 'get through' to Suharto the importance of abiding by the IMF plan. Domestic critics and officials quickly became restless, perceiving Suharto to be playing a game of brinkmanship with the IMF in order to obtain better terms than those accepted by South Korea and Thailand – under the assumption that Indonesia was too important for the international community and the United States to abandon.[108]

Treasury Secretary Robert Rubin emerged as a staunch defender of the IMF. He supported the IMF's decision to withhold additional funds, arguing that money could not solve the deep problems of excessive credit extension, monopolies, protective tariffs and wasteful infrastructure projects.[109]

The third round of talks between the IMF and Indonesia focused on two issues: restructuring of the domestic banking industry and resolving the problem of the foreign debt of Indonesia's private corporations. Several sources reported that repayment was to be handled in ways similar to the framework of Mexico's Ficorca Plan (1983) in which foreign banks offered companies extended periods to repay their loans.[110] The Indonesian economy had reached such crisis proportions that Suharto had few choices but to accept extensive terms similar to those stipulated in the second agreement, in addition to compliance measures on the monitoring and disbursement of money. In light of the desperate economic conditions, some spending allowances were made for the provision of basic necessities and humanitarian aid.

An agreement was reached in the second week of April 1998. However, riots on the eve of implementation of price increases put an abrupt end to the IMF's effort to recreate an atmosphere of credibility. Consequently, the Indonesia crisis has become predominantly one of political crisis, in which the United States was able and eager to seek resolution, with international economic assistance as the ultimate reward.

As law and order fell apart on the streets of Medan, the State Department began to assert the paramount interest of the United States in preventing a return of praetorian politics. However, debates on the floor of the House of Representative on whether the IMF was exceeding its reach and unwisely extending its obsolescent role in the Indonesian case brought doubts about whether the United States could or should supply the financial backing for IMF programmes in Asia.[111] Criticisms came from right and left: Republicans demanded the withdrawal of IMF intervention to permit the market to punish investors, while Democrats urged the addition of political conditions to the IMF agenda.

Interest groups seem less influential than geopolitical considerations, perhaps because the principal US economic interest in Indonesia was in the production of oil and natural gas, which continued uninterrupted.[112] US banks were not major creditors in Indonesia, holding only 7.8 per cent of Indonesian corporate debt (as against 39 per cent by Japanese banks).[113]

Towards the end of May 1998, newly appointed President Habibie agreed to hold an election in 1999, and tried to persuade Hubert Neiss of the IMF to resume the bailout programme. Neiss met opposition leaders, and solicited their approval for the IMF programme.[114] The fourth IMF plan called for new budgetary targets, an exchange rate target of 10 000 rupiah to the dollar, a tightened grip on credit, restructuring of corporate debt, banking reforms and restructuring, and provisions for basic necessities. Furthermore, it is estimated that an additional US$3–4 billion is needed to support the US$43 billion set aside for stabilization in the 10 April agreement.[115] Additional loans were promised by the World Bank (US$1 billion), the Asian Developmental Bank and Japan.

On 4 June a major agreement with the international banks was worked out to stretch out debt payments by Indonesian business, with a three-year grace period and payment of debt over five years.[116] The dollar value of the Indonesian private debt totalled over US$80 billion. The daunting tasks of restructuring the banking industry approached those faced by the Eastern European countries and Mexico in the 1990s, as independent accountants called in by the Indonesian Bank Restructuring Agency (IBRA) found Indonesian banks in worse shape than previously thought.[117]

Changing political perceptions of the Clinton administration provided the impetus for reaching the fourth agreement. Specifically, the agreement reflects a tentative judgment in Washington that Indonesia appears to be stabilizing politically, now that Habibie has proposed holding elections next year and started releasing prisoners. Furthermore, it conforms to the administration's view that ties the rescue plan to political improvements such as human rights, broad political inclusion and selection of pro-reform cabinet members.[118] It remains to be seen how much weight compliance with IMF economic targets carries relative to these political gains.

Secretary of State Albright's speech on 16 June was typical of the emerging US position of tying political improvements to continuation of bailout. She announced the US decision to resume support for international lending to Indonesia, the approval of US$1 billion in short-term financing through the US Export–Import Bank for the US exports to Indonesia, and further humanitarian assistance of US$65 million. In the same speech she urged Asian leaders to emulate Kim Dae Jung in carrying out political reform based on democratic principles. As she put it, 'the lesson for Indonesia is that democracies are better able to adjust to change than regimes that are autocratic'.[119]

Why is the United States carrying so large (and increasing) a share of the political burden in pressuring Jakarta? Three main reasons are readily identifiable. First, a stable and cooperative Indonesia represents a paramount strategic interest for the United States in view of its strategic position and large population. Second, there was a clear risk of 'contagion' in the region and a less certain risk of adverse effects on the US economy. Third, despite criticisms from prominent economists, there is considerable support from the mainstream for IMF policies.

CONCLUSION

This chapter has focused on debt rescheduling efforts involving primarily Mexico and other Latin American countries in the 1930s and 1940s, the 1980s, the 1995 peso crisis and the more recent Asian crises with an eye to understanding the role of creditor governments and international institutions in resolving crises. It has suggested that, when left to their own devices in the earlier period, bondholders and debtors took an inordinate amount of time to reach an accord. Indeed, accords were often only reached with significant US participation or linkages to international institution loans, with the former leading to a debtor-favourable settlement, as in Mexico, and the latter leading to quite an unfavourable agreement, as in the case of Peru.

In the 1980s, the initial efforts by the United States and the IMF, while forestalling a financial crisis, led to a long drawn-out period of roll-overs, jumbo loans and the like, resulting in high costs for Latin American debtors. Debt negotiations during this period only came to an end with the US-promoted Brady Plan that called for significant write-downs in debt. While the IMF came to endorse this strategy, it did not take any initiative in deviating from its traditional approach.

The more recent cases of the 1995 Mexican peso crisis and the Asian crises are marked once again by heavy US involvement. In the peso crisis, significant US guarantees enabled the Mexicans once again to attract capital and put their economy on a sounder footing. The Asian crises have yet to be resolved, but the initial IMF errors and the US endorsement of the bulk of the IMF's actions do not signal that much has been learned from previous efforts to cope with debt crises. It remains to be seen if the United States and the IMF will once again play a more balanced role in resolving this current crisis, as they did in the 1980s following severe political problems in Latin America.

NOTES

1. Stiglitz (1998, p. 2).
2. Eichengreen and Fishlow (1996).
3. Ibid., p. 4.
4. Ibid., p. 36.
5. Aggarwal (1996). The following discussion draws heavily on parts of Chapter 2 of this work.
6. 'Spreads' refers to the difference between the bank's cost of funds and the interest rate charged to the borrower. 'Fees' are charges for managing and initiating loans.
7. In more technical language, the bounds of the issue area can be determined by 'cognitive consensus' among actors on which issues are interlinked. For a theoretical discussion of this point, see in particular Haas (1980).
8. Lipson (1985) examines bank efforts to unite in the 1980s; Aggarwal (1987) analyses the differential success of banks and debtors in uniting.

9. Bulow and Rogoff (1989) formalize a three-way bargaining game in which sufficiently large gains from trade allow the banks and debtors to secure 'side payments' from creditor governments.

10. Naturally, creditor governments may not always see eye-to-eye on debt rescheduling issues and are likely to bargain among themselves over the sharing of costs in rescheduling. Fishlow (1985) examines differences among governments in earlier debt rescheduling episodes.

11. A more precise analysis of creditor government intervention calculations can be found in Aggarwal (1996, ch. 3).

12. Aldcroft (1977, p. 241). The following discussion of lending draws on this excellent review of financial markets in the 1920s. For other analyses of this period, see the citations in this work.

13. Winkler (1933).

14. See Felix (1984) and his references on bond defaults.

15. United Nations (1955), p. 157.

16. See United Nations (1955) for a summary of the outcomes of Latin American debt rescheduling during this period.

17. This discussion of Mexico and the following discussion of Peru rely heavily on Chapters 9 and 10, respectively, in Aggarwal (1996).

18. *Economist*, 1 July 1922, p. 15; Turlington (1930, p. 289).

19. Turlington (1930, p. 294).

20. Wynne (1951, p. 71) and Official Documents Relating to the De La Huerta–Lamont Agreement, #70, cited in Turlington (1930, p. 294).

21. See *The Economist*, 1 July 1922, p. 16.

22. For a good discussion of the terms of the USA–Mexico agreement, see Cline (1953, pp. 248–9). For other discussions, see Cronon (1960) and Wood (1961).

23. For discussion of these negotiations, see Cronon (1960), Wood (1961) and Krasner (1978).

24. Wynne (1951, pp. 97–8); *Economist*, 5 December 1942, p. 709.

25. State Department archive (hereinafter SD) 823.51/619, p. 1.

26. Werlich (1978, p. 211).

27. SD 823.51/677.

28. Carey (1964, pp. 106–7).

29. SD 823.51/1470, pp. 1–3.

30. SD 823.10/7-3151, Annex C, p. 1.

31. SD 823.10/7-3151, Annex C, p. 1.

32. SD 823.10/8-151, p. 1 of Enc. 1.

33. SD 823.10/8-1351.

34. SD 823.10/9-1351.

35. SD 823.10/12-1851.

36. The discussion in this section draws on various chapters in Aggarwal (1996).

37. Delamaide (1984, p. 1).

38. Kraft (1984, p. 7).

39. Delamaide (1984, p. 3).

40. *Washington Post*, 15 August 1982.

41. Kraft (1984, pp. 15–16).

42. Ibid., p. 18.

43. Ibid., pp. 21–2 for details.

44. *Wall Street Journal*, 25 February 1983.

45. *International Herald Tribune*, 15 December 1982.

46. *Los Angeles Times*, 28 May 1985, Part II, p. 5, op-ed article.

47. *The Economist*, 22 October 1988, p. 70.

48. *Economist*, 18 March 1989, p. 110.

49. *IMF Survey*, 20 March 1989, p. 91.

50. *Financial Times*, 14 March 1989, pp. 1–2.

51. Of the SDR3250.7 million package, SDR2797.2 million was from the EFF and SDR453.3 million was from the CCFF. The CCFF was created in August 1988 to expand the utility of the Contingency Financing Facility. The CCFF portion in this case was more compensatory

than contingent. In 1988, the decrease in prices for petroleum, coffee and tomatoes, combined with both damaged crops necessitating more imports of Mexico's main cereal imports and increased prices of these same imports, caused serious damage to the trade balance. See *IMF Survey*, 29 May 1989, p. 175.
52. *The Economist*, 29 April 1989, pp. 15–16.
53. *Wall Street Journal*, 7 July 1989, p. A8.
54. Ibid.
55. *The Economist*, 29 July 1989, pp. 65–6. For a discussion of the Mexican agreement, see Aggarwal (1990).
56. This section draws heavily on Cameron and Aggarwal (1996).
57. *The Wall Street Journal*, 28 March 1994, p. A6.
58. Ibid., 14 June 1994, p. 1.
59. Oppenheimer (1996, p. 219). For a detailed account, see Cameron (1995).
60. An official in the Mexican Ministry of Foreign Affairs suggested that the generosity of the bailout sent out a signal that the crisis was more serious than it really was. Interview, Mexico City (1995).
61. *New York Times*, 3 February 1995, pp. A1, A6.
62. Thanks are due to Lawrence Whitehead for these observations.
63. *The Economist*, 25 February 1995, p. 79.
64. Goldstein (1998, p. 1).
65. *New York Times*, 14 August 1997, p. 1.
66. *The Economist*, 15 November 1997.
67. *New York Times*, 5 July 1998, p. 1.
68. *New York Times*, 19 August 1997, p. 1.
69. See Radelet and Sachs (1998) for a complete discussion.
70. *Financial Times*, 1 July 1998, p. 23.
71. Bresnan (1998, p. 4).
72. *Asia Pulse*, 1 July 1998.
73. Fischer (1998, p. 103).
74. *New York Times*, 5 July 1998, p. 1.
75. Bresnan (1998, p. 3).
76. *White House Press Briefing*, 11 March 1997.
77. *Business Day*, 1 July 1998, p. 2.
78. Chang (1998, p. 9).
79. Feldstein (1998).
80. *New York Times*, 5 January 1998, p. 10.
81. Mr Rhodes, vice-chairman of Citibank, helped to persuade banks around the world to roll over short-term loans to Korean banks. His message to international commercial bankers: 'Let's stop the hemorrhaging and buy time to get the country back to the international financial markets' (*Wall Street Journal*, 9 January 1998, p. 10, and *The Sacramento Bee*, 2 January 1998, p. A1).
82. *Wall Street Journal*, 2 January 1998, p. 5.
83. *New York Times*, 5 January 1998, p. 1.
84. *Wall Street Journal*, 5 January 1998, p. A16.
85. Ibid.
86. Feldstein (1998).
87. Chang (1998, p. 14).
88. Ibid., p. 13.
89. *Wall Street Journal*, 26 January 1998, p. A12.
90. Ibid.
91. Ibid.
92. *Orange Country Register*, 30 January 1998, p. C3.
93. *Wall Street Journal*, 19 January 1998, p. A11.
94. *Orange Country Register*, 30 January 1998, p. C3.
95. *Los Angeles Times*, 3 March 1998, p. D-1.
96. *Wall Street Journal*, 2 February 1998, p. A16.

97. *Wall Street Journal*, 2 February 1998, p. A16.
98. *Business Times* (Singapore), 21 April 1998, p. 6.
99. *Korea Herald*, 8 May 1998, B2.
100. Ibid., 16 July 1998, B6.
101. *Boston Globe*, 14 July 1998, D1.
102. *Washington Post*, 26 June 1998, p. A23.
103. *New York Times*, 3 November 1997, op-ed.
104. Bresnan (1998, p. 2).
105. 'Economy in 1998', www.indonesiatoday.com/a3/j6/y1jan98.html
106. *The Economist*, 7 March 1998, pp. 42–3.
107. Bresnan (1998, p. 15).
108. *The Economist*, 11 April 1998, p. 29.
109. Www.pbs.org/newshour/bb/asia/jan-june98/indonesia_3–10.html
110. *The Economist*, 4 November 1998, p. 29.
111. *Washington Post*, 17 June 1998, p. A06.
112. Bresnan (1998, p. 20).
113. Ibid.
114. *Washington Post*, 29 May 1998, p. A29.
115. *Wall Street Journal*, 26 June 1998, p. A12.
116. *Washington Post*, 5 June 1998, p. D02.
117. *Wall Street Journal*, 26 June 1998, p. A17.
118. *Washington Post*, 22 May 1998, p. A42.
119. Dailynews.yahoo.com/headlines/ap/.../albright_asia_text2_1.html, p.2.

REFERENCES

Aggarwal, Vinod K. (1987), 'International Debt Threat: Bargaining Among Creditors and Debtors in the 1980s', Berkeley, IIS Policy Paper, no. 29.
Aggarwal, Vinod K. (1990), 'Foreign Debt: The Mexican Experience', *Relazioni Internazionali*, September, 26–33.
Aggarwal, Vinod K. (1996), *Debt Games: Strategic Interaction in International Debt Rescheduling*, Cambridge: Cambridge University Press.
Aldcroft, Derek Howard (1977), *From Versailles to Wall Street, 1919–1929*, Berkeley: University of California Press.
Boston Globe (various).
Bresnan, John (1998), 'The United States and the Indonesian Financial Crisis', unpublished manuscript.
Bulow, Jeremy and Kenneth Rogoff (1989), 'Sovereign Debt: Is to Forgive to Forget?', *American Economic Review*, **79**, March, 43–50.
Business Times (Singapore, various).
Cameron, Maxwell A. (1995), 'Crisis or Crises in Mexico?', *Third World Resurgence*, **57**, May.
Cameron, Maxwell A. and Vinod K. Aggarwal (1996), 'Mexican meltdown: states, markets and post-NAFTA financial turmoil', *Third World Quarterly*, **57** (5), 975–87.
Carey, James (1964), *Peru and the United States, 1900–1962*, Notre Dame: University of Notre Dame Press.
Chang, Ha-Jon (1998), 'Korea: The Misunderstood Crisis', manuscript, University of Cambridge.
Cline, Howard (1953), *The U.S. and Mexico*, Cambridge, Mass.: Harvard University Press.

Cronon, E. David (1960), *Josephus Daniels in Mexico*, Madison: University of Wisconsin.

Delamaide, Darrell (1984), *Debt Shock*, New York: Doubleday.

The Economist (various).

Eichengreen, Barry and Albert Fishlow (1996), *Contending with Capital Flows: What is Different About the 1990s?*, New York: Council on Foreign Relations.

Feldstein, Martin (1998), 'Refocusing the IMF', *Foreign Affairs*, March/April.

Felix, David (1984), 'The Baring Crisis of the 1890s and the International Bond Defaults of the 1930s: Delphic Prophecies on the Outcome of the Current Latin American Debt Crises', unpublished manuscript.

Financial Times (various).

Fischer, Stanley (1998), 'The Asian Crisis: A View from the IMF – Address by Stanley Fischer on January 22, 1998', International Monetary Fund.

Fishlow, Albert (1985), 'Lessons From the Past: Capital Markets During the 19th Century and the Interwar Period', *International Organization*, 39 (3).

Goldstein, Morris (1998), 'The Asian Financial Crisis', *International Economics Policy Briefs*, January, published by the Institute for International Economics.

Haas, Ernst (1980), 'Why Collaborate? Issue Linkage and International Regimes', *World Politics*, 32, 357–405.

IMF Survey, 20 March 1989.

International Herald Tribune (various).

Korea Herald (various).

Kraft, Joseph (1984), *The Mexican Rescue*, New York: Group of Thirty.

Krasner, Stephen D. (1978), *Defending the National Interest: Raw Materials Investments and U.S. Foreign Policy*, Princeton: Princeton University Press.

Liddle, R. William (1998), 'Indonesia's Unexpected Failure of Leadership', unpublished manuscript, Ohio State University.

Lipson, Charles (1985), 'The International Organization of Third World Debt', *International Organization*, 35 (4).

Los Angeles Times (various).

New York Times (various).

Oppenheimer, A. (1996), *Bordering on Chaos: Guerillas, Stockbrokers, Politicians and Mexico's Road to Prosperity*, Boston, Mass.: Little Brown.

Orange County Register (various).

Radelet, Steven and Jeffrey Sachs (1998), 'The Onset of the East Asian Financial Crisis', unpublished paper available from the Harvard Institute for International Development, 30 March.

Stiglitz, Joseph (1998), 'The Role of International Financial Institutions in the Current Global Economy', Address to the Chicago Council on Foreign Relations, Chicago, 27 February.

Turlington, Edgar (1930), *Mexico and Her Foreign Creditors*, New York: Columbia University Press.

United Nations (1955), *Foreign Capital in Latin America*, New York: Department of Economic and Social Affairs.

United States Department of State Archives (various).

Wall Street Journal (various).

Washington Post (various).

Werlich, David P. (1978), *Peru: A Short History*, Carbondale: Southern Illinois University Press.

Winkler, Max (1933), *Foreign Bonds: An Autopsy*, New York: Arno Press.
Wood, Bryce (1961), *The Making of the Good Neighbor Policy*, New York and London: Columbia University Press.
Wynne, William H. (1951), *State Insolvency and Foreign Bondholders*, vol. 2, New Haven: Yale University Press.

6. At the insolvency masquerade, what mask for the IMF: international bankruptcy court, mediator or insolvency law reformer?[*]

Paul D. Leake, Adam C. Rogoff and Gordon W. Johnson

The Asian crisis presents the International Monetary Fund (IMF) with an opportunity to reassess its world role in light of its original mandate to help safeguard the financial integrity of its members' economies. To date, the IMF has largely confined its role to banking, finance and macroeconomic issues, with relatively little involvement or input into its members' bankruptcy and enforcement systems. The Asian crisis has caused many to rethink the IMF's fundamental role and strategy, including the wisdom of bailout plans for the Asian economies. In our increasingly global economy, the implications of the crisis reach well beyond domestic boundaries and spotlight an issue that has nagged the international business community for decades – the void in the international insolvency framework. The IMF's new equation must take into account hitherto neglected areas, including improvement in bankruptcy and enforcement systems, credit culture and corporate sector practices.

Recent news articles report that the IMF is evaluating different options for dealing with financial crises such as Asia has encountered. According to a confidential report, considerations include the possibility of nominating standing 'creditors' committees' of banks and financial institutions in the event of a crisis, creating an international bankruptcy court, and supporting insolvency law reform efforts or 'sanctioning a temporary stay on creditor litigation'. This is the kind of proactive thinking the IMF should be doing. The triage approach, which we have witnessed in Asia, often fails to engage in a comprehensive review either of the insolvency and enforcement systems or of the credit culture and corporate sector practices. This is understandable given the nature of crisis

[*] Parts of this chapter are taken from the 'Transnational Restructurings and Insolvencies' chapter of the WGM treatise, *Reorganizing Family Businesses.*

management and the need to restore confidence in the financial systems of these countries.

To be sure, there are logical and political constraints on the kind of role the IMF should play as 'international bankruptcy court' or might play in the area of international insolvency laws. With global markets increasingly converging, with economies growing ever more complex and intertwined, with internationalization occurring on an unprecedented scale, the time has clearly arrived for the IMF to rethink its original mandate and develop a sound bankruptcy philosophy. Against the backdrop of the patchwork quilt of international insolvency law, the authors outline a role for the IMF to play in this arena and a road map to guide the way forward.

THE INSOLVENCY PARADIGM

Assessing the IMF's role in international insolvency, whether as international bankruptcy forum, international mediator or vanguard of reform, must be done against the existing backdrop of insolvency law. Insolvency laws have significance on two levels, national and international.

National Insolvency Laws

At the national level, insolvency laws serve a fundamental role in free and competitive markets. Bankruptcy laws are at the root of commercial and financial law and can play a vital role in stabilizing the commercial system of economies. Free market economies require an intricate system of laws to govern the relative property, financial and commercial rights and remedies between contracting parties. In so doing, these laws afford protections that interject certainty into commercial relationships, which create an atmosphere conducive to trade and commerce.

In a world without insolvency laws – or effective insolvency laws – as is the case in many emerging markets around the world, the typical paradigm goes as follows. When debtors default, the creditor is entitled to enforce its rights and remedies under contractual arrangements and applicable law. These remedies may involve self-help (for example, acceleration of debt, withholding performance, enforcement of a security interest, reservation of title, setting off of debts, against moneys in its possession or other claims, and the like) or judicial process. In the latter, the creditor commences legal proceedings in court for payment of debt, and execution of judgment or for repossession by foreclosure or sale. In such cases, the system is designed to give the creditor the rights for which it bargained, with the end result that the creditor ultimately may or may not be satisfied for amounts unpaid. Given such detailed rights and enforcement mechanisms, this benefit of the bargain approach elevates the law of contracts and assumes that the rights bargained for are a sufficient alternative to an insolvency system.

The above scenario works fine in the absence of insolvency and generally reflects an economy that has more sophisticated legal and enforcement systems in place to respect the rights of creditors. In the majority of non-industrial countries, legal and enforcement systems tend to be unsophisticated and in many countries judicial systems may be flawed. The end result is that, in emerging markets and less industrialized nations, the prospects for gaining the benefit of one's bargain in a non-insolvency situation may be substantially below standard. While the bargain theory works in concept if everybody plays by the rules, there are shortcomings in applying this view in the context of an insolvency. For purposes of illustration, the focus here is on corporate insolvencies.

First, a company's insolvent condition may lead to inequality in the treatment of creditors with similar rights and status. Insolvency often commences a pro-liferation of self-help remedies or the proverbial race-to-the-courthouse, as creditors seek to have first rights to a limited and generally dwindling pool of assets. Under many common and civil law systems, the first-in-time rule prevails and the 'swift of foot' get the spoils. This leads only to an increased frenzy among other creditors seeking to ensure satisfaction of their debts. With assets too few to go around, the feeding frenzy leaves many creditors unsatisfied and they must leave the party hungry. Larger and wealthier creditors are at an advantage because they can exercise more leverage and more easily expend the funds necessary to get what they want. In the end, this results in disproportionate treatment among otherwise similarly situated creditors.

Second, the race causes waste. First-in-time creditors may be willing to part with assets through foreclosure or sales at amounts that are considerably lower than a fair market value, assuming, of course, that the value is sufficient to cover the creditor's debt. The circumstances may contribute to a perception that the sale is taking place under 'firesale' conditions, resulting in a liquidation or forced sale value, which is almost always lower than the value between a reasonable seller and reasonable buyer, neither of whom is under any compulsion to sell or buy.

Third, dissolution of a corporate concern could impose burdens on employees and the economy. Although the company may have been marginally viable, the liquidation mentality of creditors will invariably result in a piecemeal dismemberment of the company's assets. Under these conditions, employees will become redundant and possibly forced onto unemployment and welfare rolls. Because the company is dissolved, the government may not be able to collect taxes that were owed, especially since governments are rarely able to respond as quickly as creditors. Finally, the company's demise decreases competition.

Fourth, while corporate failure triggers rights only among the direct creditors, enough insolvent companies could cause systemic risk, especially where businesses are intertwined (as, for example, in South Korea, Indonesia and Thailand). With a string of losses in a single industry or across industries, the erosion of capital could jeopardize the safety and soundness of a country's financial system. Of course, having a bankruptcy law is no guarantee that this will not happen (as in the savings and loan crisis in the United States), but it may provide a means of maintaining public or investor confidence to diminish the impact.

Fifth, the risk of insolvency increases the cost of doing business and financing. In a developed economy, business failures are to be expected as a natural result of competition. The healthy and efficient survive. Insolvency imposes additional risks on creditors, who either sustain losses or must incur costs to obtain the benefits of enforcing their contractual and legal rights and remedies. To remain profitable, lenders and sellers must pass their losses on to the market through increased interest rates or higher-priced goods. These measures also serve as a buffer against the risk of insolvency in future relationships, especially if this reflects a growing trend. The consequences are that financing is made available only at higher cost, which suppresses market activity.

Sixth, financially distressed debtors have been known to act in their own interests by secreting their assets away from the reach of creditors, transferring them overseas, or to friends and family. This makes it even more difficult for creditors and further increases the costs on the market.

Seventh, absent a bankruptcy system, should the government salvage or bail out an insolvent company that is vital to the economy or a significant player in the industry? The bailout subsidizes the company for economic losses that may have arisen through possible mismanagement and inefficiencies. How does this help the economy? A sufficiently strong economy may support this for a time, but it may mark a retreat from the concept of a free and competitive market system. Subsidizing one company and not others decreases competition and gives the subsidized enterprise an unfair advantage, which may encourage practices of waste and mismanagement.

Insolvency laws provide a means of addressing these abuses and inequities in several ways. The backbone of most insolvency systems entails a delicate balancing of the fundamental policies aimed at promoting equity and fostering rehabilitation.

Equity and reorganization policies
A country's insolvency laws implicate a broad spectrum of national economic and sociopolical issues. Insolvency laws are designed to balance the rights and

interests of creditors and society in reapportioning the risks of insolvency in a manner that befits a country's policies and goals. There can be no uniform or perfect solution, for countries vary significantly in their needs, as do their laws governing security interests, recordation, property and contracts rights, remedies and enforcement procedures. Nevertheless, under most insolvency regimes, these questions and issues are addressed in some fashion. Under some laws, the scale slants in favour of creditors' rights, while in others it tilts towards rehabilitation of the debtor and preserving jobs.

The overriding objective of an insolvency law is to supplant the 'free-for-all' system of individual enforcement and replace it with one that levels the playing field and balances the relative interests of creditors, debtors and the government in a suitable manner. Most insolvency laws attempt to balance two competing policies: the equity policy and the rehabilitation policy. The equity policy fosters 'equitable distribution of a troubled company's assets through the equal sharing of losses by creditors of equal rank'. Inherent in the equity policy is a respect for the relative priority of rights held by creditors. The equity policy is designed to promote equality among 'unsecured' creditors, while acknowledging and deferring to the senior rights of secured creditors then holding 'in rem' rights. In bankruptcy, creditors' rights may be suspended in whole or in part, and an official representative charged with collecting the debtor's estate for an orderly and ratable distribution to creditors. This process ensures that all creditors holding similar claims will be on equal footing.

The second policy is more difficult and has been reflected in different countries' insolvency laws in varying ways. The rehabilitation policy is premised on the concept that economically viable businesses should be salvaged and jobs preserved. In the United States, for example, the 'reorganization policy' promotes 'the restructuring of a business to preserve jobs, to pay creditors, to produce a return for owners, and to obtain for the Nation the fruits of American enterprise'. This is achieved through imposition of a moratorium or automatic injunction that prevents creditors from engaging in collection efforts or exercising enforcement remedies. As a result, the debtor or the receiver is afforded a neutral forum in which to negotiate a consensual business solution, which is hoped results in a higher dividend to creditors because the business is salvaged as a 'going concern' rather than being liquidated.

How the equity policy and rehabilitative policies are balanced in light of social objectives varies from country to country. Most countries still maintain only a form of liquidation as the sole solution for insolvent corporations. Under such systems, only the equity policy is important, although the business may be collected and sold as a unit to maximize the dividend to creditors. Because the right of 'in rem' and secured creditors are respected, these creditors are often exempt from the effect of the automatic stay. Other systems, such as that of France, are heavily titled towards reorganization. As a result, French bankruptcy law allows employees and certain administrative creditors to be paid out of the collateral of secured creditors, even if those creditors are under-secured. In like fashion, the US Chapter 11 process, which falls more on the pro-debtor side of the scale, allows a trustee or debtor to surcharge a secured creditor's collateral with administrative costs and expenses of preserving or disposing of the collateral, where such creditor has requested or consented to, or directly benefited from, acts to preserve or dispose of the assets.

Over the past decade, countries have been moving closer to the rehabilita-tion model as an apparent acknowledgment that the rescue process can return greater enterprise value to the economy, in certain cases, and serve other important economic goals, such as preservation of jobs. Even under pro-debtor or pro-rescue systems, there are mechanisms for separate treatment of viable and non-viable businesses, the latter being relegated to liquidation.

Objectives of corporate insolvency
Corporate insolvency laws address a number of objectives, some competing, others compatible. These objectives are often balanced through various mechanisms within the insolvency scheme. The following list shows some of the more commonly recognized objectives of corporate insolvency law:

- to facilitate recovery of financially distressed companies,
- to suspend pursuit of rights and remedies,
- to divest directors of management powers,
- to avoid transfers and transactions that unfairly prejudice the general body of creditors,
- to ensure orderly distribution of the estate,
- to provide a fair and equitable system for ranking of claims,
- to provide means to investigate causes of a company's failure and to impose liability on culpable management,
- to protect the public against future improper trading by delinquent directors,
- to ensure the integrity and competence of insolvency practitioners, and,
- in liquidation cases, to dissolve the company.

International Insolvency

At the international level, the problems arising from poorly developed or non-existent insolvency laws are compounded. There can be little doubt that advances in telecommunications and transport, coupled with linkages among global financial and capital markets, have caused international trade to flourish in recent decades as never before, as businesses search out new and more profitable markets. These multinational enterprises transcend national borders.

Present trends already reflect that multinationals are giving way to a new breed of 'mega-nationals' operating in numerous countries at the same time. One need only ponder the recent Daimler–Chrysler merger as another example of an international merger on a 'mega' scale.

The insolvency of companies operating in several jurisdictions gives rise to complex issues, especially if the interests of the various creditor groups and the laws of the various forums conflict, as they often do. The present framework for restructuring financially distressed multinational enterprises lags far behind in the race to internationalize. No uniform international regulations or laws govern the insolvency of a multinational corporation. No international forum exists for the resolution of claims against assets or persons located in various jurisdictions. With limited exceptions, no international conventions or treaties govern the effect of an international insolvency proceeding. It is with heightened awareness of these deficiencies that the international business community has been attempting, and lately with some success, to develop innovative and reliable solutions to achieve a greater level of cooperation in transnational insolvencies.

In the absence of international conventions or treaties, the insolvency laws of individual jurisdictions, coordinated on an ad hoc basis to the extent accepted or imposed by the individual players and courts, will continue to govern international insolvencies. The parochial nature of national insolvency laws and the complexity of the issues that cut across a wide spectrum of other equally national legal disciplines make international insolvencies especially difficult.

The typical international insolvency paradigm
An international insolvency is characteristically distinguished as involving an enterprise that has assets and creditors situated in more than one country. When an enterprise conducts business internationally, maintains employees and has creditors in multiple countries, its failure raises numerous thorny conflicts of law questions regarding: (a) the fate of the enterprise (some countries encourage rescue, while others emphasize controlled wind-up); (b) the enforcement of creditors' rights in security and remedies available on default; (c) the criteria for commencing insolvency proceedings and the effects such proceedings have upon the enterprise, and its operations, management, property and creditors, as well as upon its affiliates, and their operations, management, property and creditors; (d) the treatment of claims during the insolvency proceeding, including the effects upon the debtor's contractual relationships; (e) the distribution of the debtor's assets among its creditors and constituents and the order of preference of such distribution; and (f) the ability to set aside antecedent transactions and recover pre-petition transfers made while the debtor was insolvent or that resulted in non-statutorily recognized creditor preferences.

The failure of such multinational enterprises understandably fosters tremendous resolve in creditors concerned with diminishing prospects for repayment of debts owed them. Often this leads to a frenzied race to the courthouse at home and sometimes abroad to ensure the best treatment possible for the proactive creditors, without consideration of principles of equitable distribution. Creditor action in a foreign jurisdiction raises a host of specific questions. Frequently, the answers depend upon whether and to what extent there is foreign jurisdictional recognition of the debtor's insolvency proceedings and the consequent effect upon the debtor's assets and operations, wherever located.

By way of illustration, assume that insolvency proceedings are commenced in Country A against a corporation which has assets and creditors in Country A and Country B. Creditors in both countries immediately move to execute on assets located in Country B. If Country A espouses 'universal' jurisdiction over the debtor's assets in Country B, what effect does an injunction or moratorium entered in the debtor's insolvency proceedings have in Country B against either Country A or Country B creditors? The answer depends on the willingness of Country B ('B') to recognize and enforce the bankruptcy judgment entered by Country A ('A'), which often turns on the similarity of the two countries' laws and considerations of reciprocity. Courts in A have 'in personam' jurisdiction over A's creditors and can hold them in contempt of violations of orders entered in insolvency proceedings in A. This is not necessarily the case for B's creditors, although some may be subject to the reach of A's courts, if they conduct business or have assets located in A. Nevertheless, if B recognizes the universal reach of A's insolvency laws, then B gives full effect to A's orders against creditors from both countries.

If B takes a territorial view of the world, it will reject A's assertion of jurisdiction over assets situated in B, in which case the assets and remedies against those assets are exclusively governed by B's law. However, B may give effect to A's order by judicial decree, through a process like exequatur used in certain European countries, effectively transmuting the order to an order of Country B. That process can take considerable time, six months or more in some countries, during which neither the bankruptcy moratorium nor the order empowering the administrator to act are recognized. The assets may fall prey to the legally savvy and swift of foot. Even if an exequator order is ultimately obtained, will it have retroactive effect, thereby enabling the debtor or its representative to recover assets seized by creditors in both countries after the commencement of the insolvency proceedings? If not, only A's creditors may be compelled to return assets or, at a minimum, suffer disallowance or reduction of claims in keeping with principles of equitable distribution. If A is territorialist in approach, it may even be that A creditors are allowed to retain assets recovered outside the forum through legitimate action.

While most countries are keen to protect creditors within the confines of their own borders, virtually all consider an enterprise that does business or maintains assets within another country's borders as subjecting itself to the insolvency laws of each such host country. While rules of comity have slowly emerged in the insolvency area to facilitate cooperative resolutions with 'friendly' countries, more often than not the end result is a separate liquidation of the corporation's assets and interests in each of the countries in which it conducts business. The inevitable outcome of these multiple concurrent proceedings is expense, waste, unpredictability and inequality of treatment among creditors in different countries, though they are otherwise similarly situated. While this may seem a small price to pay to preserve a sovereign's integrity, the price paid for systemic unpredictability in defaults by multinationals translates into a higher cost of international financing.

Key principles
The cross-border corporate insolvency phenomenon entails the adjudication of competing rights in competing forums by application of competing laws. The resolution of conflicts turns on the approach taken by the courts situated within each country where the debtor's assets are located. Some adopt an approach of 'unity and universality', which is characterized by a single administration of the debtor's estate in one forum subject to universal application of the original forum state's laws over all of the debtor's assets, wherever located. Others cling to protectionist notions of sovereignty embodied in the 'territoriality' approach, resulting in multiple proceedings.

Unity v. plurality   The 'unity' principle espouses a centralized administration of the debtor's assets and interests (wherever located) in one forum, generally where the debtor has its domicile or principal place of business. 'Unity' implies that the effect of the insolvency law of the domicile jurisdiction on the debtor and its assets will be recognized wherever the debtor's assets and interests are located. Moreover, unity presupposes that all the debtor's assets and interests will be administered through the insolvency proceeding in the domicile forum. The debtor or its representative is empowered to travel to other countries to repatriate movable or dispose of immovable assets. Similarly, all creditors, wherever located, must prove their claims in a single forum. The unity approach strives for unity of administration, procedure, distribution of assets and equality of creditor treatment through a unified application of law (the latter implying universality, as discussed below). As such, it is considered by proponents of this approach the most efficient and economical means of distributing the debtor's estate. In practice, the unity principle can only be implemented by way of bilateral or multilateral treaties.

Unity provides a stark contrast with 'plurality', which demands multiple concurrent plenary proceedings in each state where the debtor's assets are situated or business is conducted. Proponents of plurality argue that 'unity' invites a sovereign to abandon its 'right to control local assets', which many consider undesirable. They argue that local creditors should not have their expectations thwarted by being forced into foreign proceedings, but, rather, should be able to rely on the predictability of their own laws and entitled to resolve their disputes with respect to local claims against local assets in a domestic forum. Critics argue that plurality encourages creditors to act hastily to gain comparatively unequal shares of the debtor's assets, and ultimately imposes on claimants the burden of greater expense, delay and injustice. Additional concerns stem from conflicting priority schemes for distribution among creditors, which are often perceived more as expressions of local interests or national policy than as formulations of rational policies for commercial transactions.

Universality v. territoriality   As unity seeks worldwide recognition of the insolvency proceeding commenced in the domicile forum, universality seeks worldwide recognition and enforcement of the law of the domicile forum. Universality presupposes that foreign jurisdictions will give effect to orders issued by the domicile forum court and recognize the representative of the debtor that is appointed in the insolvency proceeding pending in the domicile forum as having the power to collect and dispose of the debtor's assets within foreign territories. In theory, uniform application of the law leads to greater equality of treatment among creditors. In practice, however, there are considerable difficulties in applying one nation's laws to resolve all disputes in a cross-border insolvency. Which jurisdiction is the appropriate domicile forum is not always clear. Moreover, the relative ease of commencing an insolvency proceeding will have an influence over the selection of forum, as will the identity of the parties capable of commencing such proceeding. Pre-emptive petitions for relief have been filed to guarantee a choice of forum and forum law.

Creditors of the debtor have legitimate expectations that commercial laws governing their transactions will be respected, secured rights upheld and relative priorities strictly enforced, subject to overriding national interests implemented through insolvency laws. Otherwise, principles of private international law would become meaningless at the outset of commercial transactions, if a creditor's commercial expectations could be defeated by the mere chance of an insolvency within a different country. Generally, creditors make their credit decisions and assess the risks of their commercial contracts in reliance upon a particular law or set of laws that govern their contractual arrangements. Obviously, parties can and do exercise their choice of law in contractual arrangements. Nevertheless, insolvency is not a matter of private parties' contractual choices. Insolvency laws can override choice of law and have a critical impact upon commercial recoveries made by creditors in the event that their borrower or contract party suffers financial distress.

Proponents of territoriality justifiably argue that this approach maintains the integrity of legal systems and provides greater predictability with respect to assets and claims situated within a territory. In the purest sense, however, this approach 'gives no extra-territorial effect to the laws of a country'. The result is that insolvency proceedings must be commenced in each country in which the debtor's assets are located to administer those assets. Not surprisingly, this approach tends to advantage domestic creditors at the expense of foreign creditors and encourages the proverbial 'race to the courthouse'. Territoriality contravenes the spirit of international cooperation, although most systems embrace it to some extent.

The doctrine of comity No discussion of the principles of international insolvency is complete without considering the doctrine of international comity. The standard in the United States for application of the long-standing comity doctrine was set in *Hilton* v. *Guyot*, a case in which a French manufacturer obtained a French judgment against US nationals. Finding no assets in France to levy upon, the plaintiffs sought enforcement of the judgment in the United States. In holding that the judgment would not have conclusive effect, the US Supreme Court stated:

> 'Comity', in the legal sense, is neither a matter of absolute obligation, on the one hand, nor of mere courtesy and good will, upon the other. But it is the recognition which one nation allows within its territory to the legislative, executive or judicial acts of another nation, having due regard both to the international duty and convenience, and to the rights of its own citizens or of other persons who are under the protection of its law.

The Supreme Court of Canada more recently opined that the comity doctrine needs to be updated to keep pace with modern times:

> In my view, the old common law rules relating to recognition and enforcement were rooted in an outmoded conception of the world that emphasized sovereignty and independence, often at the cost of unfairness. Greater comity is required in our modern era when international transactions involve a constant flow of products, wealth and people across the globe.

In similar fashion, Lord Hoffman of the High Court of Justice in England, a strong proponent of cooperation in international insolvency, pronounced a more embracing view of the doctrine in the *Maxwell* case: 'The only satisfactory solution to the possibility of jurisdictional conflicts would be an international convention. In the absence of such a convention, the only way forward is by the discretionary exercise of judicial restraint'.

Comity recognizes a sovereign's right to establish laws over its boundaries and is premised on respect for decisions made by foreign courts on matters within the purview of their jurisdiction. The case of *U.S. Lines* represents one of the most stark examples of a company's failure to properly assess the implications of an international insolvency in the absence of comity. The company commenced a Chapter 11 proceeding in the United States to reorganize its 27-ship fleet, doing business around the world. Within a year the company had been completely dismembered, with creditors acting independently in 11 different countries.

A celebrated instance in the *U.S. Lines* case of non-cooperation between countries is *Felixstowe*. After its filing under Chapter 11, U.S. Lines sought and obtained a restraining order from the US bankruptcy court purporting to restrain all persons 'wherever located', including those outside the United States, from initiating or continuing actions against the company and its assets. In response to this action, and the subject of *Felixstowe*, two English companies and a Dutch company filed suit in England to obtain a Mareva injunction in amounts owed to the parties, which precluded U.S. Lines from removing its assets from the jurisdiction. U.S. Lines argued that, as a Chapter 11 debtor, it was a new entity, which effected a change in the ownership of the assets. The English court found this argument uncompelling. Notably, the English court stressed that 'the court would in principle always wish to co-operate in every proper way with an order like the present one made by a court in a friendly jurisdiction'. Nevertheless, because, among other things, the assets were subject to ancillary wind-up proceedings in England, the judge refused to discharge the Mareva injunction. The rest, as they say, is history.

COMMON AND UNCOMMON FEATURES OF INSOLVENCY SYSTEMS

There are a large number of features common to bankruptcy systems. These commonalities serve as a useful point for trying to conceptualize models that might lead to greater convergence in insolvency schemes. Unfortunately, there are many pitfalls for the unwary and what at first blush appears common may have nuances with significant legal implications. A discussion of the following areas serves to illustrate this point.

Directors' Duties and Liability

As a general rule, under US law a director's duties change from the shareholders to the creditors (or in some cases both) as they approach insolvency.

The same principles generally exist in other countries. However, where the dividing line is drawn and the degree of culpability of directors for failing to fulfil those duties may be more stringent. For example, in England, directors face stiff penalties if they continue to trade (do business) when they have reason to suspect that the company is or will become insolvent. Moreover, such directors must be disqualified under the Company Directors Disqualification Act of 1986 for a period of two to 15 years, if the court finds them unfit. Similarly harsh penalties or criminal liability may be imposed in other countries for reckless or improper conduct leading to or immediately before bankruptcy.

Recognition and Enforcement of Foreign Bankruptcy Judgments

While the automatic stay protects US debtors from US creditors, only in theory does it extend to foreign creditors and assets ('wherever located'), notwithstanding the universal definition of the debtor's estate contained in Section 541 of the Bankruptcy Code and the universal jurisdictional reach of the bankruptcy laws under 28 U.S.C. 1334. There is no doubt that the automatic stay applies when the US court has 'in rem' jurisdiction over the assets or 'in personam' jurisdiction over the parties. For example, if a Canadian Bank which conducts business and maintains assets in the United States attempts to seize the US debtor's assets in Canada, such creditor might be held in contempt or have its US assets frozen or seized to satisfy damages arising from its wrongful seizure of the debtor's property. This is often a very real and substantial threat for foreign financial institutions that regularly conduct business in the United States. In that regard, the *Felixstowe* decision suggests that, but for the fact of the ancillary winding-up proceeding, the English court would have had no 'in rem' jurisdiction over the assets and would have ordered their return. Assuming the US court does not have jurisdiction over the parties, some action will probably be necessary in the foreign jurisdiction to protect assets from foreign creditor enforcement activity. Some countries embrace the 'universality' theory and might readily recognize the scope of the US court's asserted jurisdiction, but even in these countries the recognition is not automatic. Proceedings to enforce or gain recognition of the automatic stay or other bankruptcy court orders are generally required. Other countries are territorial in nature and will not recognize the reach of US bankruptcy law to property within their boundaries. In these, as in most countries, it is necessary to commence an entirely new lawsuit on the merits, which hinges on the foreign country's laws or applicable law as determined under choice of law principles. This should come as no surprise, since the United States often holds the same view towards foreign debtors' proceedings. For example, the Mexican bankruptcy trustee of Aeronaves de Mexico, in the Mexican bankruptcy proceeding, commenced an ancillary proceeding in the United States under Section 304 of the Bankruptcy Code to enjoin US creditors from litigating a disputed claim in the United States in disregard of the Mexican bankruptcy court's asserted jurisdiction over claims against the debtor's estate and the debtor's assets located in the United States.

Rehabilitation v. Liquidation

The insolvency laws of most countries have a liquidation feature, with far fewer providing for corporate rescues. Few countries, but an increasing number have a functional equivalent to the US Chapter 11 process, and, of those countries, almost none incorporates the concept of the debtor in possession authorized to continue operating the enterprise following the commencement of an insolvency proceeding. Rather, most countries resort to the appointment of a representative to supervise the insolvency proceedings and implement the financial rescue or rehabilitation. The extent to which this insolvency representative for the debtor has fiduciary or other responsibilities to creditors varies, as does the extent of court supervision and reporting requirements.

In most foreign jurisdictions, this representative displaces pre-insolvency management and becomes the governing force in the enterprise. This change in control is consistent with the view that the stated objective of 'maximizing going concern value', while preserving asset value, is best achieved through a sale of the company to another entity. Moreover, the insolvency laws of most countries historically are predisposed to favour creditor rights. Such statutes are oriented to liquidation. Though some countries are coming around to the notion of a debtor-in-possession (in limited respects under Germany's new Insolvency Code to become effective in 1999), virtually all have no such concept and provide for appointment of a receiver, administrator, liquidator, trustee or other court-appointed supervisor to take control of and manage the business upon the filing of bankruptcy.

The Bankruptcy Estate

All systems have a concept of the bankruptcy estate. Debtor-oriented systems tend to be more inclusive than creditor-oriented systems. Under the former, most imaginable legal or beneficial interests of a debtor comprise the estate. Creditors must then establish to the court's satisfaction that their rights and interests are superior and should be enforced notwithstanding the equity or reorganization policies. In creditor-oriented systems, property interests of creditors holding secured and 'in rem' rights may even fall outside the estate. And then most systems vary on what property is characterized as exempt from the estate and, thereby, from the reaches of creditors.

Existence of a Moratorium

As a practical matter, the perception of the effectiveness of a jurisdiction's insolvency laws is dependent upon the extent to which (a) the insolvency laws of a jurisdiction provide injunctive protection for a debtor's assets or otherwise imposes a moratorium on creditor actions, and (b) any such relief under the insolvency laws affects secured creditors, others holding 'property interests' and the sovereign itself. In some countries, secured creditors and those holding 'in rem' rights or retentions of title may not be subject to such injunctions. Consequently, the commencement of an insolvency proceeding in such countries would not prevent secured creditors from exercising their legal remedies against their collateral. Notably, the EU Bankruptcy Convention expressly exempts creditors holding 'in rem' rights or retentions of title from its bankruptcy moratorium.

Accordingly, not all insolvency proceedings provide effective relief for debtors or unsecured creditors. The commencement of an insolvency proceeding will not necessarily protect against an anticipated enforcement of liens or otherwise be an effective pre-emptive strike to forestall creditor actions. For example, under English law, the 'floating charge' (similar in the United States to a blanket lien encompassing after-acquired property) floats until some event causes it to become 'fixed'. A floating charge can become 'fixed' upon the occurrence of a number of events, including a payment default under the debenture. The concept of 'fixing a floating charge' is significant insofar as it establishes priority as among existing and possible future liens. Of equal importance, the floating charge is generally incorporated in a debenture or other agreement that also empowers the lenders having the benefit of the 'floating charge' to appoint a receiver with little or no advance notice, upon the occurrence of a default or other agreed circumstance. Appointment and empowerment of the receiver do not require a judicial act. The receiver is entitled to possession and control of the assets subject to the lien. Accordingly, lender action to appoint a receiver may be a powerful tool to divest a debtor of an essential asset before it has an opportunity to commence an administration proceeding under the British insolvency law.

Similarly, the concept of set-off so dominates commercial law in some countries that a lender's exercise of its set-off rights could have serious implications for the rescue process. The insolvency proceedings of the Bank of Credit Commerce International (BCCI) provides an apt illustration. BCCI was placed into liquidation proceedings in Luxembourg, its place of incorporation. Ancillary proceedings were commenced in England, as well as in many other countries. Under the bankruptcy plan, the Luxembourg court approved a 'pooling arrangement' in which approximately US$1.4 billion was to be distributed to creditors around the world on a pari passu basis. The English liquidators sought instructions on the turnover of the English assets to the Luxembourg liquidators, in light of the right of set-off under English law (Rule 4.90 of the Insolvency Rule 1986). The English courts held that, before transferring funds to the foreign liquidators for the purpose of enabling a worldwide distribution to be made among creditors, the English liquidators should retain sufficient funds to honour set-off claims in the English liquidation.

In addition to offset, a number of countries have parity of distribution rules designed to further the principle of equitable treatment among similarly situated creditors. These rules level the claims recovery process by denying distributions to creditors that have already realized some recovery until other unsecured creditors have received a distribution of equal amount. Laws directing marshalling or other inter-creditor sharing or priorities may affect the likelihood and amount of recovery by creditors competing for assets in multiple jurisdictions. This is particularly true in the case of a US debtor that has some assets in a foreign jurisdiction that does not recognize the automatic stay arising upon the commencement of a proceeding under the US Bankruptcy Code. Moreover, some jurisdictions, such as England, may not recognize contractual subordination provisions in bankruptcy, which are viewed as circumventing the requirement of ratable distribution among creditors of similar rank.

Retention of Title Clauses

Reservations of title, no longer prevalent in the United States, retain their importance in continental Europe. A reservation or retention of title clause is generally found in an agreement between a buyer and seller, and provides that the seller transferring property thereunder retains the ownership of such property until satisfaction of the conditions in the agreement, such as payment in full. The reservation also extends to the proceeds of the goods if sold, to the extent traceable.

Retention of title devices are not confined to sellers, but may also be used by lenders or other providers of financing for the sale of property. Retention of title effectively provides a security for payment of the purchase price. The well-recognized effect of such clauses is to confer upon the holder of the reservation of title a prior right or security interest in the goods in question. These clauses therefore protect sellers against the rights of other secured creditors holding fixed or floating charges, as well as preferential rights. Retention of title devices frequently do not require registration or notice, and hence may operate as a 'secret lien' when such clauses may be enforced without notice or registration to any other party. These clauses can take a variety of forms and pose complex problems of private international law. Assessing one's prospects in a foreign insolvency should take into account the superior rights of such purchase money creditors.

Executory Contracts and Leases

While most countries have in place some system for dealing with contracts unperformed at the time of bankruptcy, few insolvency laws have evolved to the point of addressing the full complexion of issues. For instance, the extent to which a lease claim and other claims are limited or calculated remains an open question in many jurisdictions. Consequently, it may be difficult to gain an accurate appreciation of the impact of a foreign proceeding on the legal effect of particular kinds of contracts. Moreover, there are sometimes subtle distinctions that can have significant consequences.

For example, there are variances among countries with respect to the enforceability in bankruptcy of so-called 'ipso facto' termination clauses, pursuant to which the contract or lease automatically terminates upon the occurrence of the debtor's insolvency or the commencement of proceedings against the debtor. Some countries, such as England, routinely honour these provisions, while others, like the United States and France, treat them as unenforceable in bankruptcy. The enforcement of such rights must be carefully considered to determine what impact the commencement of insolvency proceedings will have on a company.

Employee Rights

This is another of those areas in which US law is out of step with many of the pro-employee and union laws of many countries, especially in Mexico and Europe. Next to the government, employees in these countries often enjoy the most robust rights and remedies in bankruptcy. In France, for example, employee claims can prime the rights of secured creditors. The English case of *Paramount Airways* demonstrates the potential magnitude of exposure in this area.

Section 19(5) of the UK Insolvency Act of 1986 (Section 44 for receivers) prescribes that employee claims based on 'adopted' employment contracts by administrators have priority status. For years, a widely accepted practice among insolvency practitioners in this area was to avoid the consequences of adoption by use of a 'Specialized Mouldings' letter, in effect contracting out of the Insolvency Act. The letter's contents had been meticulously scrutinized by legal experts and found sufficient to accomplish the objective, until *Paramount*. In *Paramount*, the court of appeal denounced the practice and held that administrators who maintain employees after the initial 14-day period pursuant to the terms of pre-administration contracts will be deemed to have de facto adopted the contracts. Subsequent termination of adopted contracts receive preference status, and in this case amounted to several £100 million, thereby exposing the administrators to substantial liability. Indeed, so enormous was the potential liability of administrators resulting that it threatened to halt administrations altogether. This led to an immediate Act of Parliament to rectify the problem, resulting in the Insolvency Act 1994, effective as of 15 March 1994. The House of Lords eventually upheld the court of appeal's decision by providing that the Insolvency Act 1994 would not have retroactive effect.

Financial Contracts

International transactions based on long-term commitments have increased risks based on currency and interest rate fluctuations. These risks are managed through the use of 'swap' agreements or financial contracts in which two parties exchange or 'swap' their financial obligations. In effect, the parties agree to pay each other a series of cash flows that are tied to fixed or floating interest rates in the same or different currencies.

Unlike the US case, the insolvency laws in a number of countries do not have express provisions dealing with financial and forward contracts. In the United States, set-offs in such transactions are exempt from the automatic stay. In other countries, however, exercise of set-off rights even on such financial contracts may be prohibited by the bankruptcy moratorium or similar injunction preventing creditor action. For example, notwithstanding the wide acceptance and standardization of swap agreements, prior to 1994, French law generally prohibited netting under swap agreements, interjecting significantly greater risk in transactions involving a French counterparty.

Other currency issues include differences in the calculation and application of interest rates in bankruptcy, which could make a significant difference to the amounts to be paid to creditors under a plan or arrangement. These issues also arise in the context of claims treatment under different plans and could result in disparate treatment for similarly situated creditors, albeit from different countries.

Avoidance Laws

The laws of a country pertaining to avoidable transactions and preferences also vary considerably. In international transactions it is sometimes difficult to determine which country's laws should apply when a preferential transfer has occurred. The Second Circuit's decision in *Maxwell Communication Corporation* underscores the complexity of the international conflicts of law issues in this area.

Maxwell Communication Corporation (MCC) was headquartered and managed in England where most of its liabilities were incurred. MCC's principal assets, however, were located in the United States and included, among others, two subsidiaries: MacMillan, Inc. and Official Airlines Guide,

Inc. On 16 December 1991, MCC, as a pre-emptive manoeuvre, commenced a case under Chapter 11 of the US Bankruptcy Code. The following day, MCC petitioned the High Court of Justice in London for an administration order. An administrator was appointed in the UK proceeding to take over the operation and management of MCC.

Within the 90 days prior to the commencement of the US Chapter 11 case, MCC used proceeds from the sale of the two MCC subsidiaries in the United States to repay substantial debts to three banks located in London – two English and one French. (In the case of the French bank, it was only presumed that the payment came from a US source.) The credit facilities for each of the banks were negotiated and administered in England, and expressly governed by English law. Although they had only lodged claims in the UK proceeding, each bank had branch offices in New York and acknowledged that the US court had personal jurisdiction over them. MCC filed suit in the US Chapter 11 case seeking to recover the pre-petition payments made to the banks as alleged preferential transfers under US law. The banks contested the extraterritorial application of US preference law and sought a dismissal of the action on the grounds that the connection between the transfers and the United States was too tenuous to apply US preference law.

The Second Circuit agreed with the lower courts that international comity applied where there might be conflicting results. Because of the 'intent' requirement under English avoidance law, the possibility existed for a different outcome under English law, triggering the international comity doctrine. Under principles of international comity, the Second Circuit agreed that English law governs the resolution of the dispute. The court relied on a number of facts in reaching its determination as to the 'Englishness' of the action: MCC was incorporated under English law, governed by a British board of directors and managed in London by British executives; the debtor and most of its creditors were British; most of MCC's debts were incurred in England; the credit facilities of the banks in question were each negotiated and administered in London, and were governed by English law. The only real connection with the United States was the source of the funds used for the payments, and this was known only in the case of the two English banks. In addition to the overwhelming English connection, the Second Circuit gave due regard to the high level of cooperation in the parallel proceedings.

THE PATCHWORK QUILT OF INTERNATIONAL INSOLVENCY

What has the international community done to bridge the myriad differences between insolvency laws and enforcement systems? Very little. There is no international bankruptcy code or insolvency convention. Neither is there a generally recognized international framework or agreement that binds nations to an established set of international insolvency principles and rules, such as one finds in other areas of law (such as, the General Agreement on Tariffs and Trade). Indeed, 'multilateral' insolvency conventions have been relatively sparse. Most efforts to achieve cooperation have proved ineffectual or been abandoned, outside of a handful of treaties. Bilateral treaties, though more abundant, tend to be limited to mutual recognition and enforcement of judgments, rather than agreeing an entire insolvency framework. Evidence of the difficulty of negotiating even bilateral agreements, the 1979 draft bilateral treaty between the United States and Canada sits on the shelf gathering dust.

Treaties and Conventions

International treaties and conventions generally reduce the unpredictability in cross-border insolvencies that results from disparities between the insolvency and commercial laws of the countries that are parties thereto. Most treaties and conventions attempt to strike a balance between the principles of universality and territoriality that affords appropriate deference to each country and preserves the commercial expectations of in contractual relationships. Given the obvious benefits of an insolvency treaty or convention, it is striking that such multilateral initiatives are rare and without significant effect. Bilateral insolvency treaties are more common.

This state of affairs is the unfortunate result of having widely disparate laws from one country to the next, making the task of harmonizing the legal systems virtually insurmountable. Accordingly, with the exception of the EU Convention, the handful of multilateral treaties that exist are generally limited to countries whose commercial legal systems are substantially similar.

Regional Conventions

European Union convention on insolvency proceedings
The EU Convention was opened for signature on 25 November 1995, with a signature deadline of 25 May 1996, and lapsed when the deadline passed without approval by the United Kingdom. Those closely following the process are optimistic that other member countries will agree to revive the EU Convention once the United Kingdom has signed on. The existence of the EU Convention was long overdue. Article 220 of the Treaty of Rome arguably 'mandates' implementation of such a convention. Work on the convention actually began in 1960, which explains why the Convention on Jurisdiction and Enforcement of Judgments in Civil and Commercial Matters (the 'Brussels Convention') expressly excluded bankruptcy judgments from its scope. The

original project was abandoned in 1984, when it became painfully clear that 'harmonizing' the insolvency laws of the then six (later nine) member states of the EU (now 15) was an impossible task. The project was reinvigorated in 1990 after the Council of Europe completed its largely symbolic but ineffectual and still not ratified Convention on Certain International Aspects of Bankruptcy ('Istanbul Convention'). The ad hoc working committee of the European Council modelled the EU Convention on the Brussels Convention precedent, which by then had a lengthy and successful track record. That is to say, the EU Convention contains a number of choice of law rules to be applied in specific situations. In addition, the drafters borrowed the best from the Istanbul Convention and portions from the earlier EEC version.

The EU Convention's objectives are to resolve significant legal questions common to cross-border insolvencies with respect to (a) jurisdiction of courts with regard to effects of insolvency proceedings within the EU, (b) agreeing uniform conflict-of-law rules for such proceedings, (c) recognition and enforcement of judgments entered in such proceedings, (d) opening secondary insolvency proceedings, and (e) rights of a creditor to such access to information and lodge claims. At its core, the EU Bankruptcy Convention creates a set of agreed conflict-of-law rules to be applied in typically difficult creditor relationships ('in rem' rights, set-offs, retentions of title, various contractual relationships, and avoidance actions). It also establishes the rules for the interplay between main and secondary subordinate proceedings. Rather than adopt a purely universal approach, the drafters struck a compromise between universality and territoriality.

The main proceeding must be filed within the country where a debtor's 'centre of main interests' is located, which sounds similar to a centre of gravity test. Secondary proceedings may be commenced within the territory of another EU member, if the debtor maintains an 'establishment' there, defined as 'any place of operations where the debtor carries out economic activity with human means and goods'. Accordingly, when no 'establishment' exists, the convention favours a purely universal approach governed by the laws of the forum country (as qualified by the convention). When the converse is true, however, the Convention tilts back in favour of a 'suppressed' territoriality, which is subservient to the main proceeding and can be suspended or dismissed where appropriate. Subject only to the applicable choice-of-law rules in the convention, all proceedings (main and secondary) are administered under the procedural and substantive laws of the forum.

The EU Convention is applicable to all insolvency proceedings commenced within the borders of a signatory state, when the debtor's centre of gravity is located within the EU. When applicable, the convention supersedes all other conventions and treaties between EU members and other countries, including the Nordic bankruptcy convention. Such conventions are not completely supplanted, but continue to be effective in areas not addressed by the EU Convention. The EU Convention does not come into play where the debtor's centre of gravity is located outside the EU. Thus it would not be triggered in the case of a multinational bankruptcy involving a US company, having assets in multiple EU countries, if the centre of the company's main interests is located in the United States. This is a regrettable shortcoming of the EU Convention, which could easily have provided for a single intra-EU proceeding as to assets within the EU. Interpretation of the convention falls within the province of the European Court of Justice, and decisions from this court will be binding on member countries.

The Nordic Bankruptcy Convention

The Nordic Convention on Bankruptcy (11 November 1933), executed among Denmark, Finland, Iceland, Norway and Sweden, provides for a single administration of the debtor's assets and property in the signatory country in which a bankruptcy is first filed. Moreover, the law of the forum applies to the disposition of property in other signatory countries, except as otherwise provided in the convention. The convention addresses both procedural and substantive areas of bankruptcy law, such as details on notice, and defines applicable law relating to various types of property, preferences, priorities and so on. The convention also binds the signatory countries to confirmed compositions and creditor arrangements.

Like the EU Convention, the Nordic Convention has no application where the debtor's principal place of business or the insolvency proceeding was commenced outside one of the five signatory countries. Significantly, the Nordic Convention takes precedence over the EU Convention in cross-border insolvencies between EU countries and one of the non-EU Nordic countries. In such cases, the EU Convention remains fully applicable to the EU countries to the extent that its provisions are not irreconcilable with those of the Nordic Convention.

The Montevideo Treaty

The Montevideo Private International Law Treaties of 1889 and 1940 were executed by and among Argentina, Bolivia, Paraguay, Peru and Uruguay. Commencement of a proceeding in a signatory country will be recognized and is effective for property within other signatory countries. Such countries have 60 days from the date the bankruptcy order is published to commence a separate domestic proceeding that overrides the foreign proceeding. Where only one proceeding has been filed, however, the powers of the bankruptcy representative (trustees and so on) are recognized in all signatory countries. Thus the Montevideo Treaty operates in much the same way as the EU Convention, except that subsequent proceedings are not subordinate to earlier filed proceedings.

The Bustamante Code
Signatories to the Bustamante Code of 1928 (Articles 414 to 422) include Costa Rica, Guatemala, Panama, Venezuela and certain other Central American countries. The Bustamante Code is part of a larger treaty addressing other commercial matters, and some of the signatories have made reservations so that all of the provisions do not apply. Under the Bustamante Code, commencement of a proceeding in one of the signatory countries has full extraterritorial effect in the other signatory countries. Assuming the company's domicile is in one country, a single proceeding suffices to administer the debtor's assets in all signatory countries. In other words, the Bustamante Code adopts the universality approach.

International Initiatives

With internationalism moving forward at breakneck speed and the obvious chasm in the present international insolvency framework, the international insolvency community has responded well.

The UNCITRAL Model Law
The most significant contribution to date to plug the numerous holes in the international framework involved a collaboration between the United Nations Commission on International Trade Law (UNCITRAL) and INSOL, the latter being the world's largest affiliation of insolvency practitioners. On 30 May 1997, UNCITRAL formally adopted the Model Law on Cross-Border Insolvency (the 'Model Law'). The Model Law was developed in a record-breaking two years with involvement from many of the world's leading insolvency practitioners, academics and public officials from over 40 countries. Although the Model Law has no direct binding force, such as a convention or treaty would have, it marks a long-awaited milestone in international cooperation in the context of cross-border insolvencies. Its objectives include (a) cooperation between courts and legal authorities in international insolvencies, (b) greater legal certainty for trade and investment, (c) fairness to creditors and efficiency in administrations of cross-border insolvencies, (d) protection and maximization of value of a debtor's assets, and (e) facilitating rescues of financially troubled businesses, to protect investments and preserve jobs.

Tightly compacted into 32 articles, the Model Law manages to address most of the major issues that plague an international liquidation-oriented insolvency proceeding. In essence, the Model Law will operate as a treaty among those countries that eventually adopt it, which must occur independently through each country's legislative procedures. With respect to cross-border insolvencies in such countries, the Model Law provides for direct access by foreign representatives, as well as foreign creditors. Recognition of the foreign proceeding is presumed, if it is a 'proceeding' within the meaning of the Model Law, which is broadly defined.

To protect a debtor's foreign assets from the effects of the 'grab rule', the Model Law provides for both interim and final relief. Recognition of a foreign main proceeding has the effect of staying the commencement or continuation of individual action or individual proceedings concerning the debtor's assets, rights, obligations or liabilities, as well as enjoining execution against the debtor's assets. In addition, if a foreign main proceeding is recognized, any right to transfer, encumber or otherwise dispose of the debtor's assets is also stayed. This relief is subject to exceptions for the commencement of local insolvency proceedings and steps necessary to preserve claims against the debtor under local law. Of course, the scope of the stay arising upon recognition is also subject to any exceptions, limitations, modifications or termination that may exist in the insolvency laws of the jurisdiction extending recognition.

Notwithstanding the recognition of a foreign proceeding, a foreign creditor is nevertheless free to pursue commencement of a plenary domestic bankruptcy proceeding and file claims to protect its interests, if local law provides for this. In other words, while the Model Law strives for universality, it respects the laws of a host country to protect its creditors under domestic laws. The characterization of the proceeding as a 'main' or 'secondary' proceeding may influence the court's decision in granting appropriate relief, inasmuch as the Model Law requires cooperation between courts and estate representatives to the fullest extent possible. Likewise, communication is encouraged but not mandated among courts.

Where concurrent proceedings have been commenced, the Model Law requires cooperation and coordination. A number of the provisions attempt to lay out some fundamental guidelines for cooperation and deference, depending on whether the foreign proceeding is a 'main' proceeding, and in cases where multiple foreign proceedings are pending. The concepts of access, recognition and relief are the operative characteristics of the Model Law. To underscore the objective of efficiency and cooperation, the Model Law includes an article authorizing direct communication and cooperation between a domestic court and any foreign courts or foreign representatives. If the Model Law works as intended, the spirit of cooperation should translate into some concrete mandatory guidelines that will enable courts and practitioners to administer cross-border insolvency cases with greater efficiency and predictability.

International Bar Association (Committee J)
The Insolvency and Creditors' Rights Committee of the International Bar Association, or 'Committee J' as it is more commonly known, has been involved in several noteworthy projects. Committee J developed the Cross-border Insolvency Concordat, which is designed to provide a framework for

cooperation in multinational insolvencies by setting forth common principles to encourage closer harmonization in a manner consistent with the expectations of the international business community. The Concordat has been well received and was tested in the cross-border bankruptcy case of *Everfresh Beverages Inc.*, a US-headquartered manufacturer and distributor of beverage products. The company filed bankruptcy proceedings in New York and Toronto. The judges in each case encouraged cooperation of efforts with the proceedings in the other country. Thereafter, the debtor, its major lender and creditors' committees crafted a Cross-border Insolvency Protocol using the Concordat as a model. The Concordat was also expressly recognized as 'serv[ing] to inform and provide a measure of guidance for a Court's consideration of the precatory provisions in section 304 of the Bankruptcy Code'.

Committee J is also in the process of developing a Model Insolvency Code that, when finalized, should provide a fundamental model for countries to look to for reforming and updating their insolvency laws in certain key areas. Country teams from roughly 25 countries have assisted Committee J task forces in comparing the laws of these countries in particular areas (executory contracts, avoidance actions, secured rights and so on) and to develop the model provisions addressing such matters. The Model Insolvency Code project serves only as a starting point to consider points of convergence and common elements in the insolvency schemes of the world.

American Law Institute's transnational insolvency project

The American Law Institute's transnational insolvency project, sometimes referred to as the 'NAFTA project', aims to achieve better integration of the economies of countries signatory to the North American Free Trade Agreement and to produce a framework for close cooperation, and possible integration (even harmonization to some extent), in the management of insolvencies having effects in more than one of the NAFTA countries. At present, the reporters are conducting a comprehensive study of the insolvency laws of Canada, the United States and Mexico. The study would probably be extended to include Chile, if it became a member of NAFTA.

The Group of Thirty project

In the wake of the Barings Bank collapse in 1995, the Group of Thirty, a Washington, DC-based private research and advisory group, in cooperation with INSOL, convened a working group to analyse the issues surrounding the insolvency of a global financial institution. The working group's work was premised on a long-standing recognition of systemic risks in the financial markets based on the convergence of these markets. Recently, the Group of Thirty circulated a discussion paper containing recommendations to better manage the risks, and for expeditiously addressing the failure, of global financial institutions. Many of the recommendations are not novel (encourage cooperation among regulators, take steps to reduce risks in clearance and settlement procedures, develop industry standards for monitoring, measuring and managing exposures) while others shed specific light on such failures in the insolvency context (develop a protocol to assist foreign administrators, establish standards for turnover of proprietary models by insolvent firms to potential purchasers, take the home country's insolvency regime into account when licensing foreign financial firms, encourage legislators to enact laws to assure judicial cooperation, eliminate doubts about close out netting). With the support of the Group of Thirty, chaired by Paul Volcker, the recommendations will likely have salutary effects.

DEFINING A BANKRUPTCY ROLE FOR THE IMF

The IMF's role has continually evolved over time to meet the changing needs of the world, particularly with the collapse of the fixed system of exchange rates in the early 1970s and growth of capital markets. Even so, its two fundamental goals – encouraging countries to adopt strong policies and market-oriented reforms and maintaining stability in the system – have remained the same over the past 50 years. With convergence in global financial and capital markets, and an exponential increase in the rate of cross-border mergers creating a near seamless weave of multinational enterprises, what role is most suitable for the IMF in the area of international insolvency? This chapter considers three possible roles for the IMF: (a) international bankruptcy forum, (b) international work-out mediator; and (c) international insolvency law reformer.

International Bankruptcy Forum

Could the IMF serve as an 'international bankruptcy court'? This idea has been bandied about and has an abstract allure, because it seems to plug the formidable gap in the international insolvency framework. As an international organization comprising governments from 182 countries, it would be an obvious choice. Changing the organization's Charter to accommodate this role would presumably have some immediately binding affect on its members, which account for most of the world.

On a practical level, there are many fundamental issues with this role that make it almost impossible to adopt. First, bankruptcy courts are neutral forums in which judges are bound to apply the bankruptcy laws and rules in a non-biased and consistent fashion. What would it mean to act as an international bankruptcy court? Would the role require the IMF to act as an impartial bankruptcy judge deciding over the competing rights of sovereigns and their creditors? It would be difficult for the IMF to maintain impartiality if it had outstanding loans to a sovereign. The same may be true if the forum is extended to the resolution of disputes in the private sector for multinational companies. The ability of the country to repay its sovereign debt hinges, in part, upon the prosperity of its private sector. Again, the repayment connection casts serious questions on the perception of impartiality. A second problem is equally serious. A bankruptcy forum requires a bankruptcy law. As we have seen above, international insolvencies are particularly complex because of the difficult choice of law issues. There are vast disparities in the insolvency systems around the world. Which law applies may often be outcome determinative, as was the case in the Maxwell avoidance proceeding. In addition, while the bankruptcy forum often dictates the bankruptcy law to be applied, most insolvency laws recognize contractual choice of law provisions or rights bargained for outside of bankruptcy, which cut across a wide spectrum of legal disciplines, all equally national in nature (commercial law, property rights, governance procedures and so on).

As a bankruptcy forum, whose bankruptcy, commercial and other laws will the IMF apply to resolve disputes? Does the IMF make this determination? If so, would the end result not lead to an irreconcilable conflict, with the majority vote of sovereigns comprising the IMF having the ability to erode by stages the laws of another sovereign? Yielding a sovereign's right to make determinations over its territory and the assets and persons within that territory has been one of the most significant obstacles to cooperation and integration of insolvency laws. By way of illustration, the six (later nine) members of the European Commission struggled over these questions for nearly 30 years before hopelessly abandoning their efforts. One can scarcely imagine better prospects for resolution when the number of countries involved is 20 times the size of the participants in the early EC effort. The insolvency and commercial laws of the world are far too dissimilar to enable the IMF to fulfil a role as an international bankruptcy forum or court.

International Work-out Mediator

An international work-out mediator suggests a far less intrusive role. Presumably, in this capacity the IMF would function much as the Bank of England does under the London approach to work-outs. The Bank of England's softly spoken admonitions are interpreted as resounding edicts by participants in the process. The Bank of England acts more as a facilitator to encourage compromise between divergent views and goals. This seems like a plausible role for the IMF and not too dissimilar from that which it already serves. Indeed, in connection with the debt restructuring efforts in South Korea, aided by finance ministries and bank regulators in creditor nations, the IMF 'pressured big creditors to roll over loans for troubled Korean banks'. Unlike the Bank of England, the IMF's role is not entirely impartial as it may directly or indirectly be a creditor itself.

Marking an advance in thinking, however, a recent IMF confidential report suggests the creation of a kind of permanent standing 'creditors' committee' that would act as a forum for debtors and creditors to renegotiate debts in times of severe crises. Such a panel of experts would probably serve as arbiters or mediators to facilitate debt restructuring. The report itself acknowledges that there are inherent weaknesses in this approach, such as the difficulty of determining how to avoid private companies on the committee from profiting from inside information and to ensure that contacts with market participants did not enable some market players access to the Fund's views to the prejudice of others.

Although a mediator-type role for the IMF or the panel may be workable in the context of debt restructuring, it is more difficult to implement from a procedural and substantive standpoint in a formal bankruptcy context. Would the IMF or the panel have standing to appear in a cross-border insolvency of a private company to facilitate a consensual debt restructuring? Would the role be officially recognized under the bankruptcy laws of each country? Assuming such a role were possible, would the IMF or the panel be sufficiently disinterested to serve in this capacity? For example, former Secretary of State Cyrus Vance was appointed as an official mediator in the Macy's bankruptcy case to help facilitate a consensual plan between various constituencies. The use of a mediator in this instance was viewed as a significant factor contributing to the company's successful reorganization. Vance was clearly a disinterested party, thereby satisfying the Bankruptcy Code's requirements to serve in this capacity. Where a successful outcome for rescues of private companies has an impact on the country's ability to meet its obligations to the IMF or members of the panel, it is difficult to argue that these parties are genuinely 'disinterested'.

International Insolvency Law Reformer

An IMF role in promoting reform efforts in international insolvency law probably makes the most sense. First, it is consistent with the IMF's long-standing goal of encouraging countries to adopt strong policies and market-oriented reforms. In addition to sound banking practices, market-oriented reforms can include policies and programmes to update and improve a country's insolvency laws and enforcement systems, which are equally vital to the financial health of a country. Second, the IMF's international clout uniquely qualifies it to play a role in this regard, both at the national and international levels.

At the national level, the IMF can be instrumental in promoting greater convergence in insolvency laws. The insolvency schemes of many countries are outmoded or non-existent. Given its present role, the IMF could make it a priority to encourage market reforms in the area of bankruptcy. Such reforms might be based on an adaptable set of common principles and features that exist in most insolvency schemes throughout the world, such as provisions addressing director mismanagement, the creation of an automatic stay or moratorium, a universal discharge, rescue procedures, avoidance actions and international cooperation in the context of cross-border insolvencies. A number of professional organizations have made substantial headway in this area in recent years. The International Bar Association (IBA) has developed a concordat of common principles and is working on a set of model insolvency provisions for countries interested in reforming their insolvency laws. INSOL and UNCITRAL have collaborated on the UNCITRAL Model Law on Cross-Border Insolvencies, which sets forth common principles that would be applied in the context of cross-border bankruptcies. More work needs to be done to determine how and in what fashion common principles can or should be implemented within a country's legislative framework.

Such reforms cannot be conducted in a vacuum. An insolvency law is not a panacea for financial distress in an economy. The financial health of a country depends on the interplay of many disciplines, including reliable insolvency and enforcement systems, and sound credit and corporate practices. Lax or deficient enforcement laws can lead to an improper shifting of rights in bankruptcy to the debtor, resulting in a safe haven where the debtor holds all the cards and little is accomplished. Where the credit culture of a country or the corporate/management practices in the corporate sector are flawed by abuse or deficiencies, the insolvency systems may serve as a proverbial bridge over troubled waters that leads only to more troubled waters. Accordingly, the IMF's reform proposals should take into account a disciplined review of the credit practices in the financial industry and the business practices in the corporate sector. Otherwise, at best, the insolvency system may efficiently rescue or dispose of a company through insolvency, but the larger systemic problem in the economy remains.

At the international level, the IMF's national efforts can lead to greater consistency in the fundamental principles of insolvency systems. Such similarities can encourage greater trade and investment in a country by creating predictability in the outcome of debtor–creditor relationships. Moreover, the IMF's support or endorsement of such laws as the UNCITRAL Model Law on Cross-Border Insolvency could encourage countries to adopt policies conducive to reciprocity and international cooperation.

CONCLUSIONS

The complexion of the world has changed greatly since the insolvency laws of many countries were enacted 80–100 years ago. New and innovative insolvency techniques and approaches have been developed in recent decades. Advances in telecommunications and computer technology have led to a proliferation in cross-border mergers and convergence in world markets. Such technology has also resulted in improved risk management practices across a wide spectrum of industries. With the fast-changing pace of the global market, the state of national insolvency laws still provides an inadequate framework for world commerce.

Some may argue that insolvency laws are outside the macroeconomic goals of the IMF. The recent crisis in Asia, however, reveals that such laws are integral to the financial health and stability of market economies. The IMF's role in safeguarding the financial integrity of nations calls for involvement by the IMF at some level. There are both logical, legal and political constraints on what that role can be. Certainly, a role as an international bankruptcy forum or work-out mediator raises serious questions regarding the IMF's disinterested status. Conversely, organizations like the IMF are uniquely positioned to encourage methodical and well-conceived reform efforts that have the effect of advancing these countries into the modern era while complementing international insolvency initiatives to bring about greater convergence. Such a role requires that the IMF broaden its perspective to embrace a bankruptcy philosophy.

NOTES

1. William Murray and Bob Davis, 'IMF Weighs Wider Private-Sector Role When Member Nations Face a Crisis', *Wall St. J.*, 22 April 1998, A8.
2. Martin J. Bienenstock, *Bankruptcy Reorganization* 1 (1987).
3. Ibid.
4. 11 U.S.C. ß 506(c); see, for example, *General Electric Credit Corp.* v. *Levin & Weintraub* (In re Flagstaff Foodservice Corp.), 739 F.2d 73 (2d Cir. 1984); but see *Brookfield Prod. Credit Assoc.* v. *Borron*, 738 F.2d 951 (8th Cir. 1984) (expenses incurred in the usual course of protecting collateral are unrecoverable as they do not directly benefit secured creditors).
5. For exampe, under French insolvency law, the commencement of a bankruptcy begins with the 'période d'observation' during which the company's prospects for reorganization are evaluated. At the end of this period, if the company is deemed unsalvageable, it is directed to the liquidation line.
6. The list is drawn in part from R.M. Goode, *Principles of Corporate Insolvency*, 5–10 (Sweet & Maxwell, 1990).
7. Multilateral insolvency conventions are rare. Efforts to achieve cooperation have proved ineffectual or been abandoned, outside of a handful of treaties. Bilateral treaties, though more abundant, tend to be limited to mutual recognition and enforcement of judgments, rather than agreements on a general insolvency framework. The three most notable examples of 'operative' multilateral insolvency treaties are the Nordic Bankruptcy Convention of 1933

(among the Nordic countries), the Montevideo Treaty of 1889 and 1940 (among several South American countries) and the Bustamante Code of 1928 (among mostly Central American countries). See K. Lipstein, 'Early Treaties for the Recognition and Enforcement of Foreign Bankruptcies', in I. Fletcher (ed.), *Cross-Border Insolvency: Comparative Dimensions*, (Aberystwyth Insolvency Papers, 1990) [hereinafter *Comparative Dimensions*]; J. Dobson, 'Treaty Developments in Latin America', in *Comparative Dimensions*; M. Bogdan, 'The Nordic Bankruptcy Convention', in J. Ziegel (ed.),*Current Developments in International and Comparative Corporate Insolvency* (1994) [hereinafter *Current Developments*].

There is also a multilateral bankruptcy convention of recent vintage among the Arab Maghreb Union (Algeria, Libya, Mauritania, Morocco and Tunisia), with ratification still in question. The most promising multilateral convention to date is the EU Convention on Insolvency Proceedings concluded in 1995 among the 15 member countries of the European Union, which is expected to be approved. A second, potentially more encompassing, multilateral effort is the Model Law on Cross-Border Insolvency (Model Law) formally adopted on 30 May 1997, developed by the United Nations Commission on International Trade Law (UNCITRAL). The product of the world's leading insolvency practitioners, academics and public officials from over 40 countries, the Model Law is designed to facilitate cooperation between courts and legal authorities in international insolvencies.

8. If an enterprise has only assets in multiple countries, but creditors in only one country, the assets should be susceptible to easy disposition in the country of the debtor's insolvency proceeding, by repatriation, if movable, or in the country where situated, if immovable. Where the debtor has no assets outside the forum country, but merely creditors, the creditors are generally entitled to lodge and prove their claims in the forum court. The latter situation, however, raises more complex issues of an international nature if the discharge granted in the bankruptcy is not recognized in the foreign country because the foreign creditors chose not to participate in the foreign proceeding. See generally Phillip Smart, *Cross-Border Insolvency* pp. 162–70 (1991).

9. In France, Belgium and Luxembourg, for example, only individuals that qualify as traders (commerçants) may file bankruptcy, and in Italy not even small traders may do so. See Ian F. Fletcher, 'Cross-Border Cooperation in Cases of International Insolvency: Some Recent Trends Compared', *Tulane Civ. L. Forum*, 171, at 172 n.2 (1991–2).

10. Ian F. Fletcher (ed.), *Cross-Border Insolvency: National and Comparative Studies*, pp. 280–81 (1992).

11. For a general discussion of the Exequatur process in France, Italy, Greece and Spain, see Hans Hanisch, 'Survey Over Some Laws on Cross-Border Effects of Foreign Insolvency Procedures on the European Continent', in *Comparative Dimensions*, pp. 153–5.

12. Barbara K. Unger, 'United States Recognition of Foreign Bankruptcies', 19 *Int'l Law*, 1153, 1155 (1986) (In reality, most jurisdictions tend to protect local creditors when faced with the extraterritorial effect of a foreign bankruptcy proceeding over local assets.).

13. The bankruptcy of Polly Peck, a boxed fruit to electronics conglomerate based largely in Turkey and Cyprus, is an extreme example of the inefficiencies that can occur in cross-border insolvencies where mutual recognition is absent. After nearly five years of administration, a group of unsecured bondholders challenged administrators' fees in excess of US$37 million, payable at 100 per cent, while the initial distribution proposed to unsecureds was only $US23 million, a 1.1 per cent recovery on their claims. The Polly Peck bankruptcy entailed a unique set of challenges (one administrator was shot in the leg while in Cyprus attempting to ferret out assets) and instances of alleged fraud. Many of the assets and Polly Peck's principal were located in Turkey and Cyprus, which do not recognize judgments entered by the UK courts and, indeed, have a mutual recognition pact only among themselves and Bangladesh.

14. Jay L. Westbrook, 'Global Insolvencies in a World of Nation States', in A. Clark (ed.), Current Issues in Insolvency Law, pp. 29–33 (1991).

15. Although 'unity and universality' are often coupled, and are admittedly difficult to separate, in fact they represent distinct legal notions. Unity and plurality address competing choices of forum, while universality and terroriality address competing choices of applicable law.

16. Kurt H. Nadelmann, 'The National Bankruptcy Act and the Conflict of Laws', 59 *Harv. L. Rev.*, 1025 (1946); I.J. Dalhuisen, 'International Insolvency and Bankruptcy', 2.03[3], pp. 3–183 to 3–188 (1986) [hereinafter 'Dalhuisen'].
17. Dalhuisen, *supra*, note 16.
18. Hans Hanisch, '"Universality" Versus Secondary Bankruptcy: A European Debate', 2 *INSOL IIR*, 153–54 (1993).
19. Dalhuisen, *supra*, note 16.
20. Ian Fletcher, 'Comparative Survey', in Ian Fletcher (ed.), *Cross-Border Insolvency: National and Comparative Studies*, p. 280 (1992) [hereinafter *Cross-Border Insolvency*].
21. Nadelmann, *supra*, note 16, 1025.
22. See John D. Honsberger, 'Conflict of Laws and the Bankruptcy Reform Act of 1978', 30 *Case Wes. Res. L. Rev.* 631, 634 (1980) (noting that the unity/universality approach 'was suitable to the Roman and British Empires within which there was the political reality of "one world"').
23. In the most extreme cases this practice is known as the 'grab rule' or 'ring fence' approach: local creditors attempt to satisfy their claims out of local assets before foreign creditors have access to them. In theory, this reflects the worst of a plurality approach, but in practice is not common among developed systems, which do not discriminate in treatment between similarly situated local and foreign creditors. Parity of treatment is often maintained through rules such as those contained in 11 U.S.C. ß 508, which provides that a creditor with an allowed claim under US law who has received a payment or transfer in a foreign proceeding in respect of such claim shall not be entitled to a distribution in the US proceeding until all other similarly situated creditors have first received payments in an equal amount in the US proceeding. The English rule, known as the 'hotchpot' rule, has a similar effect. See, for example, *Banco de Portugal* v. *Waddell* [1880] 5 App. Cas. 161, at 169.
24. Westbrook, *supra*, note 14, at 27.
25. One of the cardinal principles of insolvency is that 'property' rights are created before bankruptcy and follow the debtor into bankruptcy. *Butner* v. *United States*, 440 U.S. 48, 55 (1979). Property interests are created and defined by state law. Unless some federal interest requires a different result, there is no reason why such interest should be analyzed differently simply because an interested party is involved in a bankruptcy proceeding; see also Roy Goode, *Principles of Corporate Insolvency* p. 17 (1990): 'First principle: corporate insolvency law recognizes rights accrued under the general law prior to liquidation'. In some countries, such as the United States, but not the United Kingdom, national interests may override contractual rescission clauses and even rights of secured creditors in some cases, such as France.
26. Honsberger, *supra*, note 22, at 635.
27. Ibid., at 634. Examples of countries embracing territoriality are Japan, Austria, the Netherlands and Sweden. See Hanisch, in *Comparative Dimensions*, at 156. At least in Japan's case, the approach is applied both ways, inasmuch as it disclaims extraterritorial effect for domestic proceedings. See Fletcher, *Cross-Border Insolvency*, at 282 (citing Japanese B.A., 3(1)).
28. Nadelmann, *supra*, note 16, at 1025 ('Strict territoriality ... would hinder cooperation even in situations where exercise of local control is unnecessary').
29. One commentator describes the tension between protecting national interests and cooperation as follows:
The social, economic and legal policies manifested in the insolvency laws of various countries are too divergent to permit a unified approach. No country automatically gives full extraterritorial effect to a foreign insolvency law and to an adjudication pursuant thereto. Conversely, no country seems totally to disregard the effects of foreign insolvencies. (Stefan A. Riesenfeld, 'The Status of Foreign Administrators of Insolvent Estates: A Comparative Study', 24 *Am. J. Comp. L.* 288 (1976)).
30. *Hilton* v. *Guyot*, 159 U.S. 113 (1895).
31. Ibid., at 163–4.
32. *Hunt* v. *T & N*, plc [1993] 4 SCR 289, at 322.

33. *Barclays Bank* v. *Homan* (In re Maxwell) Case No. 001401 of 1991 (28 July 1992), at p. 7, aff'd CA 80 at 912.
34. Although the president was quite confident of his ability to achieve a reorganization, a year after the filing it was reported:
    Since then, Japanese trade unions seeking back wages stormed the company's offices and held a manager hostage. Creditors in Hong Kong and Singapore ignored a United States court order, seized four of [the company's] massive container ships and sold $46 million vessels at close to scrap value. And creditors in nine other nations have attached company assets around the world. (Todd Vogel, 'There's No Word for Chapter 11 in Dutch', *Bus. Wk.*, 30 Nov. 1987, at 62 (quoted in Daniel M. Glosband and Christopher T. Katucki, 'Multinational Insolvencies', in *Chapter 11 Theory and Practice* 33.01, at 33:2 (1994)).
35. *Felixstowe Dock and Railway Co.* v. *U.S. Lines, Inc.* [1989] Q.B. 360.
36. Ibid., at 376. A Mareva injunction restrains an entity from taking assets outside of the jurisdiction.
37. Under Section 214 of the Insolvency Act of 1986 (United Kingdom), 'Wrongful trading occurs if, at some time before the company's winding up commences, any person who was a director at that time knew or ought to have concluded that there was no reasonable prospect that the company would avoid going into insolvent liquidation' (Leo Flynn, 'Statutory Liability for Culpable Mismanagement', in *Theory & Practice*, p. 142; see also Janet Dine, 'Wrongful Trading – Quasi-Criminal Law?', in *Theory & Practice*, pp. 163ff.
38. See generally Sally Wheeler, 'Disqualification of Directors: A Broader View', in *Theory & Practice*, pp. 187–98; and David Henry, 'Disqualification of Directors: A View from the Inside', in *Theory & Practice*, pp. 179–85.
39. See, for example, Claes Enhrning, 'Liability of Directors Under Swedish Law', in Dennis Campbell and Anthony Collins (eds), *Corporate Insolvency and Rescue: The International Dimension*, 69, p. 71 (1993) (criminal acts include giving away assets, continuing to operate a business with a substantial loss, paying a creditor's old invoices shortly before bankruptcy, and mismanaging the bookkeeping so that the outcome of the business is impossible to follow.
40. See generally *In re Lahm Industries, Inc.*, 609 F.2d 567 (1st Cir. 1979) (appeals court reversed lower court holding of criminal contempt holding against Royal Bank of Canada for violating automatic stay).
41. It should be noted that actions taken by US creditors to ensure equal treatment with foreign creditors in a foreign proceeding present unique questions. For instance, in *U.S. Lines* a maritime creditor resident in Hong Kong caused the arrest of a number of the large cargo vessels, known as 'Econoships' that were owned and operated by *U.S. Lines*. The arrest occurred after the commencement of a Chapter 11 case by *U.S. Lines*. A bank syndicate, largely domiciled in the United States and acting through their agent, a large US bank, were the holders of the first ship mortgages on the Econoships that had been arrested in Hong Kong by a local maritime lienor, the US banks intervened in the Hong Kong foreclosure. The US banks did not seek modification of the automatic stay from the US bankruptcy court. As the Hong Kong proceeding continued the original arresting lienor and plaintiff was paid and only the US banks remained as foreclosing lienors in the Hong Kong foreclosure proceeding. The US government through its Maritime Administration (MARAD), which held junior security interests in the 'Econoships' that were subject to the Hong Kong foreclosure, sought a contempt order from the US bankruptcy court. While the US bankruptcy court was inclined to grant the relief sought, the matter was settled out of court. Nevertheless, the sequence of events in the U.S. Lines situation highlights the very difficult and complex decisions which creditors face when a multinational enterprise suffers insolvency. Should the US banks have been allowed to intervene without prior leave of the bankruptcy court? The better answer is no. They should have sought leave of court to act to protect their interests in the action commenced by foreign creditors in a foreign jurisdiction in derogation of the automatic stay. Secondly, when the protective intervention leads to a situation where only the US creditors remain in the proceeding, should such creditors be permitted to continue prosecution of the action? This question is more difficult but, given a change in circumstance, the answer may well depend on the scope of the relief from the automatic stay that was obtained to permit intervention in the foreign proceeding.

42. In *re Petition Under Section 304 of Banco Nacional de Obras y Servicios Publicos*, S.N.C., as Trustee of the estate of Aeronaves de Mexico, 91 B.R. 661 (Bankr. S.D.N.Y. 1988). US creditors/union members brought suit in a US federal district court seeking a declaration that a collective bargaining agreement existed between them and Aeronaves de Mexico. After answering the complaint in the US action, Aeronaves commenced a bankruptcy proceeding in Mexico, and the Mexican court approved the rejection of labour contracts, including those with the US union members, if any. The ancillary proceeding was commenced to enjoin the liquidation of the US creditors' claims in the United States contrary to the asserted jurisdiction of the Mexican court administering the estate of Aeronaves.

43. In addition to the United States, Canada has a proceeding outside of its insolvency laws, under the Companies Creditors Arrangement Act, R.S.C. 1970 c.C-25, which envisions a restructuring of debts while retaining existing management. Interestingly, however, CCAA proceedings frequently have what is known as an 'information officer' or other court appointee, having responsibilities to the court and creditors to monitor and report on the activities and operations of the CCAA applicant.

44. See, for example, *Re Bank of Credit Commerce International SA* (No. 10) [1996] 4 All E.R. 796.

45. See, for example, 11 U.S.C. ß 508 (U.S.); *Banco de Portugal* v. *Waddell* [1880] 5 App. Cas. 161, at 169 (English 'hotchpot' rule).

46. Marshalling, as a common law and statutory concept, operates to force a creditor having multiple sources of payment to exhaust those sources in a manner which best preserves value for junior creditors that also have a right of payment from one or more of the same sources of payment.

47. See Goode, *supra*, note 25, *Principles of Corporate Insolvency*, p. 61.

48. See Robert Pennington, 'Retention of Title of the Sale of Goods under European Law', 27 *I.C.L.Q.* 277 (1978). Its roots are traced to Roman law where a seller, having delivered goods to the buyer, retained ownership until fully paid – a rule considered critical for a non-credit society. In England, such clauses are commonly referred to as 'Romalpa' clauses, the case from which it takes its name: *Aluminium Industrie Vassen B.V.* v. *Romalpa Aluminium Ltd.* [1976] 1 W.L.R. 676 (C.A.). This is a common feature of business practice in Austria, France ('une clause de réserve de propriété'), the Netherlands (eigendomvoorbehoudsclausul) and West Germany (eigentumsvorbehalts bestimmung). See G. McCormack, *Reservation of Title*, pp. 214–15 (1990).

49. Ibid., pp. 1–2 (describing, inter alia, the five primary types of reservation of title clauses. 2 Dicey & Morris, *The Conflict of Laws*, p. 1333 (1993).

50. McCormack, *supra*, note 48, at 5. Some states (Portugal, Spain and Switzerland) require registration of such rights, especially to defeat claims by third parties.

51. In some respects, a retention of title is functionally similar to a purchase money security interest (PMSI) under US law, defined in Section 9–107 of Article 9 of the Uniform Commercial Code as a security interest 'taken or retained by the seller of the collateral to secure all or part of its price'. A significant distinction between the two rights is that the PMSI, to maintain priority over competing creditors, must be properly perfected in accordance with Section 9–312(3). For a comparison of the similarities and differences between the retention of title and the PMSI, see I. Davis, 'The Trade Debtor and the Quest for Security', in *Theory & Practice*, pp. 43ff.

52. *Re Paramount Airways* (No 3) [1994] 2 All ER 513.

53. Since their standardization in 1987, swap transactions have multiplied exponentially (from US$600 million notional value in 1987 to approximately US$55 trillion a decade later). Yet, despite the frequency of their use, there remains a lack of uniformity among countries in the enforceability of close-out netting provisions.

54. This result was the combined effect of various provisions. Article 47 of Loi No. 85–98 (dated 25 January 1985) provided for a broad injunction against creditors after commencing proceedings, specifically including 'termination of a contract on the grounds of default in payment of a sum of money'. Article 37 provides that 'Notwithstanding any provision of law or contractual clause, no frustration or termination of the contract may arise solely by reason of the commencement of proceedings for judicial reconstruction'. Article 33 'prohibits the

payment of any claim arising before the order commencing proceedings'. Presumably, this would have extended to the settlement procedure whereby the calculation of net gains or losses effectively entailed a set-off. And finally, Article 107 provides for avoidance of all payments during the 'période suspecte' (potentially up to 18 months prior to the order commencing proceedings). While the provision would probably not have affected matured debts offset by operation of law, the provision would probably have nullified payments related to terminated contracts. See translation of Law No. 85–98 in Allen and Overy (eds), *Butterworths International Insolvency Laws*, pp. 61ff. France adopted new legislation on 31 December 1993 (Loi No. 93–1444), that effectively exempts swaps and similar securities, thus rendering the current approach in France much more certain and similar to that of the United States. See Gide Loyrette Nouel, 'Memorandum on the Enforceability of Termination and Close-out Netting Upon Certain Insolvency Events Clauses of the ISDA Master Agreements under French Law', p. 2 (24 January 1994). While France no longer falls into this category, other countries that patterned their insolvency laws on the Napoleonic bankruptcy law, such as Greece, Luxembourg, Portugal, Spain and most Latin American and North African countries may still prohibit netting based on their prohibition of insolvency set-off. See P. Wood, 'Principles of Netting: A Comparative Law Study', in *NIBE-Bankjuridische Reeks*, pp. 75–6.

55. See generally Jay L. Westbrook, 'Choice of Avoidance Law in Global Insolvencies', XVII *Brooklyn J. Int'l L.* 499 (1991).
56. *Maxwell Communication Corp.* v. *Société Générale* (In re Maxwell Communication Corp.), 93 F3d 1036 (2d Cir. 1996)
57. For a discussion of parallel proceedings, see the discussion on dual, plenary cases, *infra*, following the text accompanying note 103.
58. For a detailed discussion of the EU Convention and its anticipated implications for corporate rescues within Europe, see Gordon W. Johnson, 'The European Union Convention on Insolvency Proceedings: A Critique of the Convention's Corporate Rescue Paradigm', 5 *Int'l Insol. Rev.* 80 (1,1996). For the full text of the EU Convention, see 5 *Int'l Insol. Rev.* 171–85 (2, 1996).
59. Being grounded in Article 220 of the Treaty of Rome, the Convention required unanimous approval by all 15 members of the European Union. The United Kingdom was prepared to sign the Convention when, days before its consideration in Parliament, the UK government decided to defer indefinitely all decisions on EU legislation in retaliation for the EU's embargo against British beef due to the notorious mad cow disease.
60. Treaty Establishing the European Community as Amended by Subsequent Treaties, Rome (25 March 1957). Article 220 provides in pertinent part: 'Member States shall, so far as is necessary, enter into negotiations with each other with a view to securing for the benefit of their nationals ... the simplification of formalities governing the reciprocal recognition and enforcement of judgments of courts or tribunals'. (emphasis added). One can hardly imagine a greater 'necessity' than mutual recognition and enforcement of bankruptcy judgments in cross-border insolvencies to minimize risk and increase efficiencies and economies for the benefit of creditors, not to mention stabilizing economic trade and the cost of financing within the EU.
61. The Istanbul Convention was opened for signature on 5 July 1990, and apparently has been signed by fewer than a third of the 22 countries involved. Perhaps the cause of the demise of the Istanbul Convention was its restriction to proceedings of 'disinvestment' in which a liquidator is appointed. It applies only to the European signatories and runs counter to the concept of recognizing the rights of a representative of a foreign debtor.
62. See generally Ian F. Fletcher, *The Law of Insolvency*, pp. 617–25 (1990); Ian F. Fletcher, 'Harmonization of Jurisdictional and Recognitional Rules: The Istanbul Convention and the Draft EEC Convention', in *Developments*, pp. 714–71; Phillip Woodland, 'The Proposed European Community Insolvency Convention', in E. Leonard and C. Besant (eds), *Current Issues in Cross-Border Insolvency and Reorganizations*, p. 5 (1994).
63. 'Centre of main interests' is not defined in the Convention. An early draft of the EU Explanatory Report on Insolvency Proceedings, which accompanies the Convention, states that the 'centre of main interests' will normally 'be the place of the head office in the case of

legal persons'. What is clear is that there can only be one such place. If the head office test proves unworkable in some instances, courts will no doubt rely on other factors, such as location of assets, liabilities, situs of management decisions, primary location of the debtor's operations, the place where the board of directors convenes, or a balancing of all of these factors. See Article 3(1).

64. Articles 3(2) and 2(*h*), respectively.
65. See Michael Bogdan, 'The Nordic Bankruptcy Convention', in J. Ziegel (ed.), *Current Developments* (1994). For the text of the convention, see 155 L.N.T.S. 136 (1935).
66. See Article 36 of the EU Convention.
67. For a more detailed discussion of the Montevideo Treaty, see Juan Dobson, 'Treaty Developments in Latin America', in *Dimensions*. The Montevideo Treaty is really two treaties dating from 1889 and 1940. Only Argentina, Uruguay and Paraguay signed the 1940 treaty.
68. See Article 43 (Ch. VIII).
69. For the text of the Bustamante Code, see 86 L.N.T.S. 362 (1929).
70. See Preamble to Model Law.
71. Articles 9, 11 and 12.
72. Articles 13 and 14.
73. See Articles 15–17, and 2(*a*).
74. Article 20(2).
75. Article 25(1).
76. Article 25(2).
77. Articles 28 and 29.
78. Articles 28–30.
79. Article 25 of the Model Law is entitled 'Cooperation and direct communication between a court of this State and foreign courts or foreign representatives'. Its two provisions address cooperation and authorization to 'communicate directly with, or to request information or assistance directly from, foreign courts or foreign representatives' (art. 25(2)).
80. *In re Everfresh Beverages, Inc., et al.*, Case Nos. 95 B 45405 and 95 B 45406 (Bankr. S.D.N.Y. 1995).
81. In *re Hackett*, 184 B.R. 656, 659 (Bankr. S.D.N.Y. 1995).
82. Hearing on Funding Requests for the International Monetary Fund Before the Subcommittee on Domestic and International Monetary Policy of the Committee on Banking and Financial Services, 105th Cong., 1st Sess. 6 (1997) (Statement of Mr. Timothy Geithner, Senior Deputy Assistant Secretary of the Treasury for International and Monetary and Financial Policy).
83. William Murray and Bob Davis, 'IMF Weighs Wider Private-Sector Role When Member Nations Face a Crisis', *Wall St. J.*, 22 April 1998, p. A8.
84. The confidential report, dated 10 April 1998, was apparently prepared by the office of IMF Managing Director Michel Camdessus and circulated among IMF delegates, in response to criticism about the Fund's handling of the Asian crisis.

7. Sovereign rescues: using commercial debt resolution mechanisms to reduce global public funding

Richard A. Gitlin

INTRODUCTION

The international community has faced a number of sovereign financial crises over the years, and the traditional solutions to such crises have included the injection of very substantial amounts of external public funds. The international community is now searching for ways to reduce the reliance on global public funds in such situations. A 'win–win' path for sovereign nations and the global funding sources is to maximize the use of consensual and judicial debt resolution mechanisms for the troubled commercial and sovereign obligations within the affected country. This will result in (a) reducing the size of the financial crisis at hand, (b) accelerating recovery of the local economy, and (c) causing lenders and investors to bear a greater portion of the risk of their credit decisions.

A RESCUE SYSTEM FOR BUSINESSES

A proper rescue system should save businesses that should be saved and liquidate businesses that should be liquidated, in either event in a manner that is *efficient, predictable* and is *fair* to creditors, wherever located.

The 80–20 Rule

A proper rescue system primarily emphasizes consensual resolutions, rather than legal processes. A true commercial rescue results from a business negotiation among the affected creditors, the owners of the business and others. Rescues are most successful when the negotiations take place outside court, and the court system is designed to approve a plan negotiated by most creditors and the company. The legal system defines the leverage for the negotiations.

A system would be maximized if at least 80 per cent of the process took place outside court and 20 per cent or less in court.

The London Approach

In many cases, particularly where the law and culture are oriented more towards liquidation than rehabilitation, it is helpful to articulate the preferred guidelines or principles for an out-of-court rescue negotiation and to have oversight of an appropriate governmental or administrative entity. One such set of principles was designed by the Bank of England in the 1980s to increase the number of companies in England to be saved, thereby preserving employment and increasing the return to banks on their troubled loans.

The Court Approach: Setting the Table

The significant issue in designing a local court process is not whether it follows the US Chapter 11 approach, the English administration approach, the French *redressement* approach or the rehabilitation approach of another country. It is more important that, whatever approach is implemented, that approach should set the leverage for the commercial negotiations.

The approach adopted will define the power of the owners, the creditors and labour in the negotiations. Different systems will cause the assets of a company to be distributed in varying proportions. One way to measure the economics is to determine how much shareholders will receive if there is a debt-for-equity swap in a clearly insolvent company. Today this might be 5 per cent of the distributable value in the United States, 15 per cent in England and 40 per cent in France.

The Court System: Predictability

One of the most important aspects of a rescue law is that the law be implemented in a predictable and efficient manner. A new rescue law in a country with an unpredictable court system will not accomplish the desired goals. One method to build a system in a timely way is to designate selected judges (and possibly even a specialized court as is the case in some countries) to hear 'pre-negotiated' court petitions. Where the company and the required number and amount of its creditors (two-thirds or three-quarters) have successfully negotiated an out-of-court solution, the expedited court process could be utilized predictably to cause the solution to be binding upon all creditors.

Often a company needs a new capital structure with lower debt service requirements in order to return to the market-place as a viable competitor. It is critical that a debt-for-equity swap be one of the options available in the restructuring process.

Predictability, Efficiency and Fairness to Creditors

Predictability, efficiency and fairness are critical elements of a rescue system for they encourage earlier restructuring and rehabilitation, and the development of a secondary market in distressed debt.

Earlier restructurings and rehabilitations
It is important that companies enter the rescue process before 'the patient is on its death bed'. Lenders will generally act commercially and respond reasonably to a crisis since they have a common interest with each other and the company to maximize the value of the business. This is greatly facilitated if the rules for dividing the value of the business are reasonably predictable, efficient and fair.

Development of a secondary market in distressed debt
A substantial market in the buying and selling of distressed debt obligations has developed in the United States and is rapidly spreading to other parts of the world. Morgan Stanley recently estimated that the amount of distressed debt in the secondary market is approximately US$115 billion. This amount appears to be growing rapidly as new distressed debt funds are being formed on virtually a daily basis.

The distressed debt purchasers are generally sophisticated restructuring experts who take a strong interest in the companies whose debt they purchase. They usually bring substantial business and restructuring expertise to the table and can be a substantial asset in raising additional capital after the company has been rescued.

A BANKING SYSTEM IN CRISIS

The effects of a proper rescue system and an active distressed debt market are most profound in assisting a banking system in crisis. The size of the banking crisis is in part related to the status of a bank's loan portfolio. It is often the case in times of sovereign financial crisis that the value of a bank's loan portfolio, whether the bank chooses to hold and work out the loans or to sell into the secondary market, will be directly related to the efficiency of the country's rescue system.

A purchaser of loans will significantly discount the purchase price if the rescue system is inefficient and lacks predictability. For example, if the United States had a less efficient and predictable rescue system during the US savings and loan crisis, the cost to the United States of selling off the savings and loan assets might have been another US$200 billion. This is the magnitude of additional discounts buyers of loans from the government would have required if they could not have reasonably predicted the results or the time of a mortgage foreclosure in the United States or the insolvency process.

Additional Benefits of Secondary Market Purchasers

A banking system in trouble is quite different from a corporate sector in trouble. Banking systems require quick and decisive governmental action to perform the tasks that the market-place will perform in the corporate sector.

The general rescue objectives discussed above apply equally in a banking crisis: save those banks that should be saved and liquidate those that should be liquidated, in either case in an efficient, predictable manner, treating creditors fairly, wherever located. The government must do this promptly to maximize the value of the banks to be liquidated and maintain confidence with respect to the healthier banks. A proper rescue system for corporate debt and a secondary market significantly facilitates both objectives.

It is very important that the distressed loans in a bank's portfolio be purchased at the highest prices, whether the bank is to be saved or liquidated. A proper rescue system will significantly increase the price of those distressed loans without any cost to anyone else in the system. Furthermore, most of the distressed debt funds are denominated in US dollars and the sale of a bank's distressed loans could represent a significant source of foreign currency at a time when it is desperately needed.

RESULTS OF A PROPER RESCUE SYSTEM

A proper rescue system for commercial enterprises results in a 'win–win' solution in times of sovereign crises both for the countries themselves and for global funding sources. It will result in reducing the size of the financial crisis, accelerating the recovery of the economy, and lenders and investors bearing the risks of their decisions.

Reducing the Size of the Financial Crisis

By its nature, a proper rescue system increases the value of a bank's loan portfolio in the secondary market. The 'hole' to be filled by global funding sources can be substantially reduced if the purchase price of the loans, whether sold by the remaining banks or by the liquidating agency for the closed banks, is not subject to a substantial discount for inefficiency or unpredictability in the collection process.

Also the sale of loans in the secondary market represents an immediate and significant source of foreign currency. A proper rescue system will both create marketability and enhance the amount of incoming foreign currency.

Accelerating Recovery of the Economy

Macro solutions for the salvation of a sovereign economy in crisis unfortunately do not often provide relief for businesses in trouble. The market-place must facilitate this relief. A proper rescue system will encourage early solutions to a company's financial crisis and will create a new platform for growth in its business and employment prospects. Secondly, purchasers in the secondary market may well add value to help create a proper balance sheet in a restructured company and will facilitate access to capital for growth.

Causing Lenders and Investors to Bear the Risks of their Decisions

It should be axiomatic that lenders and investors who make poor credit decisions should bear the primary risks of such decisions. This will flow naturally from properly designed creditors' rights and rescue systems. The system should define the leverage in the negotiations between creditors, shareholders and others and facilitate those negotiations. In such a system, each party will bear the weight of its decisions.

CROSS-BORDER ASPECTS OF A PROPER RESCUE SYSTEM

Many businesses have operations or assets in other countries. A proper rescue system requires an ability to preserve the status quo of the multinational assets while negotiations occur regarding a restructuring. The state of the law globally is grossly inadequate to satisfy this objective. Without an ability to preserve the status quo, the assets will probably be dissipated before their value can be captured.

It is most significant to emphasize the newly adopted UNCITRAL Model Law for Cross-Border Insolvency. This is the first global effort resulting in a workable method for courts of multiple countries to cooperate to save a business. The Model Law facilitates a holding pattern for a company's assets while the company and its creditors negotiate a rescue. The more countries that incorporate the Model Law in their own legal regimes, the more widespread the concept of multinational cooperation and rescue will be.

SOVEREIGN DEBT AND LENDER RISKS

It is beyond the scope of this chapter to explore in detail possible debt resolution mechanisms for sovereign debt. Nevertheless, a few comments are appropriate. Global public funding sources should be treated as a source of last resort in solving a sovereign financial crisis and, when necessary, should be used to produce maximum results. Funds of last resort in a private business rescue are used for two purposes, and funds from global public sources should be used for the same purposes: critical cash flow lending, and capital for growth of the restructured business.

The critical cash flow lending should not be used to pay prior lenders or creditors but should be used to maintain the value of the business. The rescue capital should not be used to pay prior lenders or creditors but should be used to facilitate the growth and value of the business.

Although analogies of private debt to sovereign debt are far from perfect, this concept of utilization of 'last resort' capital should be the goal of the global public funds. Those who have sovereign investments should bear the risk of those investments, rather than expecting a public bailout. This is an easy principle to state, but a difficult one to achieve in practice.

FINAL THOUGHTS

There is a principle that should be relied upon in designing a solution: 'Creditors will act commercially to resolve their troubled loans'. They will assess and utilize leverage available to them and, on the basis of that leverage, make a commercial decision. In essence, the solution must 'set the table' for negotiations as discussed in a proper rescue system for corporate debt. It is unlikely that the table will be set by rules of an international bankruptcy court. Therefore the rules should be set in the documentation for the purchase of sovereign debt and the laws governing the issuance and operation of those documents.

This will require collective action by the international financial community and the recognition that providing a debt resolution mechanism is critical for the future global financial architecture. Without this commitment and action, it will be impossible to achieve the desired allocation of 'last resort' capital and the goal of creditors and investors bearing the risks of their decisions.

PART III

Moral Hazard and Systemic Risk

8. Systemic risk, moral hazard and the international lender of last resort

Frederic S. Mishkin*

AN ASYMMETRIC INFORMATION ANALYSIS OF THE ASIAN CRISIS AND SYSTEMIC RISK

An asymmetric information framework described in Mishkin (1996a, 1997) is used here to analyse the recent events in East Asia, but it is worth noting that it not only applies there but to earlier crises such as the ones that occurred in Mexico in 1994–5 and Chile in 1982.

An asymmetric information view of financial crises defines a financial crisis as being a non-linear disruption to financial markets in which the asymmetric information problems of adverse selection and moral hazard become much worse, so that financial markets are unable to channel funds efficiently to those who have the most productive investment opportunities. Systemic risk is just the likelihood that a sudden, usually unexpected, event may disrupt information in financial markets so that it prevents financial markets from doing their job and can thus result in a financial crisis.

In most financial crises, and particularly in the East Asian crises, the key factor that caused asymmetric information problems to worsen and launch a financial crisis is a deterioration in balance sheets, particularly those in the financial sector. The systemic risk that caused the deterioration in balance sheets was an interaction of poor government policies with a financial structure that left these emerging market countries highly vulnerable. This perspective has important implications for the way these crises can be prevented, whether there should be an international lender of last resort and, if so, how it should operate.

A key source of systemic risk in the East Asian crises, as in the earlier financial crises in Chile or Mexico, was financial liberalization that resulted in the lending boom. Once restrictions are lifted on both interest rate ceilings and the type of lending allowed, lending will surely increase. The problem is not that lending expands, but that it expands so rapidly that excessive risk-taking

* Any views expressed in this comment are those of the author only and not those of Columbia University or the National Bureau of Economic Research.

is the result, with large losses on loans in the future. There are two reasons for excessive risk-taking occurring after financial liberalization. The first is that managers of banking institutions often lack the expertise to manage risk appropriately when new lending opportunities open up after financial liberalization. In addition, with rapid growth of lending, banking institutions cannot add the necessary managerial capital (well-trained loan officers, risk-assessment systems and so on) fast enough to enable these institutions to screen and monitor these new loans appropriately.

The second source of systemic risk that promoted excessive risk-taking was the inadequacy of the regulatory/supervisory system. Even if there is no explicit government safety net for the banking system, there clearly is an implicit safety net that creates a moral hazard problem. Depositors and foreign lenders to the banks, knowing that there are likely to be government bailouts to protect them, have little incentive to monitor banks, with the result that these institutions have an incentive to take on excessive risk by aggressively seeking out new loan business. In order to prevent this moral hazard problem, adequate government regulations needs to be in place to restrict excessive risk-taking. These include the adoption of adequate accounting and legal standards, disclosure requirements, restrictions on certain holdings of assets and capital standards. Adequate government supervision is also needed in order to monitor compliance with the regulations and to assess whether the proper management controls are in place to limit risk.

Emerging market countries, and particularly those in East Asia, are notorious for their weak financial regulation and supervision. When financial liberalization yields new opportunities to take on risk, these weak regulatory/supervisory systems cannot limit the moral hazard created by the government safety net and excessive risk-taking is the result. This problem is made even more severe by the rapid credit growth in the lending boom which stretches the resources of the bank supervisors. Bank supervisory agencies are also unable to add to their supervisory capital (well-trained examiners and information systems) fast enough to enable them to keep up with their increased responsibilities, not only because they have to monitor new activities of the banks, but also because these activities are expanding at a rapid pace.

Capital inflows can make this problem even worse. Once financial liberalization is adopted, foreign capital flows into banks in emerging market countries because it earns high yields but is likely to be protected by the government safety net, whether it is provided by the government of the emerging market country or by international agencies such as the IMF. The result is that capital inflows can fuel a lending boom which leads to excessive risk-taking on the part of banks. Folkerts-Landau *et al.* (1995), for example, find that emerging market countries in the Asian–Pacific region with large net private capital inflows also experienced large increases in their banking sectors.

The outcome of the lending boom arising after financial liberalization is huge loan losses and a subsequent deterioration of banks' balance sheets. In the case of the East Asian crisis countries, the share of non-performing loans in total loans has risen to between 15 per cent and 35 per cent.[1] The deterioration in bank balance sheets is the key fundamental that drives emerging market countries into their financial crises, and this was particularly true for East Asia. It does this in two ways. First, the deterioration in the balance sheets of banking firms can lead them to restrict their lending in order to improve their capital ratios or can even lead to a full-scale banking crisis which forces many banks into insolvency, thereby directly removing the ability of the banking sector to make loans.

Second, the deterioration in bank balance sheets can promote a currency crisis because it becomes very difficult for the central bank to defend its currency against a speculative attack. Any rise in interest rates to keep the domestic currency from depreciating has the additional effect of weakening the banking system further because the rise in interest rates hurts banks' balance sheets. This negative effect of a rise in interest rates on banks' balance sheets occurs because of their maturity mismatch and their exposure to increased credit risk when the economy deteriorates. Thus, when a speculative attack on the currency occurs in an emerging market country, if the central bank raises interest rates sufficiently to defend the currency, the banking system may collapse. Once investors recognize that a country's weak banking system makes it less likely that the central bank will take the steps necessary to defend the domestic currency successfully, they have even greater incentives to attack the currency because expected profits from selling the currency have now risen. Thus, with a weakened banking sector, a successful speculative attack is likely to materialize and can be triggered by any of many factors, a large current account deficit being just one of them. In this view, the deterioration in the banking sector is the key fundamental that causes the currency crisis to occur.

Two special institutional features of credit markets in emerging market countries explain why the devaluation in the aftermath of the currency crisis is a major source of systemic risk that helps to trigger a full-fledged financial crisis. Because of past experience with high and variable inflation rates, these countries have little inflation-fighting credibility and debt contracts are therefore of very short duration and are often denominated in foreign currencies. This structure of debt contacts is very different from that in most industrialized countries, which have almost all of their debt denominated in domestic currency, with much of it long-term, and it explains why there is such a different response to a devaluation in emerging market countries than there is in industrialized countries.

There are three mechanisms through which the currency crisis causes a financial crisis to occur in emerging market countries. The first involves the direct effect of currency devaluation on the balance sheet of firms. With debt contracts denominated in foreign currency, when there is a devaluation of the domestic currency, the debt burden of domestic firms increases. On the other hand, since assets are typically denominated in domestic currency, there is no simultaneous increase in the value of firms' assets. The result is a that a devaluation leads to a substantial deterioration in firms' balance sheets and a decline in net worth, which, in turn, worsens the adverse selection problem because effective collateral has shrunk, thereby providing less protection to lenders. Furthermore, the decline in net worth increases moral hazard incentives for firms to take on greater risk because they have less to lose if the loans go sour. Because lenders are now subject to much higher risks of losses, there is now a decline in lending and hence a decline in investment and economic activity.

The damage to balance sheets from devaluation in the aftermath of the foreign exchange crisis has been a major source of the contraction of the economies in East Asia, as it was in Mexico in 1995. This mechanism has been particularly strong in Indonesia, which has seen the value of its currency decline by 75 per cent, thus increasing the rupiah value of foreign-denominated debts by a factor of four. Even a healthy firm initially with a strong balance sheet is likely to be driven into insolvency by such a shock if it has a significant amount of foreign-denominated debt.

A second mechanism linking currency crises with financial crises in emerging market countries occurs because the devaluation can lead to higher inflation. Because many emerging market countries have previously experienced both high and variable inflation, their central banks are unlikely to have deep-rooted credibility as inflation fighters. Thus a sharp depreciation of the currency after a speculative attack that leads to immediate upward pressure on prices can lead to a dramatic rise in both actual and expected inflation. Indeed, Mexican inflation surged to 50 per cent in 1995, after the foreign exchange crisis in 1994, and we are seeing a similar phenomenon in East Asian crisis countries, particularly in Indonesia. A rise in expected inflation after the currency crisis exacerbates the financial crisis because it leads to a sharp rise in interest rates. The interaction of the short duration of debt contracts and the interest rate rise leads to huge increases in interest payments by firms, thereby weakening firms' cash flow position and further weakening their balance sheets. Then, as we have seen, both lending and economic activity are likely to undergo a sharp decline.

A third mechanism linking the financial crisis and the currency crisis arises because the devaluation of the domestic currency can lead to further deterioration in the balance sheets of the banking sector, provoking a large-scale banking crisis. In emerging market countries, banks have many liabilities denominated in foreign currency which increase sharply in value when a depreciation occurs. On the other hand, the problems of firms and households mean that they are unable to pay off their debts, also resulting in loan losses on the assets side of the banks' balance sheets.[2] The result is that banks' balance sheets are squeezed from both the assets and liabilities side and the net worth of banks therefore declines. An additional problem for the banks is that many of their foreign currency-denominated debt is very short-term, so that the sharp increase in the value of this debt leads to liquidity problems for the banks because this debt needs to be paid back quickly. The result of the further deterioration in bank balance sheets and their weakened capital base is that they cut back lending. In the extreme case in which the deterioration of bank balance sheets leads to a banking crisis that forces many banks to close their doors, thereby directly limiting the ability of the banking sector to make loans, the effect on the economy is even more severe.

The bottom line from this asymmetric information analysis is that the East Asian financial crisis was the result of a systemic collapse in both financial and non-financial firm balance sheets that made asymmetric information problems worse. The result was that financial markets were no longer able to channel funds to those with productive investment opportunities, which had then led to a severe economic contraction.

DO WE NEED AN INTERNATIONAL LENDER OF LAST RESORT?

The asymmetric information analysis in the above section indicates that systemic risk is an important feature of financial systems and can lead to disastrous consequences for the economy. Once a systemic episode triggers a financial crisis, the financial system needs to be restarted so that it can resume its job of channelling funds to those with productive investment opportunities. The asymmetric information view thus provides a rationale for government intervention to get the financial system back on its feet, thereby preventing systemic risk episodes from spinning out of control.

In industrialized countries, domestic central banks have the ability to do this both with expansionary monetary policy and with a lender-of-last resort operation. It will be argued below, however, that central banks in emerging market countries are much less likely to have this capability. Thus there is a strong argument that an international lender of last resort may be needed to cope with financial crises in these countries. However, even if there is a need for an international lender of last resort, engaging in lender-of-last resort activities does create a serious moral hazard problem that can make financial crises more likely. Thus an international lender of last resort which does not sufficiently limit these moral hazard problems can actually make the situation worse, a subject that is discussed in the next section.

The institutional structure of financial systems in most industrialized countries has two features that are very important in enabling central banks in these countries to stimulate recovery from financial crises: (a) debt contracts are almost solely denominated in domestic currency, and (b) because inflation has tended to be moderate, many debt contracts are of fairly long duration.

One way for a central bank to promote recovery from a financial crisis, given the above institutional structure, is to pursue an expansionary monetary policy by injecting liquidity (reserves) into the financial system. Injecting reserves, either through open market operations or by lending to the banking sector, causes the money supply to increase, which in turns leads to a higher price level. Given that debt contracts are denominated in domestic currency and many debt contracts are of fairly long duration, the reflation of the economy causes the debt burden of households and firms to fall, thereby increasing their net worth. As outlined earlier, higher net worth then leads to reduced adverse selection and moral hazard problems in financial markets, undoing the increase in adverse selection and moral hazard problems induced by the financial crisis. In addition, injecting liquidity into the economy raises asset prices such as land and stock market values, which also cause an improvement in net worth and a reduction in adverse selection and moral hazard problems. Also, as discussed in Mishkin (1996b), expansionary monetary policy promotes economic recovery through other mechanisms involving the stock market and the foreign exchange market.[3]

A second method for a central bank to promote recovery from a financial crisis is to pursue the so-called 'lender-of-last-resort role' in which the central bank stands ready to lend freely during a financial crisis. By restoring liquidity to the financial sector, the lender of last resort can help shore up the balance sheets of financial firms, thereby preventing a systemic shock from spreading and bringing down the financial system. There are many instances of successful lender-of-last resort operations in industrialized countries (for example, see Mishkin, 1991); the Federal Reserve's intervention on the day after the 19 October 1987 stock market crash is one example. Indeed, what is striking about this episode is that the extremely quick intervention of the Fed not only resulted in a negligible impact on the economy of the stock market crash, but also meant that the amount of liquidity that the Fed needed to supply to the economy was not very large (see Mishkin, 1991).

However, institutional features of the financial systems in emerging market countries imply that it may be far more difficult for the central bank to promote recovery from a financial crisis. As mentioned before, many emerging market countries have much of their debt denominated in foreign currency. Furthermore, their past record of high and variable inflation has resulted in debt contracts of very short duration and an expansionary monetary policy is likely to cause expected inflation to rise dramatically.

As a result of these institutional features, a central bank in an emerging market country can no longer use expansionary monetary policy to promote recovery from a financial crisis. Suppose that the policy prescription for an industrialized country to pursue expansionary monetary policy and reflate the economy were followed in an emerging market country with the above institutional structure: in this case, the expansionary monetary policy is likely to cause expected inflation to rise dramatically and the domestic currency to depreciate sharply. As we have seen before, the depreciation of the domestic currency leads to a deterioration in firms' and banks' balance sheets because much of their debt is denominated in foreign currency, thus raising the burden of indebtedness and lowering banks' and firms' net worth. In addition, the upward jump on expected inflation is likely to cause interest rates to rise because lenders need to be protected from the loss of purchasing power when they lend. As we have also seen, the resulting rise in interest rates causes interest payments to soar and the cash flow of households and firms to decline. Again the result is a deterioration in households' and firms' balance sheets, and potentially greater loan losses for banking institutions. Also because debt contracts are of very short duration, the rise in the price level from an expansionary monetary policy does not affect the value of households' and firms' debts appreciably, so there is little benefit to their balance sheets from this mechanism as occurs in industrialized countries.

The net result of an expansionary monetary policy in the emerging market country with the above institutional structure is that it hurts the balance sheets of households, firms and banks. Thus expansionary monetary policy has the opposite result to that found in industrialized countries after a financial crisis: it causes a deterioration in balance sheets and therefore amplifies adverse selection and moral hazard problems in financial markets caused by a financial crisis, rather than ameliorating them, as in the industrialized country case.

For similar reasons, lender-of-last-resort activities by a central bank in an emerging market country, may not be as successful as in an industrialized country. When the Federal Reserve pursued a lender-of-last-resort role during the 1987 stock market crash, there was almost no sentiment in the markets that this would lead to substantially higher inflation. However, this is much less likely to be the case for an emerging market country. Given the past record on inflation, central bank lending to the financial system in the wake of a financial crisis which expands domestic credit might arouse fears of inflation spiralling out of control. We have already seen that, if inflation expectations rise, leading to higher interest rates and exchange rate depreciation, cash flow and balance sheets will deteriorate, making recovery from the financial crisis less likely. The lender-of-last-resort role of a central bank must be used far more cautiously in an emerging market country with the institutional structure outlined here because central bank lending is now a two-edged sword.

The above arguments suggest that central banks in emerging market countries have only a very limited ability to extricate their countries from a financial crisis. Indeed, a speedy recovery from a financial crisis in an emerging market country is likely to require foreign assistance because liquidity provided from foreign sources does not lead to any of the undesirable consequences that result from the provision of liquidity by domestic authorities. Foreign assistance does not lead to increased inflation which, through the cash flow mechanism, hurts domestic balance sheets, and it helps to stabilize the value of the domestic currency, which strengthens domestic balance sheets.

Thus, since a lender of last resort for emerging market countries is needed at times and it cannot be provided domestically but must be provided by foreigners, there is a strong rationale for having an international lender of last resort. A further rationale for an international lender of last resort exists if there is contagion from one emerging market country to another during a financial crisis. Although the jury is not out on this one, it does appear that a successful speculative attack on one emerging market country does lead to speculative attacks on other emerging market countries, which can lead to collapses of additional currencies. Thus currency crises do have the potential to snowball, and because these currency crises lead to full-fledged financial crises in emerging market countries, the risk of contagion is indeed a serious one. An international lender of last resort has the ability to stop contagion by providing international reserves for emerging market countries threatened by speculative attacks so that they can keep their currencies from plummeting. This assistance can thus keep currency and therefore financial crises from spreading.

PRINCIPLES FOR OPERATION OF AN INTERNATIONAL LENDER OF LAST RESORT

The asymmetric information view of systemic risk and financial crises provides some broad principles for the way an international lender of last resort should operate. It suggests that there are three principles that should guide resolution of these crises: (a) the financial system needs to be restarted so that it can resume its job of channelling funds to those with productive investment opportunities, (b) balance sheets of financial and non-financial firms need to be restored so that asymmetric information problems lessen, and (c) steps need to be taken in order to limit the moral hazard created by intervention to resolve crises.

These principles are useful in thinking about how an international lender of last resort should conduct its operations to resolve crises like the ones we have experienced recently in Mexico and East Asia. The first principle suggests that an important element for success of a lender-of-last-resort operation is that it restores confidence in the financial system. Not only is the liquidity supplied by the lender of last resort necessary for this goal, but confidence that financial institutions will not go on taking excessive risk is also essential. This implies that steps to beef up the regulatory and supervisory systems in the crises countries can play a useful role in restoring confidence and resolving the crisis. Insistence by the international lender of last resort on these steps as a condition for its lending can thus be an important part of making its operation successful.

The second principle indicates that resolution of a financial crisis requires a restoration of the balance sheets of both financial and non-financial firms. Restoration of balance sheets of non-financial firms requires a well-functioning bankruptcy law that enables the balance sheets of these firms to be cleaned up so they can regain access to the credit markets. Restoration of balance sheets of financial firms may require the injection of public funds so that healthy institutions can buy up the assets of insolvent institutions, but also requires the creation of entities like the Resolution Trust Corporation in the United States, which can sell off assets of failed institutions and get them off the books of the banking sector. The international lender of last resort and, potentially, other international organizations can help this process by sharing their expertise and by encouraging the governments in crisis countries to take the steps to create a better legal structure and better resolution process for failed financial institutions.

The third principle indicates that it is necessary to limit the moral hazard created by the presence of an international lender of last resort. An international lender of last resort creates a serious moral hazard problem because depositors and other creditors of banking institutions expect that they will be protected if a crisis occurs. In the recent Asian episode, governments in the crisis countries have used IMF support to protect depositors and other creditors of banking institutions from losses. This safety net creates a well-known moral hazard problem because the depositors and other creditors have less incentive to monitor these banking institutions and withdraw their deposits if the institutions are taking on too much risk. The result is that these institutions are encouraged to take on excessive risks.

This moral hazard problem can be limited by the usual elements of a well-functioning regulatory/supervisory system: punishment for the managers and stockholders of insolvent financial institutions, adequate disclosure requirements, adequate capital standards, prompt corrective action, careful monitoring of the institution's risk management procedures and monitoring of financial institutions to enforce compliance with the regulations.

However, there are often strong political forces in emerging market countries which resist putting these kinds of measures into place. This has also been a problem in industrialized countries – for example, an important factor in the

US savings and loan débâcle was political pressure to weaken regulation and supervision (for example, see Kane (1989) – but the problem is far worse in many emerging market countries. What we have seen in the Asian crisis countries is that the political will to regulate and supervise financial institutions adequately has been especially weak because politicians and their family members are often the actual owners of financial institutions. An international lender of last resort is particularly well suited to encourage adoption of the above measures to limit moral hazard because it has so much leverage over the emerging market countries to whom it lends or who might want to borrow from it in the future.

There are two reasons why an international lender of last resort needs to encourage actively adoption of the above regulatory/supervisory measures. First is that its lender-of-last-resort actions provide governments with the resources to bail out their financial sectors. Thus an international lender of last resort strengthens the safety net, which increases the moral hazard incentives for financial institutions in emerging market countries to take on excessive risk. It needs to help strengthen the regulatory/supervisory apparatus in these countries to counter this problem. Second is that the presence of an international lender of last resort may create a moral hazard problem for governments in emerging market countries who, because they know that their financial sectors are likely to be bailed out, have less incentive to take the steps to prevent domestic financial institutions from taking on excessive risk. The international lender of last resort thus needs to make it clear that it will only extend liquidity to governments that put the proper measures in place to prevent excessive risk-taking. In addition, the international lender of last resort also needs to restrict the ability of governments to bail out stockholders and large uninsured creditors of domestic financial institutions.[4] Only with this kind of pressure can the moral hazard problem arising from lender-of-last-resort operations be contained.

One problem that arises for international organizations or foreign countries engaged in lender-of-last-resort operations is that they know that, if they do not come to the rescue, the emerging market country will suffer extreme hardship and possible political instability. Politicians in the crisis country may exploit these concerns and engage in a game of 'chicken' with the international lender of last resort: they resist necessary reforms, hoping that the international lender of last resort will cave in. Elements of this game were present in the Mexico crisis of 1995, and this has also been an important feature of the negotiations between the IMF and Indonesia recently.

An international lender of last resort must make it clear that it will not play this game. Just as giving in to your children may be the easy way out in the short run, but leads to children who are poorly brought up in the long run, so the international lender of last resort must not give in to short-run humanitarian concerns and let emerging market countries escape from necessary reforms.

An international lender of last resort must always be willing to walk away from a country that is not willing to help itself. Indeed, if it caves in to one country during a financial crisis, politicians in other countries will see that they can get away with not implementing the needed reforms, making it even harder for the international lender of last resort to limit moral hazard.

Because there is a tradeoff between the benefits of a lender-of-last-resort role in preventing financial crises and the moral hazard that it creates, a lender-of-last-resort role should only be implemented if it is absolutely necessary. An international lender of last resort must therefore resist calls on it to provide funds under normal conditions. In other words, the lender-of-last-resort role should be implemented very infrequently.

CONCLUSIONS

The bottom line of the analysis here is that an international lender of last resort may be needed to limit the damage from financial crises of the type that has recently been experienced in Asia. However, in order for the international lender-of-last resort role to be successful, it needs to focus on the microeconomics of financial markets in the crisis countries and impose strong conditionality on its lending in order to encourage governments in these countries to take the steps that limit moral hazard and make a financial crisis less likely to occur in the future. This leaves me with a fundamental disagreement with the position outlined in Feldstein (1998): the asymmetric information framework for analysing financial crises suggests that conditionality on microeconomic issues is a valid and necessary element of an international lender-of-last-resort intervention, which is exactly what the IMF has been engaged in.[5]

The analysis here also suggests that macroeconomic and microeconomic policies unrelated to the financial sector deserve less emphasis in the conditionality for the lender-of-last-resort operation. The IMF has been criticized for imposing so-called 'austerity programmes' on the East Asian countries. When a currency and financial crisis develops, what the right set of macroeconomic and non-financial microeconomic policies to pursue is not absolutely clear, and this is currently a hot topic of debate. Regardless of what the right policies are, there are two reasons why an international lender of last resort is better off de-emphasizing them.

First is that the fundamental driving the crises has been microeconomic problems in the financial sector. Thus macroeconomic policies or micro policies unrelated to the financial sector are unlikely to help resolve the crises. Second is that a focus on austerity programmes or these other microeconomic problems is likely to be a political disaster. Politicians are prone to avoid dealing with the hard issues of appropriate reform of their financial systems, and this is particularly true in East Asia, where many of the politicians' close friends, and even family, have much to lose if the financial system is reformed properly. Austerity programmes allow these politicians to label the international lender of last resort, the IMF in the East Asian case, as anti-growth and even anti-Asian. This can help the politicians to mobilize the public against the international lender of last resort and avoid doing what they really need to do to reform the financial system in their country. With conditionality focused on microeconomic policies related to the financial sector, there is a greater likelihood that the international lender of last resort will be seen as a helping hand which aids the emerging market country by assisting it in creating a more efficient financial system.

NOTES

1. See Goldstein (1998).
2. An important point is that, even if banks have a matched portfolio of foreign currency-denominated assets and liabilities and so appear to avoid foreign-exchange market risk, a devaluation can nonetheless cause substantial harm to bank balance sheets. The reason is that, when a devaluation occurs, the offsetting foreign currency-denominated assets are unlikely to be paid off in full because of the worsening business conditions and the negative effect that these increases in the value, in domestic currency terms, of these foreign currency-denominated loans have on the balance sheet of the borrowing firms. Another way of saying this is that, when there is a devaluation, the mismatch between foreign currency-denominated assets and liabilities on borrowers' balance sheets can lead to defaults on their loans, thereby converting a market risk for borrowers to a credit risk for the banks that have made the foreign currency-denominated loans. Garber and Lall (1996) have pointed out that, even with a matched book on their balance sheet, banks may also be exposed to foreign-exchange risk because of their use of derivatives, as occurred for Mexican banks during the Tequila crisis.
3. Note that not all developed countries are alike in their ability to use expansionary monetary policy to recover from a financial crisis. If a country has a commitment to peg its exchange rate to a foreign currency, then expansionary monetary policy may not be an available tool to promote recovery because pursuing such a policy might force a devaluation of its currency. This problem is of course particularly acute for a small country in a pegged exchange rate regime. Even if a country has a flexible exchange rate, an expansionary monetary policy to promote recovery might cause a depreciation of the domestic currency which is considered to be intolerable by the authorities, particularly in smaller countries. Clearly, a large reserve currency country like the United States has the most flexibility to use expansionary monetary policy to reflate the economy as a tool to recover from or reduce the probability of a financial crisis.
4. See Goldstein (1998).
5. There is, however, the serious question of whether the IMF is the appropriate international organization to take over the international lender-of-last-resort role. For example, the Shadow Open Market Committee (1998) takes the position that the IMF should not be engaged in international lender-of-last-resort operations, but that these operations would be better conducted by the Bank for International Settlements.

REFERENCES

Feldstein, M. (1998), 'Refocusing the IMF', *Foreign Affairs*, March/April, 20–33.

Folkerts-Landau, D., G.J. Schinasi, M. Cassard, V.K. Ng, C.M. Reinhart and M.G. Spencer (1995), 'Effect of Capital Flows on the Domestic Financial Sectors in APEC Developing Countries', in M.S. Khan and C.M. Reinhart (eds), *Capital Flows in the APEC Region*, Washington, DC: International Monetary Fund, pp. 31–57.

Garber, P.M. and S. Lall (1996), 'The Role and Operation of Derivative Markets in Foreign Exchange Crises', mimeo.

Goldstein, Morris (1998), *The Asian Financial Crisis*, Washington, DC: Institute for International Economics.

Kane, E.J. (1989), *The S&L Insurance Mess: How Did It Happen?*, Washington, DC: Urban Institute Press.

Mishkin, F.S. (1991), 'Asymmetric Information and Financial Crises: A Historical Perspective', in R.G. Hubbard (ed.), *Financial Markets and Financial Crises*, Chicago: University of Chicago Press, pp. 69–108.

Mishkin, F.S. (1996a), 'Understanding Financial Crises: A Developing Country Perspective', in Michael Bruno and Boris Pleskovic (eds), *Annual World Bank Conference on Development Economics 1996*, Washington, DC: World Bank, pp. 29–62.

Mishkin, F.S. (1996b), 'The Channels of Monetary Transmission: Lessons for Monetary Policy', *Banque De France Bulletin Digest*, no. 27, March.

Mishkin, F.S. (1997), 'The Causes and Propagation of Financial Instability: Lessons for Policymakers', in Craig Hakkio (ed.), *Maintaining Financial Stability in a Global Economy*, Kansas City: Federal Reserve Bank of Kansas City.

Shadow Open Market Committee (1998), 'Policy Statements and Position Papers, March 15–16, 1998', Bradley Policy Research Center Working Paper, PPS 98-01.

9.   Dealing with systemic risk

Michel Aglietta

INTRODUCTION

The aftermath of the Asian crisis has renewed initiatives to improve the functioning of the international financial system. Not lacking grandiloquence, the G-7 has put the design of a 'new international architecture' on its agenda. It is not the first time that the G-7 has been preoccupied by international financial disorders. After the Mexican crisis it was felt necessary to issue a solemn statement calling for early warning indicators, enhancing market transparency and improving prudential supervision. In the last three years there has been a follow-up to these exhortations. The Basle Committee on Banking supervision issued its core principle for effective banking supervision in early 1997, endorsed by the G-10 central bank governors. Meanwhile, the IMF has strengthened its system of macro surveillance and has been equipped with more resources to assist countries in crisis. Further work has been done on an international banking standard to adapt prudential regulation to the conditions facing banks outside the G-10 countries, but with no agreement to date.

However, the Asian crisis has highlighted the shortcomings of previous attempts at reducing financial fragility. It is now broadly acknowledged that the combination of free capital flows and badly regulated banks can be disastrous. This is why a comprehensive framework of rules has been set up. But, as Charles Goodhart forcefully argued (Goodhart, 1997), setting standards is the easier job. Implementing them so that bank behavior is effectively disciplined is a much tougher one. It requires an incentive structure to keep moral hazard in check. It is obvious from the careless short-term inter-bank lending that occurred in 1996 and 1997 in Asia that the standards are not working well, to say the least. Moral hazard has to be addressed beyond international guidelines, drawing upon advanced research on pre-commitment and the supervisory oversight built upon prompt corrective action which is implemented in the United States. This chapter will address the moral hazard problem by linking pre-commitment and prompt corrective action, thinking of ways to implement the dual procedures in the international arena.

Furthermore, there is the basic problem of systemic risk. The hot debate that has erupted from the Asian crisis has split experts into two broad categories: one points out the flawed financial systems in the Asian economies, the other emphasizes contagion that spreads panic. There is some truth in asserting that financial liberalization was too abrupt and ill-conceived. It was observed before in developed countries that banking crises had been widespread in countries where the change from a segmented to an open financial system was so brisk that the banks did not have the chance to develop a learning process for controlling new types of risk tied to new opportunities. This reasoning is conducive to the following predicaments: an orderly and progressive opening recommended to countries which have not liberalized their financial systems yet, and adopting the international guidelines for those which have done so, as well as generating better market data and promoting transparency.

From the other point of view, however, the improper handling of financial liberalization by governments falls far short of explaining the recurrence of financial crises in the last 25 years, not to mention the historical record of financial crises depicted in 'manias, panics and crashes' (Kindleberger, 1978). Global capital markets can be inherently unstable, at least under conditions of stress. This is why they need a global regulation whose linchpin is an international lender of last resort (LLR). This chapter will address the question of systemic risk in financial markets and discuss how the LLR function can best be performed internationally.

The chapter will therefore proceed as follows. In the next section some theoretical underpinnings will be introduced on the nature of systemic risk and on the reason for its presence in finance. In the third section market crises of the 1990s will be reviewed so as to stress liquidity problems and contagion phenomena in a host of financial markets and circumstances. The fourth section will draw lessons from the Asian crisis, focusing on systemic risk. The final section will discuss the need for a systemic regulator on top of prudential agreed-upon rules and national supervisors for banks. It will also inquire into the mechanisms designed to keep moral hazard in check.

SYSTEMIC RISK: SOME THEORETICAL UNDERPINNINGS

A general definition of systemic risk might be as follows: the occurrence of abnormal, that is socially inefficient, equilibria, where an economic system can be trapped because there is no spontaneous market adjustment stemming from rational individual behavior which can move the system out of the poor macroeconomic state (Aglietta and Moutot, 1993). Examples of such equilibria arise in the markets for bank deposits (Diamond and Dybvig, 1983), bank credit (Mankiw, 1993), traded assets with heterogeneous expectations (Gennotte and Leland, 1990) or extraneous beliefs (Guesnerie and Azariadis, 1982).

Therefore systemic risk per se is the latent possibility, unknown or unhedged by market participants, that a systemic event can occur (the economy actually moves towards an abnormal equilibrium). Theoreticians are prone to assign systemic events to one of two general hypotheses about the functioning of financial markets.

- *Asymmetric information in credit markets* (Mishkin, 1996) is conducive to risk undervaluation and subsequent overindebtedness which gives rise to financial fragility entailing a steep increase in the cost of financial intermediation and/or a credit crunch.
- *Asset pricing under liquidity constraints* (Minsky, 1986) depicts the alternation of euphoria and disillusionment stemming from strong subjective interactions between market participants which give rise to collective behavior (contagion and panic).

A deeper theoretical background can be provided for both hypotheses if it is understood that finance is not only information processing but also knowledge acquiring under uncertainty. Coordination failures can occur in cognitive processes, which rely on interindividual interactions (externalities). In turn, coordination failures explain why liquidity is the focus of systemic risk and why banking is the weak link of the financial system.

Uncertainty and Coordination Failures

There is a coordination failure when mutual welfare improvements are socially possible but cannot be reached by any market adjustment, because no private agent has the incentive to deviate from the existing equilibrium. The reader may notice that this concept is entirely consistent with the definition of systemic risk given above.Why may a coordination failure occur? Because of the strategic interactions between individuals triggered by cognitive processes under conditions of endogenous uncertainty.

Endogenous uncertainty gives rise to the non-independence of risks which provokes strategic interactions between market participants. Two types of endogenous uncertainty may be distinguished. The first type is the uncertainty which proceeds from each individual's attitude (ethical uncertainty). The knowledge-acquiring process depends on trust, that is, an implicit collective coordination, the lack of which entails failure. The second type is the uncertainty which proceeds from the indefinite opening of the future (epistemic uncertainty). It means that innovation cannot be foreseen from the accumulated past knowledge. The experience of past actions is radically insufficient to make future decisions. The substantive approach of risk (optimizing certainty-equivalent utility functions) no longer applies. A procedural approach must be implemented; it involves strategic interactions between market participants.

More than any other economic activity, finance, which makes wagers upon the bets of entrepreneurs and which ties those wagers to contractual commitments (debt contracts), is plagued by both ethical and epistemic uncertainty. In order to describe the procedural approach which applies under conditions of endogenous uncertainty, scholars have drawn upon theories of cognitive processes and have sorted out two hypotheses. The first is *the hypothesis of intrinsic myopia* (Guttentag and Herring, 1986). A type of risk that cannot be assessed from a well-defined probability function is liable to be treated according to a heuristic threshold. It is the psychological response to a threat whose occurrence cannot be estimated using probabilities drawn from past events of the same kind. The heuristic threshold induces a discontinuity in individual behavior since the subjective probability of the threat is zero beneath the threshold and strictly positive beyond. This myopic behavior is reinforced by the degrading memory of the last systemic event insofar as it has drifted into the past. Myopia is also self-validated by cognitive dissonance, a mental attitude which tends to stick to the undervaluation of systemic risk while the first symptoms of this undervaluation have been making their appearance.

The second is *the hypothesis of strategic complementarity* (Cooper and John, 1993). This is a positive feedback between mutually reinforcing actions of market participants. It can be demonstrated that strategic complementarity is a necessary and sufficient condition for coordination failures. It leads directly to contagion, that is, self-reinforcing collective processes. It delivers multiple equilibria and magnified responses (multiplier effects) to exogenous shocks at the macro level. Therefore multipliers are not grounded into ad hoc rigid prices, contrary to what is commonly said.

Intrinsic myopia and strategic complementarity are logically consistent. Since systemic risk cannot be assigned to an exogenous shock on a fundamental variable, but is the outcome of endogenous coordination failures, there is no independent way for market participants to gauge their heuristic threshold against mounting symptoms of an approaching threat. The only way to do so is by observing the behavior of market participants whose threshold is lower than theirs. Since reaching one's threshold triggers a discontinuous reaction, contagion can spread as a self-fulfilling process, well described as a cascade of moves (for instance selling) in the same direction.

Liquidity and Banks

Liquidity is the focus of systemic risk in financial markets. It is much more dangerous than the insolvency of individual debtors for the integrity of the whole financial system. The reason is that doubt over solvency can be circumscribed easily in the institution which originated it unless the institution is a bank; doubt over liquidity cannot. For liquidity is not an exogenous characteristic of an asset: it is a strategic relationship between market participants. Liquidity is the relationship which gives rise to coordination failures in finance.

Liquidity is a potential claim for immediate cash, the ability to acquire cash out of an asset at any time and without loss to fulfil one's commitment. Since value-generating assets are necessarily linked to production capacity, there is nothing like liquidity for a whole economy. Market liquidity holds as long as participants believe it is there. If trust wanes, making people eager to test it, liquidity becomes elusive. One-way selling pressure occurs, which can become a panic in a cascade-type phenomenon. The coordination failure can be precisely pointed out. Market participants rush to liquidate their assets because they do not know what the floor price will be. There is no floor price as long as there are new rounds of net selling. One can clearly understand the devastating effect of endogenous uncertainty.

Doubt over liquidity destroys confidence, which holds the structure of financial liabilities together. The fear of a liquidity shortage has crucial market makers stuck in involuntary positions and precipitates the demand for debt settlement instead of rolling over routine liabilities. As described in the next section, market liquidity risk may launch spillover effects from one market segment to the next. The positive feedback, which occurs because of the strategic complementarity between private agents, generates excess demand functions which are increasing market prices, causing imbalances to spill over from one market to another.

Identifying liquidity as the focus of systemic risk enables us to understand why banks are special. They are both private profit-generating units and parts of a network which deliver a collective good to the whole economy, the mechanism to make payments and settle debts. Of course, this definition is functional rather than institutional. Any unit that performs banking functions becomes a bank and should be regulated as such. Because of their dual economic role, banks are the units in which solvency and liquidity problems are inextricably entangled. They are the weak link in financial crises.

Banks have deposits, payable at a fixed price and at short notice, much higher than their reserves and liquid assets. Therefore contagion can occur faster among banks and impinge upon inter-bank balances and settlement systems. Contagion can also become more widespread among banks than anywhere else because average depositors all have reasons to believe that money is fungible.

They perceive the banking system in its collective duty of providing the service of payment, which makes them believe that banks are homogeneous in their capacity to supply cash. Thus asymmetric information is much higher between banks and their depositors than between other institutions and their creditors. So bank panics can trigger more bankruptcies and larger losses among depositors because bank capital is a much lower proportion of liabilities than that for any other firm. This is why systemic risk dynamics involve banks in a majority of financial crises.

FINANCIAL MARKET FAILURES IN THE 1990s

With capital mobility and financial liberalization expanding, a whole range of markets blossomed in the 1980s, both securities and derivatives markets. They have hugely broadened the means of liquidity and risk management. The linkages between market segments have multiplied arbitrage opportunities whose outcome is a true wholesale market for liquidity. It has been argued that a higher degree of market completeness makes risk dissemination more effective and liquidity needs are satisfied at a lower cost by a broader set of sources. This is undoubtedly true in normal conditions when systemic risk is deemed non-existent, but in the 1990s a host of disturbances have arisen in various financial and derivative markets. Repeated episodes exhibited large increases in volatility and severe liquidity problems. It is not the purpose of this chapter to provide an analytical account of the most salient episodes: this has been done elsewhere (Davies, 1995; Aglietta, 1996). It will be enough to give a synopsis of the main features (Table 9.1) as a basis for drawing conclusions on the vulnerability of present-day markets to systemic risk. Then the new role of banks as market intermediaries will be emphasized.

Lessons from the Turmoil in Financial Markets

The characteristics encapsulated in Table 9.1 might be dubbed circumstantial because they are not drawn from a large sample of crisis episodes of the same kind. Nevertheless, they illustrate the theoretical underpinnings sketched above in relation to individual behavior and contagion mechanisms in present-day market conditions. Recurrent attributes of financial fragility are hidden in the structure of international financial markets. They remain latent in normal conditions but they are activated in times of stress, often provoked by macro-economic or structural shocks. The financial disturbances occurring in fragile structures have the potential to spread over markets. The main processes conducive to systemic risk are destabilizing price dynamics, uncertainty about credit risk assessment and vulnerability to market liquidity risk. Derivatives

Table 9.1   Characteristics of selected recent financial crises

Episodes	Sources of disturbance	Nature of risks	Implication of derivatives	Potential for contagion	Prudential shortcomings
EMS (1992–3)	Exchange rate misalign-ments German shock Uncertainty about EMU	Exchange rate risk Credit risk in some countries	Put options on currencies under speculative attacks	Dynamic hedging Self-fulfilling speculation	Market illiquidity Lack of international support within ERM Heavy losses entail acute liquidity problems for international firms_
Bond market (1994)	Extensive positions on the expectation of lower long-run rates Abrupt tightening of US monetary policy	Interest rate risk	Interest rate swaps and futures	Huge increase in volatility Generalized international spillover One-way selling pressure on a wide range of bond markets	Risk management inefficient within the firm Lack of coordination between Exchanges. Lack of proper separation
Barings (1995)	Unexpected downturn of the Nikkei	Asset-price risk magnified by sensitivity of derivatives	Futures and options contracts on Nikkei 225 index	Spillover between Singapore and Osaka exchanges Uncertainty about the payment of margin calls at SIMEX	between customer and proprietary trading Massive deficiency of oversight of sovereign risk with financial liberal-ization
Mexico (1994–5)	Cumulative macro imbalances Deterioration of political situation Exchange rate peg	Exchange rate credit and liquidity risk	Swaps of *Tesobonos* between US investment banks and Mexican banks	Substantial in Latin America, especially dramatic in Argentina	Non-existent domestic supervision and implicit guarantees
Asia (1997)	Ill-conceived financial liberalization Excessive short-term credit Exchange rate peg	Credit risk (short-term overindebtedness) Exchange rate risk Extreme volatility of asset prices	Offshore trading to conceal true magnitude of exposure	Widespread in Asia: cascade of withdrawals of short-term funds and one-way selling pressure on domestic asset and foreign exchange markets	IMF delay in assessing the severe liquidity problems and the seriousness of the credit crunch

rarely start a crisis. They are nonetheless channels of positive feedback between markets under conditions of stress. Insofar as sources of systemic risk stemming from dynamic linkages between markets are concerned, the following lessons can be drawn from the episodes mentioned in the synopsis.

First, *market illiquidity on some segments of the wholesale market can force intermediaries acting as market makers to rely on dynamic hedging and effectively to convey the liquidity gap onto a broader set of segments.* Market makers are supposed to satisfy end-users and to maintain an orderly market, so that a market's overreaction can be countered by fundamentals-based traders. In their capacity, market makers are exposed to unintended large losses if they keep standing against one-way selling. If losses are too large with respect to capital, if credit is too expensive or too risky to finance an enlarging exposure in depreciating assets, market makers can give up sustaining market prices at any predetermined level (Bingham, 1992). This is a typical market failure, which causes liquidity to dry up in the particular segment and uncertainty to increase the volatility of prices substantially. As a consequence, a number of market participants have to hedge their positions dynamically. As seen notably in the 1994 bond market slump and the European Monetary System (EMS) crisis of September 1992, a concentration of option contracts, whose asking price is set at some perceived critical price according to market sentiment or to some target band, triggers dynamic hedging when the forward price exceeds the asking price. In turn, dynamic hedging creates an excess demand on the underlying asset market which is an increasing function of the market price, thus exacerbating price movements there and disturbing cash market liquidity (Brockmejer Report, 1995). Another pressure to liquidate the underlying assets comes from margin and collateral calls on derivatives which are larger the higher the volatility in prices. The Barings crisis is a good example. Absent decisive action by regulators, uncertainty could have induced dealers to forfeit their positions, causing the Singapore Future Exchange (SIMEX) to collapse.

Second, *numerous reasons account for the possibility of one-way selling in present-day markets where competition is intense and price expectations are affected by complex parameters.* Multiple equilibria of a self-fulfilling nature and asymmetric information can lead to liquidity shortage on markets which are temporarily unbalanced. This can be transformed into a full-fledged crisis by a concentrated cluster of market makers flying from unintended exposure.

Institutional investors, who play a major role in both the wholesale debt markets and associated derivatives markets, are active in speculative dynamics. Operating in very competitive markets, they respond similarly to common signals, develop the same portfolio insurance strategies and are highly sensitive to each other's performance in the market. The reason for being exposed to herd behavior is an incentive structure, which proceeds from asymmetric information in the management of contractual saving (Davies, 1995).

Fund management entails a serious principal–agent problem. Actually, there exists no long-run contingent contract capable of constraining managers to act optimally in the interest of investors. In tightly regulated financial systems, restraints were imposed on portfolio structures for the sake of risk limitation. However, those rules restricted competition and allowed fund managers to levy prohibitive commissions. The rise of contractual saving in a deregulated financial environment has enhanced ultimate investors' demands for higher yields. Shorter mandates and performance assessments, and manager earnings linked to market values have ensued.

The devices adopted to reduce the principal–agent conflict lead to herd behavior in conditions of stress. When fundamental values are highly uncertain, fund managers rationally follow market sentiment to secure their relative short-run performance, either because they mimic each other or because they receive common signals. This type of market coordination provokes one-way buying or selling of the same assets (Scharfstein and Stein, 1990). Furthermore, the relevant information in such circumstances has nothing to do with intrinsic future values of the fundamentals. What is critical to beat the market is to surmise before other market participants the news to which they are going to respond in the near future, in conformity with the rationale of Keynes's beauty contest (Schiller, 1995). Since each participant is aware that he is a source of information for others, he strategically hides his own opinion. The spreading of rumors and the design of lures to mislead competitors are features of financial markets under uncertainty. Therefore ritual calls for transparency are no more than empty wishful thinking in such market structures.

Hedge funds and mutual funds have liabilities, which can be liquidated at short notice. They are thus vulnerable to a flight to quality. They have to sell their assets instantly to redeem their own shares. This is why changes in market sentiment can trigger large portfolio shifts. When a common opinion is forming that a few currencies should be discarded, according to a mutual recognition pattern, a massive reallocation of institutional portfolios may occur.

The Nature of Hidden Fragility in Financial Markets

In his comprehensive review of historical episodes of financial crises, C.P. Kindleberger noticed that financial markets are working well most of the time. But there are circumstances where market participants' behavior has created feedback effects conveying disturbances from one market to another, instead of absorbing them in the segment of origin. One important reason is that institutional investors, the main suppliers of the bulk of liquidity, misread price signals. In an uncertain environment they may take a price slump due to a temporary shortage of liquidity for a downward revision of the fundamental value of the assets. Instead of buying the asset because its price is temporarily undervalued, thus generating the needed liquidity, they rush to sell, thus causing the price to go on sliding down. If market makers do not substitute for the withdrawal of institutional investors, the particular market segment may collapse. Dealers using that particular segment to hedge open positions elsewhere have to resort precipitately to dynamic hedging, effectively spreading the original imbalance.

According to the 1993 G-30 report on derivatives, market making on the global money markets is highly concentrated in a small number of international commercial and investment banks and securities houses. The more saving has been channeled into institutional investors, the more securities markets have been relied upon as repositories for liquidity. When institutional investors are bringing forward liquidity by buying short-term debt instruments, they will eventually hedge at least part of the market risk involved. Fast-developing over-the-counter (OTC) derivatives are suitable for providing tailor-made instruments. They are written by the international banks. These dealers must hedge their positions. The crucial question is: can they hedge in the OTC derivative markets or do they have to rely on dynamic hedging in underlying securities markets, participating in the one-way selling pressure? They can hedge directly if there are investors who want to trade risk in OTC markets. These investors become the ultimate writers of derivatives. Then market risk is effectively diversified and no dynamic externality occurs. Dealers can also hedge if their aggregate net position on OTC markets is small. Market risk is redistributed among the group of market makers according to their individual risk profiles, so that no unintended position is held. This optimal pattern of liquidity provision and risk diversification can be safely assumed to occur in stable financial conditions. However, it is extremely unlikely that the pattern holds in volatile environments when the sentiment of institutional investors is changing abruptly and collectively in response to shocks. OTC markets can become very illiquid and the whole group of market makers has to hedge dynamically in underlying markets.

The market crises alluded to in Table 9.1 and other episodes of severe losses by dealers on OTC markets highlight the fact that relatively favorable conditions are not always present. Market structures hide fragility, which is only revealed in stress situations when prices are abnormally unstable. The characteristics of a number of option-like derivative contracts make them highly vulnerable to unexpected changes in the volatility of interest rates and exchange rates. When clients tend to hedge in the same direction on a foreign exchange market, the aggregate exposure of the market intermediaries can rise sharply and their losses are huge.

As will be argued below, market illiquidity risk should be a major concern for regulators motivating organized cooperation. For doubts about liquidity destroy the confidence on which the structure of financial commitments rests. This leads to the contagion which occurred in the Asian crisis.

THE ASIAN CRISIS BEYOND MACROECONOMIC FUNDAMENTALS

The standard wisdom in explaining financial crises has been drawn from the Latin American experience of the 1980s: crises stemming from the insolvency of sovereign debtors. Crises are understood to come from a deterioration of macroeconomic fundamentals: widening in public and foreign deficits, excessive real exchange rate appreciation, low private saving, high inflation, low foreign exchange reserves and the like. Insofar as financial crises in emerging countries are concerned, little attention is given to the experience of the recurrent bank and market crises in the developed countries which have accompanied financial liberalization. The error of diagnosis originally made in the case of Asia is presumably the outcome of this bias. Yet, with the possible exception of Thailand, there is little to learn in inferring crisis factors from macroeconomic variables. No standard explanation can account for an average devaluation of 80 per cent between 2 July and the end of December 1997 in the panic-stricken countries, coupled with a 50 per cent decline in the index of Asiatic share values. The case of Korea is striking. It depicts a growth rate of more than 8 per cent on average for the years 1994 to 1996, a declining rate of inflation from 6 per cent to less than 5 per cent, a domestic saving rate as high as 35 per cent of GDP without any sign of waning, a very modest current account deficit until 1995 and a non-alarming increase of under 5 per cent of GDP in 1996, already back to 2 per cent in 1997, and a stable real exchange rate: this is hardly a deterioration of the macroeconomic situation! There is indeed a definite urge to investigate beyond the conventional view of a fundamentally induced structural crisis. The main problem is to figure out what shaped the conditions of stress which are the grounds for the ensuing panic and contagion.

A Financial Weakness Built upon an Ill-conceived Liberalization

According to the analysis of the working of financial markets, they are vulnerable to liquidity risk leading to positive feedbacks and spillover effects. The dynamics ensue from coordination failures in conditions of endogenous uncertainty. These types of uncertainty, either ethical or epistemic, make market participants perceive that multiple equilibria are possible. A pegged exchange rate, for instance, is a regime which entails at least two equilibria, since the demise of the peg leads to a flexible exchange rate, which is a feasible regime. The discontinuous break between regimes is self-fulfilling if it comes from a coordination of expectations in the belief that the speculative attack will be validated by the monetary authorities under stress (Obstfeld, 1996).

With hindsight from repeated experience in Latin America, Europe and Asia, it can be inferred that financial market liberalization is the weak link in creating the type of uncertainty conducive to unsustainable capital inflows and subsequent self-fulfilling crises. The Asian crisis is rooted in private finance, contrary to the sovereign debt crisis in the 1980s. Financial fragility developed despite favorable macroeconomic performance, as in Europe and the United States in the years 1986–9. In Asia, it occurred after a long period of high, steady growth with a debt-financed accumulation without major problems, as long as the financial systems of the countries had remained regulated. *Financial liberalization should be understood as a systemic innovation, which has destroyed the former consistency without creating a new one.* It is the grounds for an epistemic uncertainty among market participants, be they local or international.

Financial liberalization was tantamount to a brutal removal of credit control by the state, which was the pillar of financial stability in debt-prone economies. This pillar was removed without allowing time for the local financial institutions to acquire expertise in risk management and for the supervisory authorities to build up a set of prudential rules and enforcement mechanisms. The prevailing methods of management, so much despised lately by the same commentators who praised the Asian miracle earlier in the decade, were indeed incompatible with the opening of financial markets. It is true that they gave rise to credit concentration and implicit guarantees. Nonetheless, they were effective in economies whose allocation of capital was mobilized and directed by the state for the sake of growth, not shareholder's value. Systemic dissonance, much more than the so-called 'crony capitalism', makes for the upsurge of uncertainty, which feeds self-fulfilling crises.

The case of Korea is particularly telling (Table 9.2). It shows clearly that excessive risk-taking stems from inadequate financial regulation (Stiglitz, 1998). With the removal of credit control, the share of credit as a percentage of GDP going to the private sector jumped from 53 per cent in 1992 to 62 per cent in 1996. The net foreign liabilities of banks almost tripled, from US$21 billion in 1993 to US$58 billion in 1996; those of non-banks rose from US$9 billion to US$20 billion. The pervasiveness of the same behavior in the new financial environment is illuminated by the 'chaebols'. They used to compete for market shares with thin profit margins, as the consequence of an industrial policy aimed at obtaining scale economies in export industries (Yung Chul Park, 1998). This is why their relative positions depended on their investment expenditures. With debt finance they were highly leveraged. The deregulation starting in 1993 simply removed government control without reinstating any other monitoring mechanism. Subsequently, debt soared and became more short-term.

Table 9.2   Korea: macroeconomic and financial indicators after the financial liberalization

	1992	1993	1994	1995	1996	1997
Macroeconomic variables						
GDP growth rate (%)	5.1	5.8	8.6	8.9	7.1	6.0
Inflation rate (%)	6.2	4.8	6.3	4.5	4.9	4.3
Domestic saving rate (% of GDP)	35.1	35.2	34.6	35.1	33.3	32.9
Current account balance (% of GDP)	−1.5	0.1	−1.2	−2.0	−4.9	−2.0
Real exchange rate (index 1990 = 100)	87.8	85.2	84.7	87.8	86.8	—
Financial variables						
Domestic credit growth (%)	11.7	12.7	18.4	14.7	19.4	—
Credit to the private sector (% of GDP)	53.4	54.2	56.8	57.0	61.8	—
Foreign liabilities of banks (% of total liabilities)	7.6	6.9	8.0	10.1	12.8	—
Net foreign liabilities of banks (US$bn)	—	20.9	29.2	43.8	58.4	57.1
Net foreign liabilities of non-banks (US$bn)	—	9.1	11.2	14.3	20.4	23.1

Source: IMF World Economic Outlook, December 1997, Table A1.

In the early 1990s an ideological drive led by the United States and the international institutions put pressure on Asian governments to liberalize their financial sectors. Hopefully China resisted, but Korea, as a new OECD member, could not do otherwise than to conform to these demands. The forced opening without a proper preparation immediately gave rise to the amazing and unsustainable upsurge of capital inflows mentioned above. Huge exposures to maturity and market risk were taken on top of greater credit risk. Short-term borrowing accounted for more than 60 per cent of total net inflow, compared to less than 40 per cent in the 1990–93 period. Both credit trade facilities and bank borrowing substantially outpaced domestic growth and trade expansion. They were driven by the lure of high yields in the context of large interest differentials between the domestic and foreign financial markets with pegged exchange rates. Since domestic banks were piling up short-term foreign debt to make long-term domestic loans at a pace which could only be sustainable transitorily, and since the supervisory authorities were unable to enforce corrective measures, stress conditions were sure to occur, while the quality of assets had begun to be questioned. The asset side of the balance sheet of financial institutions was drastically deteriorated by the reckless investing in foreign securities and dealing in financial derivatives. Korean securities firms and mutual funds set up offshore funds to disguise their borrowing as foreign investors which reinvested in high-risk domestic securities. Huge losses ensued from these open offshore positions.

The Asian Crisis as a Self-fulfilling Process

When a boom in asset prices fuelled by a fast-growing increase in credit demand leads to higher volatility, or when heavily leveraged corporations begin to show signs of insolvency, a drastic shift in market sentiment may not be far away. Yet the bursting of the bubble is inherently unpredictable. There is a latent period when uncertainty has reached its peak. The usual set of information which normally feeds market judgment is no longer relevant. Expectations lose their benchmarks. In search for meaningful knowledge and unable to find it in fundamental values, participants turn inward. *The coordination of expectations becomes mimetic and gives rise to the formation of a collective mood.* This mood can abruptly turn around from euphoria to disillusionment; a one-way selling pressure is launched; capital inflows are reversed into capital outflows. As was demonstrated in the previous section, liquidity problems ensue which trigger a generalized flight to quality and spread contagion through herding behavior.

The foreign exchange markets were subject to an amazing turnaround of capital flows. In the five Asian crisis-ridden countries, the round trip of short-term flows amounted to over 10 per cent of aggregate GDP. Non-residents withdrew funds and residents rushed to cover their foreign exchange debts. The baht plunged on 2 July 1997. Two weeks later contagion reached Malaysia and Indonesia while the Singapore dollar drifted downwards. Trust abated all over the summer with the continuous decline of the three currencies under speculative pressure. By that time it had become evident that the markets could not found a bottom price from which liquidity would eventually be regenerated. In October the crisis gained momentum. Between 10 October and 24 December, the Won fell by 50 per cent while the rupiah collapsed entirely. Even the Taiwan dollar depreciated substantially and the Hong Kong dollar came under attack. Meanwhile, the sharp fall of the HK Stock Exchange on 23 October brought down equity markets all over the region. By that time the IMF had to repeatedly come to the rescue of the panic-stricken countries, without being able to quieten the markets.

This nutshell account of the contagion can be supplemented by a more detailed account of the Korean experience to show that the dynamics of illiquid markets was working according to the pattern depicted in the previous section. Foreign equity investors withdrew their investments from the Korean stock market as early as the first week of September (Yung Chul Park, 1998). They gave a signal to foreign banks, which refused to roll over their short-term loans to Korean financial institutions. After their reckless lending which highlighted a high level of moral hazard, international banks pressured the Korean government to seek IMF financing. As the first IMF package did not do enough to stem the liquidity crisis, the situation worsened in December, in the midst of political uncertainty.

It was not until December that a decision was reached to provide US$10 billion of emergency assistance to cover an incoming repayment default on short-term foreign loans. This was a protracted lender-of-last-resort intervention. This intervention, and not the traditional IMF policy of tight credit, imposed earlier on the Korean government, restored some confidence in the foreign exchange market. After bottoming out in early January 1998, the exchange rate recovered. It is a clue that Korea suffered from a liquidity squeeze provoked by excess short-term foreign liabilities. Alarmed by the warning signal of the slump in equity prices, banks had the incentive to rush to redeem their loans, denying their debtors the routine roll-over (Feldstein, 1998). The resulting one-way selling pressure on the Won should have been fought as early as October 1997. That is what a lender of last resort is for.

THE NEED FOR A LENDER OF LAST RESORT AND THE CONTAINMENT OF MORAL HAZARD

It is well known that lender-of-last-resort activity and moral hazard are the twin offsprings of systemic risk. Moral hazard is omnipresent in financial markets impaired by asymmetric information and externalities. Social cost comes above private cost. The main problem is that LLR intervention should be sovereign, not the hostage of the banks or debtor countries whenever the foreign debts of the private sector are de facto nationalized. This is precisely the reason why moral hazard should be contained. Contrary to what is often said, since moral hazard is involved in most financial contracts, the way to deal with this ineffi-ciency is certainly not to prohibit the LLR: it is to strengthen prudential policy to enable the LLR to assert the full sovereignty that should govern its action; this means nothing but a return to the very essence of LLR, namely safe-guarding confidence in the working of money markets.

When markets have become global, LLR assistance must also widen its scope because contagion effects spread over broad areas. If an international LLR is required, it does not follow that it should be a single supranational institution. The systemic regulator could be organized like a cooperative network of central banks taking responsibility for keeping an orderly supply of liquidity. Correlatively moral hazard prevention must be framed on the understanding that market structures involve core institutions.

The Prevention of Moral Hazard

In April 1997, the Basle Committee on banking supervision issued its core principles for effective banking supervision (BIS, 1997). It advocated consistent guidelines for financial reform to be undertaken by individual countries under the responsibility of their governments. Implementing guidelines in emerging countries will surely help make the international financial system more robust, but it will take years or even decades for the reforms to be sufficiently advanced, implemented and disseminated to affect significantly the global financial system.

This structural approach faces formidable obstacles. First, the normative view inspiring the core principles is quite foreign to the methods used to maintain financial stability in developing countries. It has been observed in this chapter that financial liberalization amounts to a systemic shock because the linchpin of financial stability, state control, has been abruptly removed. Legislating rules capable of providing an incentive structure for good behavior in free markets, instead of segmenting operations and prohibiting specific actions, represents a considerable overhaul. It will face philosophical as well as political restraints. Creating supervisory institutions capable of enforcing the rules is even more challenging. It raises the issues of expertise, desegmentation, political authority within a clear mandate and statutory independence. Then the behavioral and organizational change of financial institutions requires a lengthy cognitive process, which is going to mean strong resistance to untried management practices.

Because financial reform will likely proceed very unevenly from one country to another, cooperation among national supervisory bodies will fall short of the requirements of global surveillance by a wide margin. Meanwhile, recurrent financial crises in interrelated markets highlight the deficiencies of national supervisory agencies, which cannot take a global view even in financially sophisticated countries. In turn, private expert advice of auditing firms and rating agencies can be seriously questioned. Not much can be expected from greater transparency unless the disclosure is very drastic for international firms with multiple interlocked positions in a host of market segments. These remarks sound pessimistic, but they really point to an alternative approach which concentrates risk prevention on the core institutions of global money markets.

Focusing on the borrowers' side is not enough. If short-term foreign debt had not piled up, there would not have been a financial crisis with a potential for systemic risk in Asia. The short-term borrowing of local banks was supplied by massive inter-bank credit from the big international banks. These core institutions are supposed to be endowed with efficient internal control systems able to preclude excessive risk-taking. However, the systems cannot integrate credit risk and market risk. They also grossly underestimate potential losses in time of stress.

The Asian crisis raises a serious challenge for risk management. The high leverage in making was known of market participants. There were clues that something bad was happening, but a deep uncertainty concealed the magnitude of the problems and the time of the unfolding. The models were flashing green lights until the beginning of the crisis. The rating agencies were no more successful. Every portfolio manager assumes that diversification is fine, because financial conditions in different countries are supposed to be independent, given the information obtained from country experts. The emphasis on stress testing is not that developed, not only because of the technical difficulties but also chiefly because it is very hard to think of the unthinkable. As was observed in the second section, moral hazard is the result of the myopia about systemic risk. It is why the scenarios in the stress tests are so difficult to figure out. Self-fulfilling attacks convey a radical uncertainty. Some countries can go bankrupt without leading to worldwide turbulence; others can do it unexpectedly. But no criteria exist to discriminate between financial shocks that are self-contained and others that are not.

Sweeping conclusions can be drawn from these observations. Global capital markets need a global financial regulation, not a hodgepodge of narrow-minded national supervisors of varying quality. *Furthermore, the issue of prudential regulation for the core institutions is quite different from the macro surveillance of individual countries.* This responsibility should fall to a prudential entity acquainted with the big financial firms, with a capacity to gather data on market activity and to probe into firms' internal control systems. This points to an enlarged BIS rather than to the IMF, with the advantage of developing the expertise where it is already located and denying too large a concentration of power.

In a recent report, the G-30 contended that the most opaque risk exposures, undetected by existing monitoring systems, come from the intricacies of intermingled risks of counterparts borne by the main international firms, directly between them and indirectly through their dealings with the same customers around the world (G-30, 1997). Therefore a substantial strengthening of global supervision was much needed to induce the core intermediaries to take on greater responsibility for their risks.

A consistent framework should apply to all globally active institutions. The market-friendly approach that has been developed lately should be followed with the twin principles of internal control and delegated supervision. But the standards of quality should be much more stringent for the group of highly concentrated core institutions than for other market participants. This means the ability of internal control models to perform in extreme market conditions, the disclosure of exposures well beyond routine financial statements to determine consolidated positions, the opening to on-site examinations and the adoption of a management structure, which carefully separates operational and internal audit functions. It is also necessary to improve external auditing. Auditing firms accredited to deal with global institutions should be capable of probing into the risk profile of the auditees, meaning that there should be a single auditing firm for a core institution.

For these improved mechanisms to proceed steadily, an oversight is necessary to provide *global financial monitoring*. The BIS seems the proper place to locate this. The BIS already collects the reports of international banks. It houses a banking committee which gathers together the national supervisors of most or all international banks. This committee has already conducted a substantial dialogue with the financial community, sheltered from governmental interference. The BIS is also the hub of a network of central banks. Under its auspices, or closely related to it, an institute could be created for the study and the diagnosis of systemic risk.

Nonetheless, a better framework for preventing conduct which induces systemic risk will not be completely safe. If moral hazard is to be fought effectively, there should be sanctions imposed by the supervisor or the network of supervisors. Two frameworks are advocated to link the sanctions to an incentive structure acting as a deterrent against deliberately accepting heavy losses (Goodhart *et al.* 1998). One is a *rating scheme* for core institutions granted by the supervisor of the home country of the institutions, according to a rating method agreed upon by the supervisors as part of the global financial monitoring. This in-depth rating will have the further advantage of forcing the rating agencies to come up with much better methods themselves. The other framework is a *pre-commitment approach* whereby a financial institution pre-commits itself to a maximum loss on its trading or global portfolio and undergoes a sanction if the pre-commitment is overstepped (Kupiec and O'Brien, 1997).

The advantage of pre-commitment for the supervisor is that it does not have to assess internal control systems. But it also has serious drawbacks. The pre-commitment is not just a self-evaluation regarding the level of risk. It is a mix of the level of risk, the appetite for risk and the cost of capital weighted according to each firm's culture. The consequence is that there is no consistency in pre-commitment levels across institutions. They will vary widely and still embody excessive levels of risk. Moreover, if the penalty for overstepping the pre-announced maximum loss is of a financial nature, it can be circumvented by using option strategy. For the penalty is like an option put on the earnings profile of the bank.

Therefore the best strategy for the supervisors must be to devise a rating scheme coupled with sanctions of a non-financial nature. A direction that might be promising to investigate further is to define the sanctions as graduated responses by the supervisors in an extended framework of prompt corrective actions. A degrading of the rating by supervisory authorities would entail an injunction on the bank to undertake actions designed to reduce its exposure to risk. The greater the speed and the larger the magnitude of the deterioration, the more drastic and the more prompt the required measures.

The Issue of the International Lender of Last Resort

Originating in Thornton's writings as early as 1802, the doctrine of the lender of last resort acquired operational characteristics in the last two decades of the 19th century. Since that time is has undergone significant changes. However, the basic framework of systemic risk which gives its raison d'être spells out the conditions and purpose of its actions. Restating the principles is the best way to take up the problem raised by the requirement to give an international scope to this function. It then makes it possible to define what type of institution might best implement the LLR function in the present-day globalized financial setting.

The LLR is a sovereign attribute of a monetary authority, which avoids the propagation of a liquidity crunch due to coordination failures in money markets. In the period before the First World War, when financial crises had been frequent and had spread internationally, LLR was labeled 'the art of central banking'. Lending in last resort is not a contract but a discretionary decision of a central bank having diagnosed that a whole economy is about to fall into an abnormal equilibrium because of a liquidity shortage.

This sovereign discretion entails a constructive ambiguity in the markets. Because a liquidity crisis can be self-fulfilling, the amount of liquidity assistance needed to contain it cannot be predetermined. Only a sovereign institution creating money can mobilize unlimited resources. The boundless elasticity of central bank money in a liquidity squeeze is what restores confidence among banks. It is thus possible to exert LLR assistance by inducing some core banks to keep their credit lines or deposits with other banks, without actually spending central bank money. This is all the more likely if the central bank can rely on good financial monitoring to contain moral hazard and to assess the deteriorating state of liquidity early enough.

To be operational and not conducive to moral hazard, the doctrine must distinguish between illiquidity and fundamental insolvency. Institutions can indeed become insolvent because of the slump in asset prices and the withdrawal of credit lines ensuing from the liquidity crisis itself. But, had their portfolio been valued at pre-crisis levels and liabilities been routinely rolled over, they would have been perfectly solvent. Therefore the classical doctrine of LLR recommended lending freely to institutions capable of mustering good collateral when valued at 'normal' prices and lending at a penalty rate to discourage moral hazard. It is well known that a clear-cut distinction between illiquidity and insolvency is not feasible in the midst of a full-fledged crisis. This is precisely why moral hazard arises in sympathy with LLR assistance. Be that as it may, a basic insight of the classical doctrine is pervasive: *in a world of free financial markets, the lender of last resort is the only institution capable of setting a bottom price in critical markets beset by panic sales.*

Furthermore, the big market intermediaries can be enrolled in liquidity rescues only if a LLR is standing ready behind them. With this collective insurance, they can be induced to make buying pools of assets or to lend to institutions ready to buy the assets sold by all the other market users who are rushing for liquidity.

Such interventions, which assert the LLR's presence without actually spending money, are commonplace in national markets. We need only recall that, on 20 October 1987, when the futures market on stock indexes had threatened to collapse entirely, the Fed urged the big city banks to go on lending to market dealers and issued a statement announcing that it was standing ready to provide whatever amount of liquidity was needed.

In global financial markets, the visibility of the LLR has been more elusive and has never been institutionalized. Nonetheless, recent episodes of crisis highlighted its efficacy. In late September 1992, the French franc came under a self-fulfilling speculative attack. A solemn joint statement by French and German monetary authorities reasserted the relevance of the central parity as regards fundamentals and its importance for the transition to economic and monetary union (EMU). The statement added that the parity would be defended with all the means available under the EMS agreement. This unusual and symbolic address had a great impact on the market. It gave credence to the official scenario and debased the rival one, effectively stifling speculation. In late 1994, it appeared that the Mexican authorities would face an unmanageable liquidity problem in the first half of 1995. The huge demand for dollars triggered a panic sale of pesos. The decline of the exchange rate was turning into a full rout and the stock market was on the verge of collapsing entirely because no one knew which value would be a floor for the dollar price of the peso. After some procrastination, the Fed and the Treasury stepped in and arranged an emergency loan to the Mexican government, effectively restoring confidence and stopping the free fall of the peso. The market failure was successfully fought down because the US monetary authorities had credibly convinced the market that they wanted a reasonable floor price for the peso. With this benchmark safeguarded it was possible to resume trading activity, some international investors betting on the recovery of the peso on the basis of this bottom price.

A deeper historical view can give more insight on the international LLR in practice, looking back at the global financial markets of the pre-First World War era. A controversial debate has recently been raised between economic historians. One view holds that the cooperation between central banks was a decisive contribution to the working of the classical gold standard (Eichengreen, 1995). Another view points out that cooperation was rather episodic (Flandreau, 1997). The two views can be reconciled if one admits that the gold standard took care of itself in normal times, thanks to the strong mean-reverting capital flows close to the gold points, expressing a faith in the convertibility rule. Yet, in time of stress, acute shortages of gold could arise because of the same convertibility rule. The Bank of England was shackled in its international LLR role by the tight restraint imposed under the Official Act of Peel. On the contrary, the Bank of France had accumulated a considerable amount of gold which allowed it to participate in emergency lending to foreign banks or in smoothing liquidity conditions on the international money market.

Two episodes were remarkably noticeable. In the 1890 Barings crisis, the Bank of France, jointly with the Bank of Russia, lent gold as part of an international rescue package arranged under the auspices of the Bank of England. In the autumn of 1907, the liquidity crisis was in full swing in the New York money market. J.P. Morgan shipped to London to request assistance on behalf of its members. The Bank of France made a critical contribution, directly providing gold and discounting London bills.

Both modern and historical episodes show that international LLR interventions are central bank actions, either unilateral or bilateral, whenever the central banks involved have an interest in keeping orderly conditions in money markets they care about. Central banks are not entitled to make losses in their LLR capacity. This is why they have to find good collateral. In Asia, no member of the powerful club of the G-10 central banks cared enough to step in. The markets were scared and the losses triggered by the panic were unnecessarily high. Had the Federal Reserve and the Bank of Japan intervened to support the Won in the critical days of October, eventually swapping the acquired claims for SDR assets with the IMF thereafter, they would have sent a powerful signal to the market. The liquidity crisis would have been stopped, most likely as early as October 1997.

The conclusion to be drawn is that the function of the LLR cannot be fulfilled by the IMF, unless its mandate is transformed into a full-fledged supranational central bank. The LLR deals with markets and private financial institutions, the IMF deals with governments. The LLR acts in full discretion to preserve the constructive ambiguity necessary to keep moral hazard in check. The IMF operates at governments' request after a lengthy negotiation under conditionality. The international LLR and the IMF are complementary, not substitutable. One is a central bank prerogative to thwart contagion in money markets; the other is a political mechanism whereby the international community leads some of its members to good behavior according to a liberal doctrine, by means of structural adjustments backed by concessionary financing. One is an early short-term move, which leaves no persistent track record in the financial structure, if properly conducted; the other is a long-run process, which alters irreversibly the financial structure of the countries involved.

Therefore the proposal to assign a LLR function to the IMF is seriously flawed. Besides the exorbitant and dangerous concentration of power its implementation would create, it would mix in a single political institution two quite different functions. Such a proposal is completely at odds with the doctrine of separation and independence pursued by the financially advanced countries in designing the institutional structure of their monetary and prudential authorities. On the contrary, for market acceptance in the global financial system, the safety net should be developed applying the best practices available.

A market-friendly regulation must be enforced in the global financial system. It entails both a strengthened financial monitoring of the core international intermediaries and an international lender of last resort. There are the realms of a club of bank supervisors and central banks, open to new members, housed in the BIS. The international lender-of-last-resort function is not to be institutionalized. It should remain an ad hoc cooperation between the central banks most concerned by a particular crisis. But central banks should become more dedicated to precluding the destabilizing disturbances in global money markets than they were in addressing the Asian crisis.

REFERENCES

Aglietta M. (1996), 'Financial market failures and systemic risk', working paper, CEPII, 96.01, January.

Aglietta, M. and P. Moutot (1993), *Cahiers economiques et monétaires*, **41**, Banque de France.

Basle Committee on Banking Supervision (1997), *Core principles for effective banking supervision*, Basle, April.

Bingham, T. (1992), 'Securities markets and banking: some regulatory issues', in H. Cavanna (ed.), *Financial Innovation*, London: Routledge.

Brockmeijer Report (1995), 'Issues of measurement related to market size and macro-prudential risks in derivatives markets', BIS, February.

Cooper, R. and A. John (1993), 'Coordinating coordination failures in Keynesian models', in G. Mankiw and D. Rowen (eds), *New Keynesian Economics*, vol. 2, Cambridge, Mass.: MIT Press.

Davis, E.P. (1995), 'Market liquidity risk', in D. Fair and J. Raymond (eds), *The Competitiveness of Financial Institutions and Centers in Europe*, Kluwer Academic Publishers.

Diamond D. and P. Dybvig (1983), 'Bank runs, deposit insurance and liquidity', *Journal of Political Economy*, **91** (3), 401–19.

Eichengreen, B. (1995), 'Central bank co-operation and exchange rate commitments: the classical and interwar gold standards compared', *Financial History Review*, 2, 99–117.

Eichengreen, B., A. Rose and C. Wyplosz (1996), 'Exchange market mayhem: the antecedents and aftermath of speculative attacks', *Economic Policy*, 21, 249–312.

Feldstein, M. (1998), 'Refocusing the IMF', *Foreign Affairs*, March–April, 20–33.

Flandreau, M. (1997), 'Central bank co-operation in historical perspective: a sceptical view', *Economic History Review*, L, 735–63.

Folkerts-Landau, D. and C.J. Lindgren (1998), 'Toward a framework for financial stability', *International Monetary Fund*, January.

Gennotte G. and H. Leland (1990), 'Market liquidity, hedging and crashes', *American Economic Review*, December, 999–1021.

Global Derivatives Study Group (1993), *Derivatives: practices and principles*, Group of Thirty.

Goldstein, M. and C. Reinhart (1998), *Forecasting financial crises: early warning signals for emerging markets*, Washington, DC: Institute for International Economics.

Goodhart C. (1997), 'Setting standards is just the first step: maintaining them is the hard part', International Finance Group, University of Birmingham, October.

Goodhart C., P. Hartmann, D. Llewellyn, L. Rojas-Suarez and S. Weisbrod (1998), *Financial Regulation: Why, How and Where Now?*, London: Routledge.

Group of Thirty Study Group Report (1997), *Global Institutions, National Supervision and Systemic Risk*, Group of Thirty.

Guesnerie, R. and C. Azariadis (1982), 'Prophéties créatives et persistance des théories', *Revue Economique*, 33, (5), September, 787–806.

Guttentag, J. and R. Herring (1986), 'Disaster myopia in international banking', *Princeton Essays in International Finance*, 164, September.

Kindleberger, C.P. (1978), *Manias, Panics and Crashes*, New York: Basic Books.

Krugman, P. (1996), 'Are currency crises self-fulfilling?', *NBER Macroeconomics Annual*, 345–506.

Krugman, P. (1998), 'Currency crises', mimeo.

Kupiec, P. and J. O'Brien (1995), 'A pre-commitment approach to capital requirements for market risk', *Finance and Economics Discussion Series*, 95-34, July.

Minsky, H. (1986), *Stabilizing an Unstable Economy*, New Haven: Yale University Press.

Mishkin, F. (1991), 'Asymmetric information and financial crises: a historical perspective', in P. Hubbard (ed.), *Financial Markets and Financial Crises*, Chicago: University of Chicago Press.

Mishkin, F. (1996), 'Understanding financial crises: a developing country perspective', *NBER Working Paper*, 5600.

Obstfeld M. (1996), 'Models of currency crises with self-fulfilling features', *European Economic Review*, April, 1037–47.

Orlean, A. (1989), 'Mimetic contagion and speculative bubble', in *Theory and Decision* 27, Kluwer Academic Publishers.

Pritsker, M. (1997), 'Liquidity risk and positive feedback', in *The Measurement of Aggregate Market Risk*, Basle: BIS.

Radelet, S. and S. Sachs (1998), 'The East Asian financial crisis: diagnosis, remedies and prospects', *Brooking Papers on Economic Activity*, 1, spring.

Scharfstein, D. and J. Stein (1990), 'Herd behavior and investment', *American Economic Review*, 80 (3), June, 465–79.

Shiller, R. (1995), 'Conversation, information and herd behavior', *American Economic Review Papers and Proceeding*, **85**, May, 181–5.

Stiglitz, J. (1998), 'The Role of International Financial Institutions in the Current Global Economy', Address to the Council on Foreign Relations, World Bank, Chicago, 27 February.

Wyplosz, C. (1998), 'International capital market failures: sources, costs and solutions', mimeo.

Yung Chul Park (1998), 'The financial crisis in Korea: from miracle to meltdown?', Conference on coping with financial crises in developing and transition countries: regulatory and supervisory challenges in a new era of global finance, FONDAD, The Hague, Netherlands, 16–17 March.

10. Creditor panic, asset bubbles and sharks: three views of the Asian crisis[*]

Marcus Miller and Lei Zhang

High on the list of possible causes of the East Asian financial crisis, Radelet and Sachs (1998a) put bank runs and creditor 'grab races', so we begin this chapter with a brief overview of liquidity crises arising from the failure of collective action among creditors. We consider creditor panics affecting both bank depositors and bondholders, and outline institutional arrangements to prevent them. We then provide an explicit model for bond valuation which is used to illustrate the case for forced roll-overs and debt guarantees.

In the second section we turn to the sharply contrasting view, espoused by Dooley (1997) and Krugman (1998a), that implicit government insurance attracts unsustainable capital inflows which are reversed in a financial crisis. This view emphasizes the moral hazard problems inherent in deposit insurance and lays the blame for crisis at the door of poor regulation of domestic financial markets. We illustrate this using the approach of Dewatripont and Tirole (1994): depositors have a money-back guarantee, but limited liability gives the bank managers a put option in the face of losses, so they are free to gamble with other people's money, leaving the government to bear the costs.

In the third section we focus on the potentially destabilizing role of large players: in particular, we analayse the attacks on the Hong Kong dollar in a strategic setting where there are economic incentives for large creditors to attack a currency with sound fundamentals. Finally, in the light of three contrasting views, we discuss in the fourth section, albeit briefly, specific measures for crisis prevention and management, concluding with five steps for improving the international monetary system in the light of the East Asian crisis.

[*] This chapter draws on joint work with Pongsak Luangaram and has benefited from discussions with T.J. Bond and Luisa Corrado, and from comments at the Conference on 'The Aftermath of the Asian Crisis' organized by the World Bank and The Reinventing Bretton Woods Committee in May 1988. Financial support from the ESRC, under project No L120251024, 'A bankruptcy code for sovereign borrowers', is gratefully acknowledged.

LIQUIDITY CRISIS: AN OVERVIEW

Liquidity Crises as Shifts of Equilibrium

Radelet and Sachs (1998b, p. 4) explain recent crises essentially as 'failures of collective action' on the part of creditors:

> Our preferred explanation of [recent crises] turns on the critical distinction between illiquidity and insolvency. An *insolvent* borrower lacks the net worth to repay outstanding debts out of future earnings. An *illiquid* borrower lacks the ready cash to current debt servicing obligations, even though it has the net worth of repaying the debt in the long term. A *liquidity crisis* occurs if a solvent, but illiquid, borrower is unable to borrow fresh funds from the capital market in order to make current debt servicing obligations. ... The unwillingness or inability of the capital market to provide fresh loans to the illiquid borrower is the nub of the matter.

Bank deposits

If credit is supplied in the form of bank deposits the failure of collective action shows up as a bank run. The most widely cited paper on bank runs is that of Diamond and Dybvig (1983). It is important to note that, in this model, bank runs are caused by exogenous stochastic demands for liquidity by some depositors and *not* by fear of imprudent lending. Banks lend prudently and are essentially solvent, but their investments are illiquid; and it is the conflict between the liquidity needs of some depositors and the illiquidity of the bank's assets that can precipitate a bank run. (Of course, if the bank run is not checked, illiquidity can become insolvency as banks seek to dump illiquid assets.)

Two ways of averting bank runs are discussed by Diamond and Dybvig: first is to provide *deposit insurance*, as the Federal Deposit Insurance Corporation (FDIC) has done in the United States since 1934, and second is for the central bank to act as a *lender of last resort* (LLR), as Walter Bagehot recommended to the Bank of England in the 19th century. If deposit insurance is available, there is no need for depositors to withdraw their funds just because they fear others may do so. By providing liquidity for banks faced with sudden withdrawals, the central bank relieves them of the pressure to dispose of illiquid asset at a loss – and this can also reduce risk of contagion. (Note, however, that Walter Bagehot insisted that only solvent banks should be provided with such liquidity.) These two institutional responses are indicated in the top row of Table 10.1. The second row is concerned with liquidity crises in bond markets, to which we now turn.

Bonds

A creditor who does not receive agreed debt service payments on time may be able to 'accelerate' the debt and demand payment in full, which can trigger the closure of a solvent firm as assets are sold to honour such claims. A key objective of modern bankruptcy laws is to avoid premature closure of viable firms: under the provisions of Chapter 11 of the US Bankruptcy Code, for example, debt may be 'rolled up' as creditors are forced to lend into arrears (or it may be converted into shares as part of debt–equity swap).

Table 10.1   Liquidity crises and measures to prevent them

Type of creditor	Failure of collective action	Institutional responses
Depositor	'Bank run'	Deposit insurance
		Lender of last resort
Bondholder	'Grab race'	Debt roll-overs
		Debt guarantees

Similar problems of creditor coordination may arise in the context of international lending (where the operation of appropriate bankruptcy procedures is much more problematic). As Radelet and Sachs (1998b, p. 5) argue, 'International loan markets are prone to self-fulfilling crises in which individual creditors may act rationally and yet market outcomes produce sharp, costly, and fundamentally unnecessary panicked reversals in capital flows'.

To see this, assume that creditors as a group would be willing to make a new loan, but no individual creditor is willing to do so unless other creditors do the same; then, with a failure of coordination among creditors, it is quite possible that there will be no lending to an illiquid borrower. Technically, the source of multiple equilibria is payoff externalities; that is, the payoffs to an agent adopting an action increase in the number of other agents adopting the same action (see Devenow and Welch, 1996, pp. 605–7.) Table 10.2 provides a simple illustration of the argument (assuming only two creditors). The setting is one in which each of two creditors has lent 50 to a borrower who is solvent but illiquid: solvent because the project will pay 120 in a year's time, illiquid because there are no dividends in the meantime. At the beginning of the year, however, the borrower is required to provide a total of 20 as debt service. If each creditor is willing to relend the 10 of debt service received, the project will continue and each will receive future payments with a present discounted value of 50. But if neither creditor is willing to roll over the loan, the debtor will default and the project will be scrapped, with each creditor receiving only 30 from the scrap value. The payoffs in these two cases are shown in the top-left and bottom-right of the table.

Note that, if creditor 1 is willing to lend 10, but not creditor 2, the project will still be scrapped and creditor 1 will be worse off (with a net return of only 30–10 = 20: see top-right corner of the table). Likewise, if only creditor 2 is willing to roll over the loan, the payoffs will be shown at bottom-right. What are the equilibrium outcomes?

Table 10.2   To lend or not to lend?

		Creditor 2	
		Lend	Not lend
Creditor 1	Lend	(50, 50)	(20, 30)
	Not lend	(30, 20)	(30, 30)

The cases of *both* creditors lending and *neither* lending are the two Nash equilibria of this game, where a Nash equilibrium is defined as a situation where no creditor has the incentive to deviate from his or her strategy given that the other does not deviate. Clearly, continued lending is the more socially efficient equilibrium, but a failure to coordinate will lead to a self-fulfilling liquidity crisis where the debtor is pushed into default, the project is scrapped and each creditor concludes that it was right not to put extra money into a failing project.

Deposit insurance together with the prudential regulation of the banking industry is generally sufficient to avoid bank runs. But what about the bond market? In circumstances where continued lending is in the interest of the creditors, an *enforced roll-over* may be an appropriate way of handling the liquidity crisis. The coordinated roll-over which saved Korea from default at the end of 1997 provides a topical example of this policy.[1]

An alternative proposal, indicated in the second row of Table 10.1 as 'debt guarantees', is for an International Bondholders Corporation (BIC) to provide insurance of international bonds issued by developing countries in return for a premium paid by bond purchases. In the view of William Cline (1995, p. 483) such an institution 'could be housed in the World Band family ... and would seek to do for bonds what the Multilateral Investment Guarantee Agency (MIGA) does for direct investment'. How would it work?

> One approach would be simply to apply binary criterion: the IBIC either would or would not stand ready to insure new bonds issued by a country in a given year ... A better design would probably be to have the IBIC provide alternative levels of coinsurance for a standard premium, with the differing coinsurance rates reflecting greater or lesser risk. The top rate might be, for example, 80%. The IBIC would pay a claim of 80% of missed interest or principal payments on insured bonds in a country judged in the highest creditworthiness category. The lowest rate might be, for example, 20%. The premium might be 50 basis points in either case. (Ibid.)

In the midst of the East Asian crisis, George Soros (1997) also recommended such an agency to avoid the breakdown of international finance.[2]

Liquidity Crisis, Forced Roll-overs and Debt Guarantees

We use a deterministic version of Bartolini and Dixit's (1991) model of sovereign debt to illustrate both the coordinated equilibrium and what happens when creditor coordination fails. As mechanisms to offset collective action failure among bondholders, both forced roll-overs and debt guarantees are discussed.

Assume that the country's capacity to pay, X_t, grows with a percentage trend μ so that

$$dX_t/dt = \mu X_t dt. \tag{10.1}$$

The present value of capacity to pay, the country's gross international wealth W, is

$$W(X_t) = \int_t^\infty X_s e^{-r(s-t)} ds = X_t / (r - \mu). \tag{10.2}$$

where r is the real interest rate and we assume $r - \mu > 0$ to ensure the existence of this solution. If debt is less than gross wealth, that is $D \leq W = X/(r - \mu)$, then the country is technically 'solvent'; and in this deterministic case market value of debt will equal its face value. (Even where $D > W = X/(r - \mu)$ and the country is technically 'insolvent' creditors may nevertheless have a shared interest in keeping things going, as we discuss below.)

Why does creditor coordination matter if the country is solvent? It may be necessary to avoid a liquidity crisis. It is true that there is no risk of such a crisis if $X_t \geq rD$ (and μ is positive) and the country is always able to honour its debt service obligations in full out of current earnings. But consider the case where $X_t < rD$ and full payment of interest to existing creditors would require the issue of new debt to satisfy

$$rD_t = X_t + dD_t/dt, \tag{10.3}$$

where dD_t/dt is the amount of new borrowing. Alternatively, of course, existing lenders could simply roll over the debt. In either case, because the country is solvent, debt stands at par if creditors coordinate to inject new funds. This is shown in Figure 10.1, which plots the average value of debt against the current ability to pay. The former, denoted as $v \equiv V(X_t, D_t)/D_t$, is the ratio of market to face value of debt; the latter is measured as $x \equiv X_t/D_t$. For a solvent country, with $x \geq r - \mu$ and debt at par, the outcome will lie on the line segment *CFP*. As indicated by the arrows, x will be increasing, at the rate μ to the right of F

but more slowly between *C* and *F* as debt and capacity to pay are both growing. as the latter grows faster, the country is 'growing out of debt'; see Appendix for the dynamics of *x*.

In the insolvent case, the outcome will lie on the *SC* where $w = W/D$. Here, *x* is decreasing as debt grows faster than the capacity to pay. The debtor is playing a Ponzi game, but as long as *v* exceeds the value of assets that may be siezed (shown as α in the figure), coordinated creditors will allow the game to continue. Seizure of assets will not occur until *S*, when $v = α$. (Note that, under strict sovereign immunity, $α = 0$ and *S* is at the origin.)

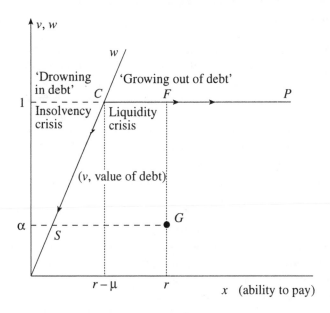

Figure 10.1   Debt value with and without coordination

Coordinated equilibrium is by no means guaranteed. Let us now look at a game between the two creditors each with an equal share of the debt, assuming $r - μ < x < r$ (where the coordinated solution lies on *CF*). Suppose in particular that the current cash flow is just below the required interest payment and neither creditor can supply sufficient new lending for current interest payments to be met, though together they can. (In terms of (10.3), it is when $X_t < rD_t$ and each creditor can, for example, only supply new lending of $\frac{1}{2}dD_t/dt$.) While the coordinated solution (where each party provides new funds believing the other will do so) is one possible equilibrium; the case that neither provides new funds is another, with each creditor hesitating to inject new lending for fear of non-cooperation. (This is analogous to the multiple equilibria in Diamond and Dybvig's (1983) model of bank behaviour.) Coordinated outcomes lie on the line CF; but the failure of collective action pushes bond values down to α.

As can be seen from the figure, the collapse in the market value of debt (from F to G) caused by failure of the collective action can be substantial.[3] For the two-creditor case, the substantial gain to coordination may well ensure that both parties agree to supply the additional funds. But if the number of creditors is large, and if the liquidity crisis could be resolved without all creditors rolling over their lending, each individual creditor may have an incentive to 'free-ride' and coordination will collapse.

It follows logically that a liquidity crisis can be avoided by a *forced roll-over*, where the debtor is given more credit by all lenders. If each and every lender is forced to lend into arrears, that solves the coordination problem![4] Another strategy, which may seem more attractive for both lenders and borrower, is for a third party with a 'deep pocket' (for example, the government) to give lenders a guarantee. This is illustrated in Figure 10.2; the dashed line $G'G'$ gives the value of the guarantee designed to check creditor panic by limiting the downside risk. If in the region of potential liquidity crisis, CF in the figure, creditors are now willing to lend into arrears, crisis will be averted and the government will not be called upon to deliver on its guarantee. This is an attractive outcome: but is there a catch somewhere?

Unfortunately, yes. Unconditional guarantees can have 'adverse incentive' effects which diminish the capacity to service debt (so-called 'moral hazard'). Assume for example, that these adverse incentives reduce the expected growth of earnings, and move the valuation function down from Ow to Ow'. This will make things worse, not better. At the point where x equals r, for example, the moral hazard effects of a guarantee designed to protect an illiquid borrower imply that the guarantor has to bail out an insolvent borrower, which could prove extremely expensive. And if the guarantee was too costly to be credible, it could well trigger the creditor panic it was supposed to avoid! These issues are taken up in more detail in the next section.

Lastly, consider a case of mistaken identity, namely, the Latin American debt crisis of the 1980s, a solvency problem which was treated initially as a liquidity problem. Figure 10.1 may be used to illustrate in broad-brush fashion two phases of this crisis. In the first phase, 1986–8, the Baker Plan sought to achieve creditor coordination on the mistaken assumption that debtor countries would 'grow out of debt'. But it was progressively recognized that they were in fact 'drowning in debt' (that is, to the left of point C in Figure 10.1, and not to the right). To remedy this situation, the Brady Plan of 1989 included 'debt and debt service' reductions (Cline, 1995, p. 237) that is, debt write-downs. In terms of

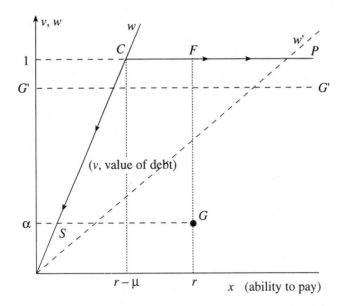

Figure 10.2   Debt guarantees and moral hazard

Figure 10.1, a debt write-down which increases *x* (and also *v*) can shift debtor
countries to the right of point *C*, giving them a realistic chance to grow out of
debt. In his re-examination of this episode, Cline (1995) writes as follows:

> A debt strategy originally intended to orchestrate lending until countries could
> increase exports and restore credit-worthiness (the Baker Plan) [gave] way to a
> forgiveness plan that had the predictable effect of cutting off new long-term lending
> from the banks (the Brady Plan). However, the broadly cooperative, market-oriented
> nature of the forgiveness plan contributed to an atmosphere of confidence for other
> categories of creditors, including bond holders, so that renewed capital flows through
> other channels accomplished the return to the capital market.

The moral of the story is that creditor coordination may be necessary but not
sufficient to solve debt problems!

DEPOSIT INSURANCE, LIMITED LIABILITY AND
MORAL HAZARD

As has just been noted, illiquidity is often the close cousin of insolvency. But
efforts to bail out those close to insolvency may face serious problems of moral

hazard. How relevent is this for events in East Asia? Radelet and Sachs (1988b) argue that, because external debt was substantially short-term and the regional growth had been so strong, the problem was one of illiquidity and not insolvency. An alternative view (Dooley, 1997, 1998; Krugman, 1998a) is that money-back guarantees for depositors and limited liability for lenders had generated excessive spending in real estate in Thailand, for example, and over-investment in Korean manufacturing, so insolvency was just around the corner.

How severe moral hazard problems can arise when illiquidity slides into insolvency is addressed in this section taking banks as an example.[5] Assume that domestic banks have invested both local and foreign currency deposits in domestic interest-earning assets with stochastic returns, X. Let D indicate the value of total deposits being invested and D_F the amount of foreign currency deposits. Let the equity value of bank, that is the value of assets less deposits, be given by the schedule MN in Figure 10.3 where MN is an increasing function of loan returns, X, plotted along a horizontal axis. (MN has a slope of $1/r$ where r is market rate of interest.)

For values of X close to X_B, the net equity of the bank is close to zero. This is when observers predict that loan managers will 'gamble for resurrection'. This is because they can increase the net equity value of the bank by increasing

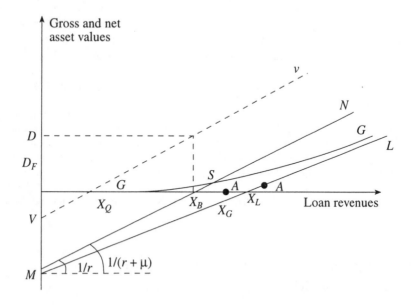

Figure 10.3   Moral hazard in banking: 'gambling for resurrection'

the variance of returns: high returns will enhance bank profits but low or negative returns will be written off through bankruptcy.

To illustrate, let the alternative investment available to loan managers have higher risk but lower mean return, $(-\mu)$, as indicated by the line ML in the figure whose slope is $1/(r + \mu)$. Note that ML lies everywhere below MN, the value of investing safely. Why would managers ever be tempted to switch to such high-risk, low-yield assets? Would they not prefer to close the bank down at the point X_L where ML crosses the horizontal axis? To do this would be to ignore the way expected profits depend on the variability of returns and the limited liability of the bank shareholders: together they imply that the net equity of the bank is given by the schedule GG when deposits are invested in risky assets. So risky investment is more probable than safe investment when bank capital is low (that is, to the left of S where GG crossed MN).

(We can see this by the following argument. Assume that X_L is chosen at the close-down point and consider returns fluctuating above and below this level. Note that, if returns go above X_L, this will increase the bank's profits, as shown at the point A; but if returns fall below X_L, profits only fall to zero as a result of limited liability: see point A'. The expected value of profits (at that point above X_L on the ray joining A and A') is positive, so why close down? Is it not better to wait? Yes, because the economic value of waiting before closing down is in fact captured by schedule GG which lies above ML by the put value implicit in limited liability. The schedule GG is tangent to the horizontal axis at X_Q and approaches ML asymptotically to the right as X goes to infinity where X_Q is the point at which the loan manager would like to exercise the option of going bankrupt.)

Given the possibility of switching from safe to lower-yielding high-risk assets, loan managers will be tempted to gamble when net returns of the safe portfolio are at X_G or below. Who is to prevent loan managers from behaving in this way? Without deposit insurance, it would in principle have to be depositors who monitor portfolio manager when X is close to X_G and promptly punish any sign of gambling (by firing the manager, for example). But as Dewatripont and Tirole (1994) point out this is a counsel of perfection; most bank deposits are small and most depositors are uniformed and unsophisticated. Consequently, to protect small depositors exposed to the moral hazard of loan managers who gamble, the government usually guarantees deposits and takes upon itself the task of monitoring portfolio allocation decisions and punishing mismanagement.

What if the state provides the guarantee but fails to check the moral hazard (which seems to have been true in several East Asian countries)? Certainly, local taxpayers must expect substantial tax charges as required to cover the losses of the insurance agency, as US experience with savings and loan institutions clearly demonstrated. But provided the agency will be bailed out, local currency depositors can rest assured.

The same may not be true for foreign currency depositors.[6] They see local banks mismanaging their portfolios without any regulatory response and they can forecast bank insolvencies. They also know that, while the local central bank can print domestic currency, it cannot print dollars. So, if foreign currency reserves are low (relative to foreign currency deposits), they can have no assurance that there is an effective lender of last resort. This is a recipe for a bank run as foreign currency depositors head for safety. And the central bank, having lost all its reserves, will be forced to float the currency.

In short, *if returns fall to the critical value, (X_c), and this does not trigger an appropriate regulatory response, it can be the signal for the exit of foreign depositors and a full-blown financial crisis.* The danger of allowing or encouraging substantial short-term capital inflows to pour into a weakly regulated banking system is only too apparent. Short-term deposits may easily exceed foreign currency reserves and low bank returns trigger exit rather than regulation.

Note that for assets in fixed supply the combination of deposit guarantees and limited liability can also give rise to rapid asset price inflation. As Krugman (1988a) observes, fixed assets may be priced on the basis of the best possible outcomes (that is, at 'Pangloss values') with the government covering losses in all other cases. In Krugman's assessment, the crisis was the bursting of an asset price bubble created by moral hazard in banking.

Lastly, we note that the willingness of the IMF to act as a lender of last resort in foreign currency terms is necessarily hampered if there is unchecked moral hazard in local banking system. Unconditional lending into this situation will not avoid the problem. It may even lead to greater losses to local taxpayers (as the US savings and loans experience confirms).

ARE THERE SHARKS IN THE SOUTH CHINA SEA? STRATEGIC ASPECTS OF THE ATTACK ON THE HONG KONG DOLLAR

There can be multiple Nash equilibria – either everyone lends or no one lends – without any individual being in a position to shift the equilibrium (see Cooper and John, 1991). By using two-creditor examples to illustrate the coordination problem, it may appear that we have overplayed the strategic aspects of the situation. But the attack on the Hong Kong dollar in the summer of 1998 suggests otherwise. Players big enough to move markets were, it seems, able to place bets so as to reduce the number of equilibria from two to one: that is, to attack the currency.

Table 10.3 below illustrates the payoffs to each of two players considering whether to speculate against the Hong Kong currency, which has been pegged against the US dollar for 15 years. If neither attacks, the peg is sustained. Any player attacking on its own will fail (with a loss of 5). But if both attack, the HK dollar will be forced to devalue, giving profits of 20 each. So there are two Nash equilibria the speculators may choose. For sharks to make a killing, they have to hunt in packs.

Table 10.3   Payoffs to a speculative attack on the HK dollar

		Player 2		
		Attack		Not attack
	Attack	(20, 20)	←	(−5,0)
Player 1		↑		↓
	Not attack	(0, −5)	→	(0, 0)

The payoffs in Table 10.3 do not incorporate the benefits of what has been described as the 'double play in which speculators push up the local interest rates by selling HK dollars and benefit from short positions in the stock market' (*Financial Times*, 7 September 1998). Assume that any player who sells HK dollars drives up interest rates and makes a profit of 6 on the short position taken in the stock market before the attack. The payoffs, *including the benefits of the 'double play'*, are shown in Table 10.4. What is the effect of adding 6 to the payoff of any attacker? A successful attack is, of course, more profitable, but even an unsuccessful attack now pays dividends as the double play more than covers the costs of the attack. There is only one Nash equilibrium: attacking is the dominant strategy.

Table 10.4   Payoffs with the 'double play' of 1998

		Player 2		
		Attack		Not attack
	Attack	(26, 26)	←	(1, 0)
Player 1		↑		↑
	Not attack	(0, 1)	←	(0, 0)

It is, we believe, for this reason that the Hong Kong Monetary Authority (HKMA) has gone to such drastic lengths to defend the peg, using its reserves to buy a substantial fraction of the shares in the Hang Sheng Index and impose a 'bear squeeze' on speculators. The effect has been to replace the profits of the double play with losses, so attacking the peg is no longer the dominant strategy. (In addition, by increasing bank liquidity the HKMA has reduced the risk of interest rates rising sharply when large amounts of HK dollars are sold and has made it much more expensive for speculators to manipulate the territory's money markets.

One of the most disturbing features of the East Asian crisis has been the destabilizing role of capital flows. Could it be that the payoffs to short-term creditors – after adding in the benefits of government guarantees and 'double plays' – have made capital flight the dominant strategy? (If you can pull your money out of Thailand with a dollar guarantee, and profits on short selling the baht to boot, why keep on lending?)

CRISIS PREVENTION AND MANAGEMENT

What can be done to avert further financial crises or at least to mitigate their consequences?[7] One step upon which most commentators are agreed is to improve the regulation of financial institutions in emerging countries, so as to ensure greater transparency and proper monitoring of bank portfolios,[8] and taking prompt corrective action when danger threatens. Beyond that, commentators differ widely. We outline three contrasting views.

Go with the flow: the US Treasury View

We begin with the 'liberal', or free market, view of the US government as recently put by Larry Summers (1998), deputy secretary of the US Treasury. 'The case for capital account liberalisation', he argued, 'is a case for allowing capital to seek the highest productivity investments', though he warned that 'inflows in search of genuine economic opportunities are one thing. Inflows in search of government guarantees ... are quite another'. In view of the acknowledged danger of liberalizing capital flows when incentives are distorted, he concluded that 'the pace of opening up should be matched by the pace of developing a sound domestic financial system'.

What changes (if any) are needed at international level? Summers acknowledges that 'there will never be enough money in the world to respond as an official lender of last resort to all the crises that can appear ... as capital flows increase'; but he dismisses proposals for 'speed bumps or other forms of capital control' as more likely to do harm than good. Three suggestions are made for improving the global financial system. The first two are familiar and uncontroversial: greater transparency and improved prudential standards; third is the proposal to 'ensure that policymakers do not confront the choice between uncontrolled chaos and confusion, on the one hand, and large bailouts, on the other'. (It is not made clear how these can be achieved, though the reference to bankruptcy law implies some sort of work-out procedure: see below.)

International Monetary Reform: a First Best Approach

The appropriate counterpart to globalized capital markets would in principle be the globalization of controls developed at the national level: mechanisms like deposit insurance and the lender of last resort. The former could well be delegated to national central banks, but not the latter. This poses the key question: can the IMF as currently constituted act as an effective international lender of last resort?

Even those in favour of substantial reform answer 'no'. In Sachs's view, for example, current IMF procedures are too slow to stop bank runs in any case; and he is against enhancing their resources and discretion because, according to him, the IMF is already too powerful and too unaccountable (*Financial Times*, December 1997). Krugman too is sceptical: instead of 'a sort of super-IMF with the huge resources needed to act as a full-fledged lender of last resort and with extensive direct regulatory powers over the banks of member countries', he reckons that 'we will be lucky if the existing, far-from-super IMF gets the modest funding increase it is seeking' (*Financial Times*, 'Start taking the Prozac', 9 April 1998). What about second best?

International Monetary Reform: Second-best Approaches

Noting that financial liberalization preceded the dangerous build-up of short-term foreign currency exposure in East Asia, Radelet and Sachs (1998b, p. 36) conclude that

> the rapid push towards fully open capital markets among the developing countries would seem to be misguided. There is certainly no strong empirical evidence that economic growth in middle-income developing countries depends on unfettered access to short-term capital flows from abroad ... The policy goal ... should be to support long-term capital flows especially foreign direct investment, and equity portfolio flows, but to limit short-term international flows mainly to the financing of short-term trade transactions.

Two mechanisms for doing so are discussed: inflow controls (as in Chile) and explicit supervisory limits. Though the authors concede that the former are more attractive on economic grounds, they argue for the latter in terms of practical enforcement (administration and monitoring).

Since Korean debt default was avoided by an involuntary roll-over on the part of Western banks just before Christmas of 1997, Radelet and Sachs (1998b) make the case for generalized orderly work-out arrangements. (The

Korean negotiations demonstrated that such a mechanism could work in practice. Now, we suppose, we will have to discover whether it can work in theory!' p. 38). In other words, besides prudential limits on capital controls, they are hinting at another institutional innovation, the equivalent of an international bankruptcy court. The strategic case for a payments standstill is made in Miller and Zhang (1997) and in the BIS annual report (1998) which emphasizes the need to get creditors to the negotiating table to restructure (and write down) debt.

In the disastrous circumstance of the current crisis, Krugman (1988b) has recommended stabilizing exchange rates with widespread exchange controls on capital account transactions, leaving interest rates free to help stabilize domestic demand.

In the light of the crisis in East Asia, we end by proposing steps to resolve the burden of outstanding debts and to change the international rules of the game to prevent recurrent crisis. We suggest that two steps are needed to resolve the current crisis:

1. for the Asian central banks to quantify the losses resulting from deposit insurance and to devise appropriate packages for financial reconstruction (as Thailand has recently done);
2. for creditors and debtors, in Indonesia for example, to get together to negotiate the write-down of debts that are beyond the capacity to pay. To bring creditors to the negotiating table, debtors might consider a unilateral stay of payments with continued lending by international financial institutions subject to appropriate conditionality.

The following steps are needed to reform the international monetary system:

1. establishing a *surveillance mechanism* of countries' financial regulations and supervisory systems, jointly staffed by the IMF and the World Bank (which can also devise financial sector reforms for countries in crisis);
2. devising a set of administratively practical *capital inflow controls* and regulatory procedures along the lines of Federal Deposit Insurance Corporation Investment Act (FDICIA) (1991) to reduce the financial vulnerability of emerging market economies;
3. *not* writing the requirement of capital account liberalization into the Articles of the IMF for the foreseeable future;
4. Instead, convening a working party of the G-10 to recommend changes in the Articles of the IMF needed to protect debtor countries trapped in liquidity crisis and to consider the case for capital controls as a defensive measure for countries in crisis.[9]

Without prompt action to renegotiate debts, countries in crisis will be condemned to prolonged recession; without reform of the international monetary system, these crises will recur.

NOTES

1. But the fact that half-a-dozen of the 'chaebols' have gone bankrupt suggests that the problem was not simply one of illiquidity.
2. Soros's proposal is, however, roundly criticized by Eichengreen (1999, ch. 5) on the ground that 'to assert that the international community would be able to stand aside in the event of default on uninsured loans, in disregard of the systemic consequences, is to assume a solution to the problem'.
3. What happens if the debt is short-term? In terms of Figure 10.1, this corresponds to a higher interest payment by the country, so point F moves to the right while the critical level of $x = r - \mu$ remains the same. So shortening the maturity of the loan increases the range of liquidity crisis (that is, the horizontal distance between C and F).
4. This was what happened in December 1997, when central banks of G-7 countries pressured their own national lending institutions to roll over their debts and thus prevented unilateral default by Korea.
5. The moral hazard problems arising in the banking industry are analysed by Dewatripont and Tirole (1994), assuming that financial panic can be avoided by a deposit insurance. In their monograph on the prudential regulation of banks, they treat the problem as one of corporate governance and discuss how effective the BIS capital adequacy ratio may be as triggers for regulatory action. The same model is also used in Bond and Miller (1998).
6. 'The effective functioning of deposit insurance depends on the deposits being in domestic currency: countries with dollarized banking systems often leave themselves exposed to creditor runs even when some deposit insurance arrangements are in place, because such deposit insurance often lacks adequate reserve funds and therefore credibility' (Radelet and Sachs, 1998, p. 9).
7. This section is largely based on Miller and Luangaram (1998). For later and more detailed assessments see Bhattacharya and Miller (1998), Eichengreen (1999) and Griffith-Jones (1999).
8. Canada and Britain have proposed a new surveillance structure for this purpose: this would combine the World Bank financial operations unit with staff from the IMF and be responsible both for general surveillance and for devising financial sector reform for countries in crises (*Financial Times*, 17 April 1988).
9. Bearing in mind the strictures laid at the door of global financial markets by George Soros (1998), for example, other devices worth considering in a crisis include (a) more public disclosure of the position taken by hedge funds, as proposed by Malaysia; (b) banning borrowing in local currency by hedge funds and other foreign banks: see the actions of the Hong Kong Monetary Authority against speculators (Dieter, 1998); (c) including hedge funds and merchant banks in a target group of creditors whose exit will attract regulatory censure, by increasing the withholding penalties in Chilean capital controls, 'exit taxes' or by regulatory action in their G-7 host countries, for example; (d) two-tier exchange rates, with a floating rate on capital account.

REFERENCES

Bartolini, Leonardo and Avinash Dixit (1991), 'Market value of illiquid debt and implications for conflicts among creditors', IMF Staff Papers, **38** (4), 828–49.

Bhattacharya, Amar and Marcus Miller (1998), 'Coping with crises: is there a "silver bullet"', mimeo; forthcoming in R. Agenor *et al.* (eds), *The Asian Financial Crisis: Causes, Contagion and Consequences*, Cambridge: Cambridge University Press.

BIS (1998), *Annual Report*, Basle: Bank of International Settlements.

Bond, Timothy J. and Marcus Miller (1998), 'Financial bailouts and financial crises', mimeo, International Monetary Fund, January.

Cline, William (1995), *International Debt Reexamined*, Washington, DC: Institute for International Economics.

Cooper, Russell and Andrew John (1991), 'Coordinating coordination failures in Keynesian models', in N.G. Mankiw and D. Romer (eds), *New Keynesian Economics: Coordination Failures and Real Regidities*, vol. 2, London: MIT Press.

Devenow, A. and I. Welch (1996), 'National herdling in financial economies', *European Economic Review*, **40**, 603–15.

Dewartripont, Mathias and Jean Toole (1994), *The Prudential Regulation of Banks*, Cambridge, Mass.: MIT Press.

Diamond, Douglas W. and Philip H. Dybvig (1983), 'Bank runs, deposit insurance and liquidity', *Journal of Political Economy*, **91** (3), 401–19.

Dieter, Heribert (1998), 'Crisis in Asia or crisis of globalisation', *CSGR Working Paper*, No. 15, Centre for the Study of Regionalisation and Globalisation, University of Warwick, Available at http://www.CSGR.org.

Dooley, Michael P. (1997), 'A model of crisis in emerging markets', *NBER Working Paper* No. 6300.

Dooley, Michael P. (1998), 'Are capital inflows to developing countries a vote for or against economic policy reforms?' mimeo; forthcoming in R. Agenor *et al.* (eds), *The Asian Financial Crisis: Causes, Contagion and Consequences*, Cambridge: Cambridge University Press.

Eichengreen, Barry (1999), *Towards a New International Financial Architecture: A Practical Post-Asia Agenda*, Washington, DC: IIE.

Eichengreen, Barry and Donald Methieson (1998), 'Hedge funds and financial market dynamics', *IMF Occasional Paper* No. 166, Washington, DC: IMF

Griffith-Jones, S. (1999), 'A new financial architecture for reducing risks and severity of crisis', mimeo, IDS, University of Sussex.

Krugman, Paul (1998a), 'What happened to Asia', mimeo, MIT, January.

Krugman, Paul (1998b), 'Saving Asia: it's time to get radical', *Forture*, 7 September, 33–8.

Miller, Marcus and Pongsak Luangaram (1998), 'Financial crisis in East Asia: bank runs, asset bubbles and antidotes', *CSGR Working Paper*, No. 11/98, University of Warwick.

Miller, Marcus and Lei Zhang (1998), 'Sovereign liquidity crises: The strategic case for a payments standstill', *CEPR Discussion Paper*, no. 1820, February.

Radelet, Steven and Jeffrey Sachs (1998a), 'The onset of the East Asian financial crisis', mimeo, Harvard Institute for International Development, March.

Radelet, Steven and Jeffrey Sachs (1998b), 'The East Asian financial crisis: diagnosis, remedies, prospects', *Brookings Papers on Economic Activity*, **1**, 1–90.

Soros, George (1997), 'Avoiding a breakdown: Asia's crisis demands a rethink of international regulation', *Financial Times*, December 31, p. 12.

Soros, George (1998), *The Crisis of Global Capitalism*, New York: BBS.

Summers, Lawrence (1998), 'Go with the flow', *Financial Times*, March 11.

APPENDIX

The Dynamics of x in the Deterministic Case

Let the value of assets that may be seized be proportional to the debt level $S_t = \alpha D_t$; then the debt value is determined by

$$V(X_t, D_t) = \int_t^\tau \min\{X_s, \tau D_s\}e^{-r(s-t)}ds + e^{-r(\tau-t)}S_T \qquad (10.4)$$

where τ is the time that the debt value falls to that of the collateral assets.

It can be seen from (10.4) that $V(X_t, D_t)/D_t$ is a function of the ratio $x \equiv X_t/D_t$. The dynamics of x_t is given as follows. If $x \equiv x(0) \geq r$, then

$$dx_t = \mu x_t \qquad (10.5)$$

and the average debt value is equal to par, so $\mu = 1$. If $x < r$, then

$$dx_t = x_t[x_t - (r - \mu)]dt. \qquad (10.6)$$

The solution for (10.6) is

$$x_t = \frac{(r-\mu)x}{x - [x - (r-\mu)]e^{(t-\mu)t}} \qquad x = x(0). \qquad (10.7)$$

The solution is increasing over time when $x > (r - \mu)$ and decreasing when $x < (r - \mu)$.

Debt Valuation in the Case where x is Stochastic

Adding uncertainty gives broadly the same qualitative results as in the deterministic case, and we briefly sketch the solutions in Figure 10.4. To capture the short maturity of loans, assume the debt repayment $c > r$. Let us first look at the coordinated solution. When x is very large, the firm is expected to have little difficulty in repaying the debt, so the debt value v goes asymptotically towards par c/r. The fact that v lies below c/r is because there is always a positive probability for the debt to be restructured (its value reduced). When x is very low, the debt value approaches the scrap value α. Debt value v joins the horizontal line α smoothly at L because creditors can trigger liquidation optimally. The value of debt without coordination is shown as the first passage option v' which joins the scrap value at $x = c$ and asymptotically goes to c/r as x increases. It is clear from the figure that *the region of liquidity crisis* (the range between $r - \mu$ and c) *increases if c increases* (when the maturity of the debt decreases). Since v is monotonically increasing in x, *the shorter the maturity of the debt the larger the losses to both borrowers and lenders if collective action fails*. So forced roll-over becomes even more important in preventing the failure of collective action when debts are predominantly short-term.

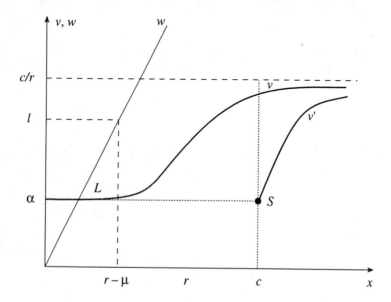

Figure 10.4   Debt value under uncertainty

Index